ROADS THAT MOVE

ROADS THAT MOVE

A Journey through
Eastern Europe

WALTER PERRIE

MAINSTREAM
PUBLISHING

First published in Great Britain in 1991 by
MAINSTREAM PUBLISHING COMPANY (EDINBURGH) LTD
7 Albany Street
Edinburgh EH1 3UG

British Library Cataloguing in Publication Data
Perrie, Walter
  Roads that move: a journey to Eastern Europe
  1. Eastern Europe. Visitors' guides
  I. Title
  914.7

ISBN 1 85158 318 1 (cloth)

Typeset in 11/13pt Bembo by
Falcon Typographic Art Ltd, Edinburgh and London
Printed in Great Britain by Mackays of Chatham, Chatham

Rivers are roads that move, and carry us whither we desire to go.
Blaise Pascal

No man is an Island, *entire of it self; every man is a piece of the* Continent, *a part of the* main; *if a* clod *be washed away by the* sea, Europe *is the less, as well as if a* promontory *were, as well as if a* manor *of thy* friends *or of* thine own *were; any man's* death *diminishes* me, *because I am involved in* Mankind; *And therefore never send to know for whom the* bell *tolls; It tolls for* thee.
John Donne

To my father and mother

I want to thank all those who have helped make this book possible. Most obviously, all those who are mentioned in it whose generosities of time and hospitality made the journey worth while. In addition, I want to thank Walter Cairns and the literature committee of the Scottish Arts Council who provided a grant towards the cost of travel. Trevor Royle provided unfailing encouragement and good advice. Other friends provided information and help of all kinds: Robert Bringhurst, Robin Magowan, Susan Greenoff, Tony Rudolf, George Szirtes, Jascha Kessler, Myron Grindea and, not least, my friends in Dunning.

I GREW up between two households, my father's and that of my mother's father and mother. My father had one especial hero: William III, King of Great Britain and Ireland and Prince of Orange. To my father the Dutchman, by smashing the forces of James II at the Boyne and, more decisively, at Aughrim on 12th July 1691, saved the country from an Irish-Catholic tyranny of popish servitude, idolatry and nameless superstition. Those battles were not events of long ago which no longer mattered. Rather, they were of decisive moment in how we lived from day to day and deserved the commemoration of daily objects, so that William's figure, seated on his prancing white charger, sword-arm raised in a gesture of advance, decorated tea-towels and plates. William's victories served to divide us for ever from those wretched people whose popish sedition would undermine the fabric of our world and who were known to hate everything Britain was and stood for. *Their* sympathies automatically lay with Britain's enemies, whoever they might be; a range of people from Hitler's Nazis, to the Kennedy tribe in America. Nor was my father in any way unusual in his opinions, though he was unusually fierce in the vehemence with which he expressed them. On the Twelfth of July each year, he would be one of tens of thousands who marched to display their common purpose and faith. And of those tens of thousands the overwhelming number were decent, god-fearing men and women.

The Twelfth of July parades, actually held on the Saturday nearest to the date in Scotland, were days of high excitement. The order of events was the same each year: first, the bus or train ride to whatever town The Walk was to be held in; then being stationed somewhere from which I could see the parade. It was a tremendous spectacle, part carnival, part mystical communion of the Elect. At the front of the parade, the solemn men in dark suits and bowler hats, one of whom carried a Bible on a purple cushion. Then came the ranks of the individual lodges, men's and women's lodges separate, all in good order, with parade marshals keeping to the side of the ranks. Each lodge had its own brightly coloured banner, mounted on heavy poles and carried by two strong men. The long tasselled ropes which could keep the banner steady in a breeze were carried by four others. And on the banners scenes from the common story; William of Orange, or a secret conventicle; or the face of some favoured hero such as Lord Edward Carson. Hour after hour the great multicoloured sails swept past.

Best of all, of course, were the bands; flute, accordion or pipe and their wonderful marching tunes, some of which, like *Lilibulero,* had taken British armies into battle for centuries. Those traditional marching tunes of Ulster must be among the most stirring and spirited airs any child could wish for: the melodiousness of *Derry's Walls,* the bravado of *The Sash* or, best of all, the sweet austerity of the pipes playing *Rowan Tree* or some of the gentler hymns as four/four marches.

After the parade, along to the park where the speeches boomed from ancient public address systems to an audience more intent on its flasks of tea and sandwiches or, for the men, bottles of beer or whisky. Here my mother or grandmother would meet up with my great-aunts and uncles, cousins and second cousins. The whole day's spectacle was an affirmation that a common history mattered and would be maintained. I knew even then that I inherited a history which defined who I was. In the villages where I grew up, we did not play with Catholics. My father's father, a soldier in the Black Watch, had helped put down a rebellion one Easter in Dublin.

In my paternal grandparents' house, things were ordered differently. Religion was more a background, a context. My grandfather was a miner, a staunch socialist and very anti-Tory. His and my granny's stories and memories centred round the struggles they had come through, especially the terrible days following the collapse of the General Strike in 1926 when the miners stayed out for many months. My granny would tell how her mother, Jane Blackley, née Sharp, would bring a basket of potatoes, eggs and ham, or how my grandfather and his brother-in-law operated an illicit mine and sold the coal to local farmers on the sly, for there were young children to be fed. My grandfather would tell how he and some village musicians persuaded a local sympathiser to part with a lorry with which they toured round Scotland to raise money for the village. My grandfather was the singer. The tour travelled up the west coast to Oban, round the far north and down through Inverness to Aberdeen and Edinburgh, finishing up in Dumfries. As the last concert was held in a field in a howling wind, my grandfather sang one of his favourite Burns songs; *O' aa the Airts the Wind can Blaw*. And both, but most often my grandmother, would speak of her brother, Nethan (Nathaniel); of his good looks, of his skill as a musician, of how he had tried several times and failed to persuade my grandfather to enlist. Here was another history, intimate and intensely alive.

It was not until my teenage years that my notions of which history was mine began to be complicated. One history teacher, more imaginative than the others, not content with facts and analyses, supplemented these by reading aloud lengthy passages from the diaries or memoirs of people who had witnessed the events we were studying. Two such passages stand out in my memory: one was of a forced march during the Crimean War; the other, an account by someone who had travelled in the west of Ireland in the years of the Great Hunger. Famine, we were told, was what happened when there was no food. However, in the years when the population of Ireland was halved through starvation, disease and emigration, we learned that there had been food; eggs and beef, grain, butter and pork, but that much of it was exported to England to pay rents. Gradually, over the years, I would piece together another family history; of those who had come to Scotland in the terrible years of the 1840s, some of whom, indeed, had even been Irish Catholics.

Later still, living in Canada, travelling in the United States and working with Americans, I came to understand that not everyone lived history in the same way; that for many Americans, history was only a bunch of dead stories. Maybe we Scots and Irish have paid a high price for our long memories, but who in Scotland or Ireland has not some attitude to the Great Hunger, or the Clearances, or just to a vague morass of names, Culloden and Robert the Bruce and Rebel Songs?

There was, too, another, more private, childhood. My favourite stories were of exotic places, of Fawcett exploring the Amazon or of Arctic whalers. And my favourite fantasies were of walking across country after country until I reached some strange place no one had ever visited. I would trace out the courses of rivers in my school atlas and imagine following them to their sources or to some foreign sea. Where and when I first heard the names 'Rhine' or 'Danube' I cannot now remember. Wherever it was, they have always had a more than casual fascination for me, and when I read

11

Patrick Leigh-Fermor's splendid books recounting his year-long walk down the Rhine and along the Danube, those childish fantasies resurfaced like long-forgotten toys rediscovered.

For anyone interested in history, 1989 was clearly a year to match 1789 or 1914 in the momentous import of events in Eastern Europe. As revolution followed revolution, I recalled Neville Chamberlain's infamous remark in the days after he sanctioned Hitler's partition of Czechoslovakia: 'A distant people of whom we know nothing.' I wanted to see something of those countries which were so much part of what Europe has been and will become, and which were yet so unknown. This book is the result of that journey.

I had for company a silver-grey, two-litre Volvo and the *Pensées* of Blaise Pascal. The latter I had been intending to read for years and, by happenstance, had come across a cheap edition in a book sale just days before setting out. When a friend asked me the car's name I answered at once – Anastasia Fyodorovna Romanova, Princess of all the Russias. Perhaps a teenage fascination for Russian history had resurfaced in my pre-journey efforts to revive a too-long-neglected language. Whatever the reason, the name stuck and Anastasia she remained.

The journey was conceived and prepared through a Scottish winter with the idea of setting out in the spring. I once knew by heart a poem by the Russian, Fyodor Tyuchev entitled *Vyesna* (Spring). It began: '*Already in the fields the snow is melting and the swollen rivers herald Spring.*' After the terrible decades of Cold War and such near approaches to Hot War as the Cuba crisis, after decades in which the whole of Eastern Europe was a remote and hostile armed camp, the sudden thaw in which all of Europe seemed caught up was more than a political event. It was a load lifted from the heart, a load we had not even known weighed us down. So it was that with high spirits I packed Baedekers and prejudices, boots and a bootload of assumptions and set out for Dover.

THE roar of Dunning Burn in its January spate fills my house. This reddish-brown turmoil of turbid waters is the run-off from the grazing lands of Middle Third, Pitmeadow and Balquhandie, gushing over the clays and old red sandstone of Dunning Glen to swirl down the ford behind my study window. From here, along with many other tributaries from the north-eastern corner of the Ochil Hills, the waters thrust into the Earn and thence, between Rhynd and Newburgh, into the slower-moving waters of the Tay to merge and circulate, ever-so-slowly, in the world sea.

Dunning. It is half past three of the afternoon and already the houses across the burn are fading into a sodden gloom. Rain gusts at the kitchen window and the outer door, its wood swollen by damp, has to be wrenched open. Outside, in my strip of garden, the shrubs are tilted north-eastwards by the storming wind and bits of tree and deadwood waltz past on the surface of the spate.

It was another kind of January, a January of sudden snow storms and hard frosts at the end of the month, when a rabble of Catholic Jacobite clansmen under the nominal control of John Erskine, Earl of Mar, came to burn the protestant villages of Dunning, Muthill, Blackford, Auchterarder and Crieff. That was in 1716. It was the 1730s before the government stumped up compensation for those whose houses had been damaged or destroyed and among them was one James Sharp, ancestor of Jane, my great-grandmother, whom I still remember being taken to visit as a child.

One man who, greatly to the relief of his family and parishoners, did not see the burning, for he died while the rebels were on their way, was the minister, William Reid. He was a fierce old Covenanter and an unrelenting opponent of the Jacobite cause. Hours before the rebels arrived his body was hurriedly wrapped in a blanket and secreted in a shallow grave. As a young man, in 1679, Reid had fought in the protestant fiasco at Bothwell Bridge when their armies were smashed by Monmouth. Fleeing the slaughter, he hid himself in Hamilton Kirk where: 'A number of other fugitives following him into the church were pursued by the dragoons, who, regardless of their cries for mercy, butchered them in the sacred place.' Reid watched the mess from his hidey-hole in the roof-space where he hid for three days.

It was at Hamilton also that, early in 1916, Nathaniel Blackley became Private Blackley 40639 in the 9th battalion, The Cameronians (Scottish Rifles), the regiment whose origins lay in standing guard over the meetings of the Covenanters. Nathaniel Blackley was named after his maternal grandfather, Nathanael Sharp, who had

13

been raised by *his* grandfather on the family farm at Tillicoultry, just west of the head of Dunning Glen. The Blackleys were a ferocious tribe of Orangemen from the County Down who had settled in Scotland in the 1860s.

Nathaniel was the favourite son, fair-haired and blue-eyed, and his sister Annie, my grandmother, kept a lock of his curls until she died. He was a gifted musician and the army used his talents as a bugler on recruiting drives. Eventually he went with his battalion to France. On his last leave before sailing he had said his goodbyes to his mother and gone out but, stopping at the gate, turned and gone back in again, leaving with her his signet ring and pocket watch. Six weeks later, on 23rd October 1916, he was killed, shot through the head by a sniper's bullet in one of the endless and inglorious messes on the river Somme. He was twenty-two.

> . . . after the War the Army Graves Service were unable to locate his grave and he is therefore commemorated by name on the Thiepval Memorial, France, on which the names of the casualties from the Cameronians appear on Pier 4, Panel D . . . This memorial is 8 kilometres north-east of Beaucourt-Hamel railway station and south of Thiepval village. It records the names of some 70,000 of the Forces of the British Commonwealth and Empire who fell in the battle in the neighbourhood and have no known grave.

From Calais to Albert, the nearest town to Thiepval, is but a two hour drive.

IT is warm for April. Somewhere distant, faint, off to my right, I can hear a cuckoo calling as he moves among the coppices and hedgerows. Springtime flatters this part of the Somme country-side, undramatic with its flat fields and scattered villages. The largest object for miles, dominating the shallow depression which is the valley of the Ancre, is the Thiepval Memorial. You approach the park down a long avenue, past lawns carefully tended and set in a girdle of trees. The massive triple-arch of dark-red brick, each leg of the arch four piers deep, each pier with its four high panels of dun-coloured marble on which the names of the dead are engraved, is, for all its height, a squat, graceless thing.

Climbing the steps through the central arch to the altar-like plinth, I see that someone has left a pot of red begonias. A wreath of artificial poppies has been held down by a brick. I place my three long-stemmed, red roses beside the begonias. There is not another soul in sight and no sound. From the plinth you look down long rows of white crosses and plain headstones on the far side of the memorial; some say *inconnu*, others 'A Soldier of the Great War'. Beyond them, beyond this enclosure, the lush countryside meanders to its low horizon.

Nathaniel's name is high up on an inner wall of one of the piers. The dead are listed by regiment, then by rank and then alphabetically – nothing disordered here. This dismal monumentalism is the apotheosis of impersonality, a confirmation rather than a denial of the mindset which led to such slaughter in the first place, though the architect intended no irony. The monument was raised by the power of the state as a piece of political theatre extravagant enough to be seen from miles and years away, as it was by my father when he passed on the Bapaume Road in the summer of 1944.

'Shambles': Latin; *scamnum*, a bench or stool, or table from which meat is sold, hence; a meat-market, a slaughter-house or, figuratively; *a place of carnage*.

On 1st July 1916 at 7.30 a.m., to the sound of exploding mines and a massive artillery barrage, British and Commonwealth forces attempted to storm these low hills around Thiepval. The dead and wounded in that one attack amounted to 59,000. Thiepval and Beaumont-Hamel were not taken until September and November respectively. Between July and November 1916 on this front there were on both sides three million men in arms, of which the dead, wounded and shell-shocked would amount to one million two hundred thousand. I left Thiepval having had enough of cemeteries. But the landscape here is a charnel-house and graveyard follows graveyard.

Only a few hundred yards to the north-west of Thiepval is the Ulster Tower, commemorating the soldiers of the 36th (Ulster) Division and across the road is the Connaught Cemetery. A little to the west lies the village of Hamel. Here are commemorated the

15

Scots of the 51st (Highland) Division who set out, pipes playing, on that morning of 1st July and who suffered high casualties. Here also are commemorated the men of the Newfoundland Regiment whose monument is a splendid bronze caribou, looking out over the trenches of *Camp Terre Neuve*. The trenches here have been left untouched, eroding away year by year. The stanchions to which the rolls of barbed wire were attached are still here, rusted now. The mud and corpses and rats have gone. That was three-quarters of a century ago when most of those who fought here were not much more than boys. On my way back to Anastasia, I catch sight of a tree-creeper and watch him flit from tree to tree, scurrying mouse-like up their trunks as though nothing else had ever happened here.

When the Battle of the Somme began, Czechoslovakia and Yugoslavia did not exist; Hungary was twice its present size and Austria was the centre of a ramshackle empire which had lasted for centuries. The Sultan, the Kaiser and the Tsar still sat on their thrones.

The world changes and the world does not change. Formal logic cannot cope with even so simple a contradiction, though we live with such conflicts as matters of course. Part of my process of becoming who I am involved rejecting some of what I had been born into. What Nathaniel was born into was perhaps a boring life in the pits. Perhaps the war offered adventure, travel, a use for his gifts. Perhaps, like so many others, he sincerely believed that it was a just war and fought for his values in righteousness. Therefore the nostalgic gloss my grandmother cast backwards upon her own childhood and on her favourite brother, cannot be separated from their histories, and our easy condemnations of slaughter miss the complicated realities. As a soldier, Nathaniel was no longer Nathaniel. He was a name, rank and number, his individuality merely an accident, irrelevant to the great machinery of a war between states, not persons. And yet it was persons who died in such numbers, without ever necessarily subscribing to the consequences of their own actions. That impersonality is the essence of war and the Thiepval Memorial attempts to disguise that fact by pretending to commemorate persons. But what it truly commemorates is the *surrender* of individuality by all those persons. The horrible irony is that it is in that very surrender that community itself is founded.

16

THE town of Albert was reduced to rubble in the First World War and rebuilt in the 1920s. Now it is a prosperous place, making its living from light industry and the visitors who come to tour the battlefields. A light cloud cover in the late afternoon had given way to a lovely, pale, evening sky as I wandered through the town to its main tourist attraction, the red-brick basilica of Nôtre-Dame de Brebières. Its two-hundred-foot-high tower is surmounted by a dome on which stands a golden Virgin holding aloft the Christ-child. In January 1915 a shell struck the base of the dome, toppling the fifteen-foot-high statue which hung horizontally above the town until 1918, becoming known as The Leaning Virgin. Postcards of the 'then and now' variety were on sale in the vestibule, showing the rubble to which the basilica had been largely reduced.

Albert has two hotels and, there being nothing in the guidebook to distinguish them, I settled on the Grand Hôtel de la Paix, sight unseen. It was not long before I was ensconced in the dining-room with a pastis and looking forward to dinner. The *patron*, M. Duthoit, was a comfortable sort of fellow with his green and blue patterned cardigan and spectacles dangling at his breast. I expected slippers but he was more spruce than that and clearly businesslike in the way he ran this family hotel. From his slight paunch he also looked as though he enjoyed his own cuisine.

French restaurants, real ones, are indefinably different from anything one finds in Britain. It shows in the lack of fuss about décor. The dining room of the Hôtel de la Paix had a red-tiled floor. The walls were wood-panelled for most of their height and the old wicker and wooden chairs were well worn. The linen was good quality, plain white. Eating here is a mundane but important matter. It is not an excuse for social display. For a small-town, one-star hotel, the menu was more ambitious than anything likely to be found in its British equivalent and included such delights as scallops and sweetbreads. I settled for the *terrine du chef* followed by *rognons d'agneau* and *pommes vapeur*. To drink, I settled on a half bottle of Passetoutgrain.

Tomorrow I shall be in Germany, France's traditional enemy and new-found friend. Before sleeping I wonder what Pascal had in mind when he wrote in the *Pensées*: 'Time heals griefs and quarrels, for we change and are no longer the same persons. Neither the offender nor the offended are any more themselves. It is like a nation which we have provoked, but meet again after two generations. They are still Frenchmen, but not the same.'

I DO not remember that as a child I played cowboys and Indians very much. Our usual game, played in the woods behind our house, was Germans v. British. The trouble was that, naturally, no one wanted to be a German. Germans, therefore, had to be selected on an 'eeney, meeney, miney mo' basis. If you did end up as a German, however, you still played to win and I can remember a kind of perverse pleasure in being determined to win, *even though* I was a German, which was something of a contradiction.

A cousin of my granny's lived only a few hundred yards from us. He had been injured in the pits many years before and supplemented his income by hunting and fishing. He was a regular provider in our house of burn trout and other delicacies. His wife, Vera, who had left Germany just before the war, was very nice. I still wondered though, how it must feel to be a German. It had to be very different.

Thirty and more years later, those underlying attitudes persist as unthinking sympathies and antipathies far below the level of articulate rationality. They require a kind of check placed upon them, in order that one should not be captured by them. Prejudice is like that. It is not rational. All too often, what follows from it is rationalisation; the justification of what we feel against all the evidence of our intelligence. A whole history has been assimilated long before conscious self-criticism is a realistic option. It cannot simply be thought away. It is part of the fabric of one's being. One is *also* that cluster of prejudices.

Germans were not, of course, the only targets of our childish hostility, nor was hostility the only bias we absorbed. School atlases in the 1950s were still coloured half in red. The Empire might have become the Commonwealth, but that was just a new name for the same thing as far as we were concerned. It proved that, in the whole world, British was best. Luckier still, out of the British *pot pourri*, Scots were definitely the best of the lot. The Empire and the superiority it evidenced, was just the way things were, entirely natural. Not that I knew any foreigners, though I recall thinking that there were two kinds. The good ones were those like the Gurkhas and Queen Salote who were part of the Empire and the baddies were nasty little creatures like the Japs or Koreans - or Germans.

As we get older and perhaps more worldly, it is sometimes awkward to admit that we ever believed such nonsense, and even more difficult to admit that not everything we imbibed was bad or wrong. Pascal knew all this very well. He wrote:

> For we must not misunderstand ourselves; we are as much automatic as intellectual; and hence it comes that the instrument by which conviction is attained is not demonstrated alone. How few things are demonstrated? Proofs only convince the mind. Custom is the source of our strongest and most believed proofs. It bends the automaton, which persuades the mind without its thinking about the matter. Who has demonstrated that there will be a tomorrow, and that we shall die? And what is more believed? It is, then, custom which persuades us of it; it is custom that makes so many men Christians; custom that makes them Turks, heathens, artisans, soldiers etc.

MUCH of that European history which came to so terrible an ending in and around the battlefields of the Somme had its beginnings in the north Rhineland town of Aachen, Charlemagne's capital, Aix-la-Chapelle; because it was here, for more than half a millenium, that the Holy Roman Empire celebrated its mysteries. Between 936 and 1531 no less than thirty-two kings and emperors were crowned in Aachen.

Driving across the flat and prosperous farmlands of Picardy and through the shabby industrial suburbs of Charleroi and Liège to the German/Belgian frontier on which Aachen sits, the first thing you notice is its novelty. Having had the misfortune to have good rail links, a large aerodrome and to be within easy reach, Aachen was a regular target for Allied bombing raids, so that much of it *is* recent. French towns, large or small, have a raffish, down-at-heel quality which shows up as a relaxed attitude to their urban fabric. Exterior plaster and paintwork, whether on public buildings or private housing, is allowed to flake and crumble. Not so in Aachen, or anywhere in the old Federal Republic where the townscapes are sprightly and well kept, the public parks devoid of litter and the shopping malls reek of prosperity. The downtown antique shops which clustered in the streets off the Marktplatz sold the bric-a-brac, not of the nineteenth but of the fifteenth and sixteenth centuries. It is less a question of efficiency or cleanliness than a refusal to let past and present blur together. Some anxiety keeps them distinct, the past properly categorised and preserved, the present carefully renewed. Whatever the cause, decay is not a feature of Federal townscapes.

Ancient Aachen was, above all, the site of an idea and the idea was *empire*. Charlemagne made it his capital because it was a defendable town in his own territory. There he built his palace and chapel, part of which survives in the present cathedral. There in 796 the Avars, nomad warriors who roamed the Pannonian plain before the Magyars came, made their submission to Frankish arms. There too came Greek envoys from Constantinople to acknowledge Charles's claim as Western Emperor. But after Charles's death, his empire dissolved in a turbulence of Frankish feud. The real founders of the Empire were the Saxon emperors, Otto the Great and his son and grandson. They married the fact of a German kingdom to the theory of Italian churchmen and the offspring survived for nearly a thousand years.

Originally, in early Republican Rome, *imperium* meant that power exercised over individuals by officers of the state and that power was specific in its limits and granted by the people. So at least ran the theory, and, for a time, it did operate that way, very much along the lines of the Athenian *polis* in its democratic phase. By the time of Pompey, the distinction between the powers granted to an *office* and the authority of the man who held that office had begun to blur. By the time of Constantine, who christianised the empire, it had ceased to exist. Power had grown absolute and derived not from the people, but from God. That concept of authority deriving from God was, above all, the claim of the bishops of Rome and, as their influence grew, it was they who nourished the idea of a unitary empire. It was the popes of Rome, those caesars of the Christian churches, who insisted on a continuity not just from Christ, but from Constantine.

They wanted one over-arching political structure which would be their temporal instrument. If they could not exercise that power themselves, or count on the eastern empire to do it for them, then they would find it where they could. For a time the eastern empire was able to maintain itself in Italy, but thereafter the popes had to look to the new Frankish power in the north for their temporal defences. Charlemagne's empire was German and tribal. That of the Ottos' was, at least in its ideology, universal and feudal. Much of the history of the Middle Ages follows from that fact, as the papacy struggled to separate the concept of the Empire from the property of any one dynasty, and the emperors strove to make of the Church an instrument of state.

For Otto the Great, crowned in Aachen in 936, Charlemagne and his capital were key elements in his effort to legitimise his ascendancy over a rabble of dukes, princelings and petty kings. He understood the value of public relations. For his coronation he did not just go to Aachen to be 'elected' king of the Franks in the old way, but dressed up in Frankish costume for the occasion. By fostering an image of himself as the inheritor of Charlemagne's empire, he did much to create that image of Charlemagne which dominated the later middle ages.

Otto's authority rested on the success of his armies, most spectacularly in 955 at the battle of the Lechfeld when he defeated the Magyar hosts who were attacking Augsburg. That defeat closed the west to the Magyars who then set about colonising the Pannonian plain and founding the state we now know as Hungary. More curiously still, by promoting the figure of Charlemagne, Otto has also been seen as contributing to the creation of the French state: 'The notion that there was such a country as France, at a time when the royal authority was very little recognised outside the narrow boundaries of the royal domain, the Île de France, was fostered by the legend of Charlemagne.'

Once Otto had consolidated his hold over Germany and secured his external frontiers, he went to Rome in 962 for a second coronation, following again in the steps of Charlemagne. His new imperial title did not change the basis of his power. It did, however, enhance his prestige and set precedents which drew German and Austrian rulers southwards for a thousand years. Otto III, his grandson, went further still in his pursuit of the imperial idea by establishing his capital in Rome itself. In the year 1000 Otto III had Charlemagne's tomb opened and removed from it the gold cross which hung round the neck of the skeleton and the marble throne on which the body had been placed. That cream-coloured stone chair can still be seen in the cathedral treasury in Aachen. It became the coronation seat of the emperors. Eventually, of course, the empire *was* captured by a dynasty, the Habsburgs, whose first emperor, Rudolf, was crowned in Aachen in 1273. But by that time there had been two centuries of strife between Empire and Papacy and the Empire no longer had any special connection to the City of Rome.

It was Voltaire who observed that the Holy Roman Empire was neither Holy, nor Roman, nor an Empire. By the eighteenth century, no one believed in it. Nevertheless, that Empire which, as Dryden said, 'is no more than power in trust', provoked a world war. What was it that so introverted a man as Ludwig Wittgenstein thought he believed in, when he volunteered to fight for the Emperor? Or was he, like so many millions of others, caught up in a swell of mindless sentiment which hardly knew what it was doing?

Having performed my duty and wandered around the coronation hall of the fourteenth century Rathaus with its dreadful nineteenth-century frescoes on the life of Charlemagne, and gazed at Charlemagne's marble throne in the Cathedral, it was time to sit in the sun for a while and eat an ice-cream. Whatever Aachen may have been in the past, it has settled down now to being a prosperous commercial town with few pretensions.

FROM Aachen to Bonn, the ancient to the modern capital, is but an hour's drive. From where I am sitting on the Rhine embankment I can see the Siebengebirge and the Drachenfels, named for the dragon which guarded the treasure-hoard of the Nibelungs. After killing it, Siegfried bathed in its blood, thereby rendering himself invulnerable. As he bathed, a sycamore leaf fell between his shoulder blades so that, like Achilles, his perfection was flawed and it was there that the treacherous Lord Hagen thrust his spear. That the *Nibelungenlied*, the Ur-epic of both Rhine and Danube, should have as its ending the annihilation of the German army at the court of King Etzel (Attila) in Hungary, sounds like the over-stretched irony of some modern tragedian.

The hills are wrapped in a shawl of pink light gradually fading into dusk. A thin moon is already hanging over the river and the swallows are feeding very high, a sign of continuing fine weather. The pollarded limes along the promenade look like irregular candelabra. At this hour it is still pleasantly warm and numbers of elegantly dressed strollers are converging on a pleasure cruiser, the *Filia Rheni*, moored just upstream. Further out in the channel the *Petite France* is heading upriver with another freight of day-trippers. Although the lights of the pleasure cruisers sparkling from the water make the river look attractive, Baedeker's advice is forthright: 'Bathing in the Rhine should be avoided at all costs.' By day it is a fast current of murky water. Though it once supported salmon and sea-trout runs, little flourishes in it now.

Bonn is usually taken to be the dividing line between the upper and lower Rhine, western Europe's longest river at 1,320 kilometres. From Bonn it heads north across the relatively flat north German plain, but southward it has to cut its way through the hard rocks of the Taunus range where narrow gorges once made the upper reaches of the river dangerous to navigate. The Rhine is one of the central facts of European geography and has always marked a boundary. It was a frontier to the north-east for the Romans who had a camp here, *Castra Bonnensia*, where they suffered a defeat at the hands of the German tribes in AD 70.

From the late thirteenth century it was the residence of the Archbishop Electors of Cologne. The Holy Roman Emperors were elected by three lay and three clerical Electors plus the King of Bohemia, a title always held by the Habsburgs after the Thirty Years War. There were no elections after 1794 when the town was occupied by French troops of the Revolutionary Army for, in 1805, under pressure from Napoleon, the emperor Francis II gave up his imperial title and became just plain old Emperor of Austria. At the Congress of Vienna in 1815, Bonn, like Aachen, was given to Prussia. In 1949 it became the capital of the Federal Republic which grew out of the amalgamation of the French, British and American zones of occupation.

Bonn is a handsome town but, far as it is from the historic centres of German power, it seems an odd choice for a capital, even allowing for the Allies' post-war policy of de-centralisation. Still, Germany has no very long history as a unitary state (less than a century) and has had three capitals since 1918 – Weimar, Berlin and Bonn. One reason why Bonn became the capital was that it was favoured by Konrad Adenauer, *der alte Fuchs* (the Old Fox), the Federal Republic's first post-war chancellor who had his political base in the North Rhineland. He had been mayor of Cologne before being expelled by the Nazis. He became mayor again after the war only to be dismissed by a British officer of the occupying forces, who found him as awkward to deal with as the Nazis had.

Adenauer was chairman of the parliamentary council which drafted the constitution and the basic law for the new state and, with the success of his party in the 1949 elections – he was a Christian Democrat – he was the obvious candidate for chancellor. After the Potsdam agreement, by which Germany lost a fifth of its territory to Poland and the Soviet Union and with the Oder-Neise line as its eastern border, eleven million refugees were expelled from Eastern Europe, principally from the Czech Sudetenland, East Prussia and the Banat in north-east Yugoslavia. When Adenauer took over domestic administration from the occupying forces in 1949, an estimated seven million of those found themselves in the new Republic. In the course of a few years Hitler had managed to undo a thousand-year-long German expansion eastwards. It was the largest movement of peoples since the tribal wanderings of the first millenium.

Adenauer's other achievement was to build up a personal relationship with Charles de Gaulle which made possible a Franco-German *rapprochement* of real depth and made the European Economic Community a reality. Now that the Federal Republic has vanished, François Mitterand's efforts to lock Germany into a system of political as well as economic interdependencies seems the only secure way to stabilise Western Europe.

Given the political will, a primitive nationalism can be generated by governments in a remarkably short space of time, certainly in less than a generation. The Thatcherite view of a loosely associated

Europe, including some of the Eastern European states, rests on a nationalistic suspicion of things European. More importantly, it fails to lock Germany into a European confederation. Many sophisticated Germans such as Günter Grass have regarded the unification process with dismay, arguing that a return to the traditional German pattern of a confederation of states would be healthier. But it is too late for that. The young research scientist with whom I chatted in a Bonn café was not worried about nationalism. His anxiety was that the cost of unification would cripple the West German economy, an anxiety I was to hear expressed on several occasions. Unfortunately, economics and nationalism are profoundly linked.

The Scottish poet Hugh MacDiarmid, who was expelled from the British Communist Party for his nationalism and from the Scottish Nationalist Party for his communism, thought that economics and nationalism could not be separated. In that he was wiser than Marx and his Eastern European successors, though the root issues go deeper than either economics or nationality. Marxism grotesquely underestimated the power of nationalism, as it did that of religion. But that is because both those phenomena address human problems of identity and motivation at an individual level in a way that Marxism cannot. Marxism has no philosophy of the individual. Marx never interested himself in how individuals arrive at their sense of themselves or in what motivates them to behave well or badly. Marxism has no psychology of experience, an omission which warped its radicalism from the outset.

As Federal capital Bonn is naturally a political town. In warm afternoon sunshine I spent a pleasing hour wandering the narrow *Gassen* (lanes) round the Münsterplatz. At one end of the Square, presided over by the statue of Beethoven, a group of Vietnamese were staging an anti-communist demonstration complete with public address system. They waved their banners, sang songs, made speeches and shouted slogans in unison, mostly in Vietnamese. A few yards away, a group of police motorcyclists in their olive-green leathers lounged by their bikes and chatted with friends. On the other side of the Square, attracting a much larger crowd, a fire-eater was doing his thing watched by amazed children as he threw his head back and spewed flame a couple of yards into the air. One little girl dropped her ice-cream in the excitement of it all and began to howl like a banshee. It was the run-up period to a series of local elections, which were being widely viewed as a test of chancellor Kohl's handling of the unification issue. But the only posters I could see disfiguring the town were those of the ecology party.

By far the most attractive part of the town was the area between the university and the Rhine embankment with its splendidly kept lawns and gardens and a huge magnolia tree in full bloom, a riot of purple-tinged blossoms. But it is the university itself which gives the scene its elegance. A three-storeyed neo-classical frontage of immense length, the ground level is in grey stone, the upper storeys in pale ochre. The great sweep of lawn and stone, is not overwhelming, imposing though it is, being softened by paths and trees, the former much frequented by courting couples and idling students.

When Bonn's old-town fortifications were dismantled in 1717, the stone was used to build a new palace for the Elector, Joseph Clemens. When the electors became redundant the buildings were turned into a university. It was in the Elector's private chapel here that Beethoven, a native of Bonn, gave his first public performance.

It was here too that the young Friedrich Nietzsche came to study philology and theology in 1864, though he quickly abandoned the latter. Nietzsche is hardly read now as a serious philosopher and his influence on writers and artists was always greater than on philosophers. Sadly, it was not confined to writers and artists, for though it may be unfair to blame Nietzsche for his appropriation by Nazi ideologues, there is no question but that his doctrine of the superman and his apparent anti-semitism provided them with fertile soil. There is, in any case, a tradition of romantic nationalism among German philosophers extending long before Nietzsche. Its seeds can be found in Hegel's glorification of the Prussian State, but its chief exponent was Johann Fichte. Hugh Seton-Watson has some perceptive things to say about it:

After the defeat of the German Revolution of 1848 German Nationalism lost much of its original liberalism. Worship of State and Race . . . began to predominate over the principle of Liberty, taken by the Germans from the French Revolution . . . The Austro-German bourgeoisie of Vienna and Bohemia turned its back on liberalism, and plunged into an orgy of intolerant romantic nationalism. Liberalism was left more and more to the Jews who, as a socially inferior group, were naturally more inclined to see the value of individual liberty and equality than the Germans, intoxicated since the victory of 1870 (over France) by a sense of the strength of the German people . . . *(Eastern Europe Between the Wars).*

Nietzsche's achievement is rather to have prefigured so much of twentieth-century thought. He is a precursor of both existentialism and psychoanalysis even if both have turned out to be disappointing by comparison with the hopes once placed in them. I found it difficult to associate the storms of either Beethoven or Nietzsche with this douce façade and pleasant park.

THE following morning dawned bright and warm and, being weary of towns, I settled on driving some way down the Rhine and then exploring one of the country roads. Following the left bank of the river, you are rarely out of sight of the water. First, you follow the Adenauer Allee out of Bonn through the suburb of Bad Godesberg where Neville Chamberlain came for his chats with Herr Hitler in the days before Munich. Now it is largely the diplomatic quarter of Bonn with a mixture of new office buildings and elegant old villas. By half past seven the sun was just surfacing above the silhouette of the mist-shrouded Siebengebirge, looking like a vast behemoth shouldering its way up into the light. The scene was sufficiently oriental that one could easily imagine some Hokusai image of a dragon rising into the skies above the Drachenfels.

The riverside landscapes were startlingly beautiful, a riot of castles, châteaux and towers perched on any available rock high above the wooded slopes. Many of the trees, chestnuts, thorns, an occasional lilac, were already in blossom and the river glittered in the sunlight. Around Remagen you cross from Westphalia into the Pfalz, the old Palatinate, so much fought over in the Thirty Years War.

At Koblenz the Mosel enters the Rhine – wine country –

and, wherever possible, the hillsides have been terraced. The soil between the long rows of vines is kept weed-free, so this early in the year the hills look rather bare. It is also fruit-growing country and the vineyards are interspersed with orchards of apple, plum and pear. The little towns through which the road runs may once have been important, but are now picturesque backwaters. Boppard, for example, was a royal residence of the Merovingian Franks and later became a Free Imperial City. Now it is a pretty village, much frequented by tourists. After the narrows at St Goar and the infamous Lorelei, the river opens out again and begins to look a little cleaner, as though it might even, once upon a time, have been blue. Pausing long enough at Bingen to have a coffee and look at maps, I decide it is time to abandon the Rhine for a while and cut up the valley of the river Nahe towards Idar-Oberstein and the Palatinate Forest.

A few miles outside Idar I found a meadow by the side of the Nahe where I could picnic. Lunch was a collation of local salami, black olives, spring onions and dark soft rye-bread. On the opposite bank, not much more than a stream at this point, the hillside was thick with scrub hazel and thorn. Further over, in the dandelion-dotted meadow, a man and a boy were kicking a football through the foot-high grass while two women laid out a picnic lunch. The only other sound to be heard was the chirping of birds. Dunning and its January tempests seemed a world away.

The smallest road I could find on my not-very-good road map headed south-east from Idar towards Kaiserslautern, through the hill country of the Bergland. Near Wolfstein the roads run along a valley floor, the hills on either side rising to above 1,000 feet. It is a rich dairy-farming district of lush pastures and scattered woodland. Just outside Wolfstein I found an attractive-looking Gasthof at the tiny settlement of Reckweilerhof which is no more really than two large farm steadings, one of which has been turned into a guesthouse. The steadings had been built three sides of a square, with the fourth side open to the road. They were big, comfortable-looking farm buildings, not much different from what one might find in parts of Perthshire, except that the upper floor had a roofed balcony running along one side. That the farm opposite was still in use was obvious from the great mound of steaming manure in the middle of the courtyard. For thirty-eight marks (about £12) I had a large, modern double room, pleasantly furnished.

As the day began to cool in the later afternoon, I walked up the hill road behind Reckweilerhof through twelve hundred feet of gently sloping sward. The meadows were scattered with wild flowers some of which I did not recognise. There were certainly forget-me-nots, violets, white wood anemones, huge numbers of dandelions and some buttercups. At a muddy little pond halfway up the hill swallows were dive-bombing its insect life and three brown pigs browsed at the further end of the meadow. High overhead, a buzzard circled lazily on a column of warm air and on the roadway a butterfly with big white-ringed, russet-coloured eyes staring from its black wingtips, opened and closed its wings. I had certainly found the rural setting I had been hankering after.

A couple of miles on, just over the rounded summit, lay the village of Einöllen, a settlement of two or three hundred souls. The village was built on a fairly steep hillside and on a terrace which functioned as the village square a party was getting under way with a barbecue and a band consisting of sound-system, drums, electric guitar, bass guitar and electric keyboard. Crates of beer were stacked ready for consumption. The tunes were in a slow waltz time but played with that characteristic thump which accentuates the first beat of the bar so strongly as to obliterate everything else, reducing any melodic line to a tribal dance. In the north-east of Scotland it would be described as 'playing wi' a guid dunt'. It looked as though it would be a good party.

Some of the houses had a curious cruciform shape, with mottoes carved into the lintels, usually invoking God's blessing. Since all of them were built in traditional style, it was difficult to tell which were old and which new. The deep-sand colour of the plasterwork, the dark-red tiled roofs with the little balconies and shuttered windows looked like the kind of house one might be content to live in. A few new houses were under construction, using breeze-blocks rather than the traditional brick. But their complete conformity to traditional styles gave the village a coherence one would rarely find in Britain and never where much new building was involved.

Back at Reckweilerhof in time for dinner, an old man was leaving the restaurant with a couple who were probably his son and daughter-in-law. He beamed widely as he was helped down the steps and said to me: 'O, gib's nichts mehr' (Don't give us any more). He had clearly had a splendid day out.

I sat in the evening twilight with a glass of straw-coloured wine in its traditional glass of heavy amber stem and base. The glass must have held nearly half a pint and I thought I too had had a splendid day out.

S INCE I was in the Palatinate, I spent the evening with C.V. Wedgewood's great account of the Thirty Years War. That struggle shaped Germany for the subsequent two centuries and it also determined much of the shape of Europe prior to the First World War. The Palatinate was a major player in the war which was both political and religious with alignments changing as events developed. It is a difficult tale to tell simply. After the early years of the Reformation, a settlement between the Lutherans and Catholics had been arrived at in Augsburg in 1555. The gist of it was summed up in the formula *cuius regio, eius religio* which meant that each king or prince had the right to choose the religion of his subjects. A decade later, however, Calvinism appeared on the scene to make an already complicated matter more so. The Calvinists detested the Lutherans almost as much as they did the Catholics but, as Wedgewood has observed: 'The fundamental issue was between revealed and rationalised belief.'

The Counter-Reformation really began with the formation of the last great 'military' order of the Catholic Church, the Society of Jesus, in 1534. Its leading European supporters were the Spanish and Austrian Habsburgs. So if the Protestant camp was divided between Calvinist and Lutheran, the Catholic Camp was divided between the Habsburgs and all those who opposed the ambitions of that dynasty, a group which included the 'Most Christian Majesty' of France, the popes of Rome, the Protestant powers such as the Dutch, English, Bohemians and Swedes and assorted Protestant princes of Germany concerned to preserve the 'German Liberties'. It is worth recalling that there were some three hundred autonomous legislative powers in what we now call Germany in the years during which the war took place, 1618-1648.

The Habsburg Ferdinand of Styria became King of Bohemia, by election, in 1617. Of all the Habsburgs, he was perhaps the least attractive of that long line. Educated by the Jesuits, he was a fanatical bigot, determined to crush heresy wherever he could. The immediate trouble began in Prague. When the Bohemians realised the mistake they had made in electing Ferdinand, they deposed him and elected in his place the Palatine Elector, Frederick V, a weak if romantic figure. From his father he had inherited the leadership of that association of Protestant princes known as the Party of the German Liberties. Their aim was to keep the Catholic Habsburgs from swallowing them up. Frederick and his queen, Elizabeth, daughter of James VI and I, held court in Prague for a brief season as The Winter King and Queen. Through his mother, a daughter of William the Silent, Frederick was also a prince of the House of Orange.

At the battle of The White Hill, near Prague, Frederick's forces were utterly crushed. That defeat effectively extinguished the independence of the Bohemian kingdom which did not find expression again until 1918 in the new state of Czechoslovakia. Ferdinand was ruthless in victory and made the Bohemian kingship hereditary in the House of Habsburg. Frederick had to flee and the Palatinate was over-run by Spanish armies and the forces of the Catholic League headed by Maximilian I of Bavaria who coveted the Electoral dignity and to whom it was awarded in 1623.

Too late, those who should have been Frederick's allies realised their mistake in letting him be crushed. Thereafter, and for more than a generation, Germany was the stage on which the rival powers played out their conflicts. Armies from Sweden and Spain, France, the Netherlands and from as far away as Transylvania contended for superiority. The results were catastrophic. The German economy, already in difficulties before the war, was ruined. Plague followed the armies like a faithful dog. It is estimated that about a third of the population of Germany perished in the struggle. The countryside lay half-deserted and stricken by famine.

As in the period following the Black Death in the fourteenth century, the acute shortage of labour led to a tightening of feudal restrictions on the peasantry. Together with the wreck of the economy, it produced a chasm between the aristocratic/military caste and a peasantry bereft of any opportunity for social mobility through a bourgeoisie. The militarism and caste rigidity which has been the bane of Germany in Europe, has its roots in the Thirty Years War. Thereafter, the divisions between north and south Germany also became fixed and the balance of influence

31

in Germany began to shift away from Austria and towards the rising power in the north, Brandenburg-Prussia, under whose aegis Germany was eventually united.

Ironically, it was the last great European conflict in which religion played a dominant role. Thereafter, religion became increasingly impotent to sway political history. As Wedgewood concludes: 'The war solved no problem. Its effects, both immediate and indirect, were either negative or disastrous. Morally subversive, economically destructive, socially degrading, confused in its causes, devious in its course, futile in its result, it is the outstanding example in European history of meaningless conflict.'

DRIVING in the early morning sunshine along quiet country roads through the Palatinate Forest, was a fine start to the day. Most of the villages, often with charming names like Schwanheim (swan-home) or Petersberg, looked more or less intact. Many of the houses were eighteenth century or earlier with steeply sloping red-tiled roofs and half-timbered gables painted white or pale green. At Karlsruhe, the Rhine had finally turned blue and the river here is the boundary between the Palatinate and Baden-Württemberg. Having decided to press on southwards and finish the day somewhere in the region of Freiburg, I joined the autobahn at Karlsruhe. Driving on German motorways can require strong nerves and does not leave much attention for observing the countryside. By mid-afternoon I was almost at Freiburg and left the motorway to look for a village in which to stay, preferably near the Rhine. I soon found myself at the Gasthof Löwen in the little village of Sasbach.

Sasbach is really no more than a scatter of houses, a couple of shops, a garage and a church set down in the middle of vineyards and orchards. From it, one road crosses the Rhine into France and Colmar, the other takes you to Breisach and Freiburg. It is a pretty village. The houses are pink or yellow with white sills and dark shutters. Even prettier was the petite brunette of about seventeen who showed me to my room. Her name was Annette and she seemed to do all the serving and running up and down while her rather dour and unhealthy-looking mother issued the orders. Father looked after the bar. Annette was studying English at school but was too shy to try using it. Her parents spoke only German. I asked whether they did not find it inconvenient, living so near the French border, not to speak French, but they said not. There seems to be a profound antipathy between the French and Germans about learning each other's language. They would rather converse in English.

The Gasthof Löwen was spotlessly clean and the Gute Frau obviously intended, by her acerbic tone and more acerbic expression, that it would be kept that way. Situated on a corner opposite the church, one could survey much of Sasbach from its little courtyard where three tables had been set out under three chestnut trees. The trees, two white and one pink, were an extravaganza of blossom which floated down onto the chequered tablecloths. Having refreshed myself with a glass of one of the excellent local wines and a vision of two large ladies at the adjoining table munching their way through what looked like several pounds of ice-cream, I decided it would be fun to walk to France. Half a mile along the road, however, I was diverted by a nature-trail which wound up the side of a hill and promised a fine view. From the summit one looked beyond Colmar to the hills of the Vosges and east to the hills of the Black Forest. But what one chiefly saw was a landscape patterned by the long lines of vine running up to the wooded hilltops, a supremely domesticated landscape.

This bounty was reflected in the Gasthof Löwen's wine list on which there were eleven local wines. I accompanied the asparagus I had for dinner (over-cooked) with a couple of glasses of the Sasbacher Scheibenbuck Müller Thurgau (trocken). Despite its name, the wine was easy to drink, fruity and a greeny-yellow colour and served in a traditional long-stemmed wide glass. The 'trocken' part is just 'dry'. Müller-Thurgau is the grape variety, an early ripening and highly flavoured variety, much favoured along the Upper Rhine. For 'Scheibenbuck' I have not a clue, though it is probably the name of the vintner. Scheibe is a wheel or disc and bücken is the transitive verb for 'to bend' so I would like to think it meant 'wheel-buckler' though I greatly doubt it. I revised my estimate of the Mother that evening when an elderly man arrived, one of whose arms was in a sling. She cut up his dinner for him in a charming, solicitous way. The bar was well patronised by the locals. Mostly, they drank beer, so much of it that one old man stumbled out into the night entirely on automatic pilot and a middle-aged, tired-looking woman with a wooden leg lapsed into a coma. On one wall hung a large framed text in black-letter Gothic. It read:

A History of Wine	*Lebenslauf des Weiners*
From the grape into the tun	*Aus der Traube in die Tonne*
From the tun into the barrel	*Aus der Tonne dann ins Faß*
From the barrel then, o joy,	*Aus dem Fasse dann o Wonne*
into the bottle and the glass.	*In die Flasche und ins Glas.*
From the glass into the throat,	*Aus dem Glase in die Kehle,*
down the gullet into the gut	*In den Magen in den Schlund,*
and then as blood into the soul	*Und als Blut dann in die Seele,*
and as speech then to the mouth.	*Und als Wort dann in den Mund.*

Village communities anywhere are notoriously conservative, so when two young cyclists wandered in to the Gasthof Löwen with shoulder-length hair and matching headbands, they received some doubtful glances from the table where five farm-workers sat steadily drinking their way through the evening. Their long, slurred vowels rendered their German almost incomprehensible to me, though it was impossible not to listen in as they argued more loudly and grinned more broadly at each other's jokes as the beer did its work. I cannot resist quoting C.V. Wedgewood on German drinking habits: 'The Landgrave of Hesse founded a Temperance society but its first president died of drink; Lewis of Württemberg, surnamed the Pious, drank two challengers into stupor and, being himself still sober, had them sent home in a cart with a pig. The vice ran through all classes of society . . ..'

Later in the evening when the place had quietened a little and the cyclists had eaten, I invited them to join me for a glass of wine. They were clearly impecunious and I was curious. The elder of the two, Kurt, was in his late twenties and his companion, Wolfgang, was perhaps twenty-three. With their youthful good looks and bronzed faces they were an attractive couple. It emerged, they were from a small town in the former German Democratic Republic near the Polish border. It was their first time in 'the West' and they intended to cycle on into France and thence home via Belgium, the Netherlands and North Germany. Kurt was a physicist. He had worked for a year in the Ukraine and said he liked the people there more than those he had met in the West – they were more open and friendly. Both were scathing about the failures of state socialism in the DDR which they referred to as 'the Russian system'. Ultimately, they said, it broke down because it simply could not deliver the goods. They were not, however, impressed by what they found to be the 'superfluous materialism' of the Federal Republic which they said was 'rather stupid'.

Kurt and Wolfgang's main worry was that large-scale unemployment among people not accustomed to a winners-and-losers system, which capitalism is, would create lasting resentments with dire social consequences. When Kurt had finished his training as a physicist, there had been sixteen other graduates on his course. But there had been eighteen jobs on offer. While that might also be true in Britain for people with such sought-after qualifications as physics, Kurt pointed out that that was the norm in East Germany. What he found difficult to accept was the size of the gap between winners and losers in a system in which inheritance could automatically make one a winner.

Corruption in the DDR was, they said, rampant. The entire system depended on 'arrangements' and favours if you wanted to get hold of any particular commodity. The corruption went unchecked because the system could not afford to acknowledge the extent of its own inefficiencies and failures. The other cyclist, Wolfgang, taught Russian and spoke good English. His enthusiasm was to visit Ireland and he had read whatever he could get hold of by Irish writers, but especially by Flann O'Brien. His view of Ireland, a highly romanticised one, had been initiated by his reading of Heinrich Böll's *Irisches Tagebuch* which, coincidentally, I had just read as a way of getting into German again after two decades of neglect. It was late by the time we had finished chatting and they cycled off to find somewhere to pitch their tent. They were an intelligent and charming pair. I hoped they were not to be disappointed by the rest of their tour and wondered whether that residue of egalitarianism which their culture had instilled in them, for all its dreadfulness, might not in time lead them to question whether unification was wholly to their advantage.

ONE of the great advantages of villages over cities for chronic insomniacs, such as I am, is that late at night there is nothing to do in a village except read. Sasbach was no exception and I made good progress with Pascal's *Pensées*. Perhaps almost by definition, travel, like philosophy, is for those who find themselves in some sense displaced. The cult word would be 'alienated'. Perhaps some component of Pascal's restless questioning was due to his displacement through recurrent ill-health, but what makes his questionings still worth reading, is that they confront the foundations of our existence and that despite the fact that he is sometimes seen merely as a Catholic apologist.

Like Heidegger, he understands that the root of the problem is not that we are born black or Jewish or rich or blind, but that we are born at all and much of his best writing deals with that most fundamental of displacements. His response is to try to see clearly what we are in the scale of things:

> Man is but a reed, the most feeble thing in nature; but he is a thinking reed. The entire universe need not arm itself to crush him. A vapour, a drop of water suffices to kill him. But, if the universe were to crush him, man would still be more noble than that which killed him, because he knows that he dies and the advantage which the universe has over him; the universe knows nothing of this.
>
> All our dignity consists, then, in thought. By it we must elevate ourselves, and not by space and time which we cannot fill. Let us endeavour, then, to think well; this is the principle of morality.

And there is all the critique we need of the notion of empire.

By 'thought', however, Pascal does not mean that somewhat shallow notion of Reason which became fashionable in the eighteenth century and which has become fashionable again in the twentieth in the guise of formal logic. Rather, he means the workings of a live intelligence which draws on experience and intuition as much as on a more narrowly conceived logic. The twentieth century has become notorious for its rejections of rationality, but that is not a case, as with Pascal, of pushing thought to its limit and finding it wanting. More often, it is a case of a rejection of serious thought for the sake of some prejudice or desire. The pernicious notion that we can believe whatever we feel like believing may not be unique to the twentieth century but it has certainly found great popularity in it.

One other respect in which Pascal is a modern thinker is in his view, which he shared with the Jansenists, that language had proven too strong for mystery, so that theology had become merely a branch of rhetoric. That scepticism about language – especially when it is divorced from the purposes of daily life – has become a hallmark of much contemporary thought. Philosophy, if it is anything, is a linguistic activity which teaches us to be critical about linguistic categories. There is a Dunning story of the Canadian who asked where Dunning was and was told that it was next to Forteviot, a village only a tenth the size of Dunning. What we answer to 'what am I', categories like *Scot* or *Jew* or *Protestant* are vague by comparison with *Dunningite* or *excellent-maker-of-baskets* or *enthusiast-for-books-about Ireland*. Pascal's insistence that rigorous, self-searching thought is the basis of morality needs as much hammering home now as it did three centuries ago.

He cannot have been an easy man and had, at least, a ferociously sober intelligence. Maybe at the end of our enquiry we shall decide that no philosophical sense can be made of the world – and the world does not seem to be primarily linguistic. But, Pascal tells us, we need to make the effort: 'Imagination cannot make fools wise, but she can make them happy, to the envy of reason which can only make its friends miserable.'

T HE war memorial in Dunning, as in most Scottish villages, occupies a conspicuous place. Erected in 1919, it has an addendum for those who died in the Second World War. In Albert, the memorial was large and conspicuous, draped with the *tricouleur*. In the little churchyard in Sasbach, by contrast, two inconspicuous marble tablets are set into a wall. They list the names of those killed in Hitler's war. Below the list of names is the legend: *Unser Opfer/Eure Verpflichtung/Frieden*. (Our sacrifice is your duty to peace.)

Though there is nothing to commemorate the fact, one of Europe's greatest soldiers died in Sasbach; the Vicomte de Turenne, marshal of France, in 1675. A cousin of Frederick, the Elector Palatine, he was a physically feeble young man who by dint of self-discipline transformed himself into a vigorous soldier. In 1630 he entered the service of Richelieu, despite the difference in their religious convictions. In 1643 he was made a marshal of France and his first command with that rank required him to reorganise the army of Weimar which had been smashed at the battle of Tüttlingen. That done, he crossed the Rhine at Breisach and in four extraordinary campaigns brought an end to the Thirty Years War. The most important engagement of that first campaign was the fiercely contested battle at Freiburg against Bavarian forces. Louis XIV offered to revive the office of Constable of France for him if he would become a Catholic but he declined the offer (1661). In 1668, however, persuaded by Bossuet, he did join the Catholic church. In the summer of 1675, in the course of Louis XIV's Dutch War, he found himself up against the great imperial general Montecucculi, who in the previous year had outmanoeuvred Turenne to capture Bonn. This time Turenne forced him to battle at Sasbach but was struck by one of the first shots fired. He was buried with the kings of France until Napoleon had the remains removed to the *Invalides* in 1800. Napoleon claimed that Turenne had 'grown bolder as he grew older'; not a bad epitaph.

Dunning and Sasbach, two inconspicuous villages which happenstance has made part of my experience. Neither of the least strategic value and yet, wherever you go in Europe, there is no escape from the fact that every atom of the continent has played some part in an interminable saga of warfare and violence. Turenne's death in Sasbach is, for me, a fact of negligible emotional gravity. More touching was the sad list of names in Sasbach churchyard, each of them representing a large loss in a small community. What we do not know passionately, offers us no resistance, we pass through it as through air.

F ROM Sasbach my next target was the Danube, a drive that took me through the Black Forest. The first part was splendid, since on the west side the Forest rises steeply to about eight hundred metres before the high plateau slopes gradually down to the Danube basin. Climbing the steep mountain roads round hairpin bends was quite dramatic and more than once I had glimpses of distant eagles. In striking contrast to the Scottish hills which are often exposed rock and almost infertile at higher altitudes, the Black Forest plateau is prime cattle country with lush pasturage. Many of the pastures looked as though dandelions were being grown commercially, for they formed carpets of unbroken yellow.

The source of the Danube has been the subject of vigorous debate and in his *Danube*, Claudio Magris devotes several droll pages to the matter. I am content with the orthodox view that the spring which flows into the Brigach in the Schlosspark at Donaueschingen, and which shortly thereafter is joined by the Breg, constitutes the source of the greatest of European rivers, all 2,840 kilometres of it. The Danube has a different name in every country through which it flows: in Germany it is the Donau, in Slovakia, Dunaj, when it reaches Budapest it becomes the Duna, at Belgrade it is the Dunav and in Romania it is the Dunărea. Only the Volga is longer, though less voluminous. Like the Rhine it also marked a boundary for the Romans; beyond it – unknowable nomads!

As a route into Europe the Danube valley has been a funnel for migrating peoples since before history. Celts, Goths, Visigoths, Huns, Avars, Magyars, Cumans, Pechenegs, Tatars, Mongols, Turks have all had to take or occupy its key fortresses; hence the importance of Belgrade, of Budapest, even of Vienna, for that gap between the Northern Carpathians and the Eastern Alps which lies between Vienna and Bratislava has to be traversed to gain access to the German plain.

The Schlosspark at Donaueschingen was laid out for the Princes of Fürstenberg in the eighteenth century. In the nineteenth the little stream which, when it joins the Brigach in the palace grounds becomes the Danube, was channelled underground. However, an elaborate Baroque-style stone basin has been constructed, seven or eight yards in diameter, through which the stream flows. A couple of hundred yards downstream it gushes out below a ceremonial arch into the Brigach. Here one can run one's hands through the limpid water, at one moment in the Brigach and at the next in the Danube.

The handsome park adjoining the palace was almost empty of people but two screaming peacocks on a little island provided company enough. As I walked round the lake, a flotilla of ducks paddled furiously after me, hoping to be fed, while fieldfares fluttered about on the lawns. Until now the greeting I most often heard had been *G'Tag* or *Morgen*. Here it began to be replaced by the South German *Grüss Gott*.

T HE rest of the day was less pleasing. Stopping for lunch near Messkirch, *en route* for Ulm, I discovered that my three days' neglect of the groceries in the car boot, together with the intense heat, had reduced some of them to a suppurating, soggy mess. Having gingerly discarded over a hedge bits of rotted fruit and suspect cheese, I lunched on olives and mineral water in the shade of a great oak wood. Thereafter, someone had decided to make it well-nigh impossible to get to Ulm from Messkirch and had constructed an obstacle course of road-works, diversions, traffic jams and misplaced signposts which did my temper no good at all in the sweltering heat. Arriving, triumphant, in Ulm in the late afternoon, I had within half an hour found the worst hotel I had been in in years, with the rudest staff and a parking ticket to boot. Deciding to cut my losses, I fled Ulm and promptly got lost in one of its industrial suburbs. By now it was after six o'clock and time to find somewhere to stay. A few miles outside Ulm in the little town of Rammingen I got the last available room in the Landgasthof *Adler* (Eagle).

Rammingen, near Langenau, lies just over the Baden-Württemberg border in Bavaria and the *Adler*, run by an Italian family, was decked out in full Bavarian kitsch. The rooms were 'done' in Loden-green wood, ornamented with floral motifs. This extended to the headboards of the bed, the ashtray, the mirror-frame and anything else with a paintable surface, including the milk-churns and cartwheels which littered the hallway. Nevertheless, it was a relief to have found anywhere, since the *Adler* was my fifth attempt since Ulm. Having changed from sweat-sodden clothes, I found that, as the hotel had been taken over for the evening by a wedding party, I and an English couple had a dining-room to ourselves. After a reasonable dinner: watercress soup, steak with a peppercorn sauce, a shared bottle of Barolo and insipid conversation, I excused myself and sank into oblivion for ten hours.

INGOLSTADT was having a kind of festival, a *Projectwoche*, entitled *Eine Welt für Alle* (One World for All). It was, naturally, heavy with lectures and discussion groups but there was also a series of film shows and plays as well as street theatre, concerts and exhibitions. It was very much a local affair with the town's voluntary groups playing the largest part in the proceedings. Although the town centre is quite compact, Ingolstadt has extensive suburbs and a population of ninety thousand. Those suburbs house most of the industry, which is largely oil-refining and motor-car manufacture. Along at the High School where the films were being shown, Charlie Chaplin was starring with Paulette Goddard in *The Great Dictator* (1940) and at the Statdtheater George Tabori's *Mein Kampf* was playing in the evenings while, during the day, there was a week-long symposium entitled *Mein Kampf – Theatre after Auschwitz*.

The downtown area was a strange mixture of the very modern and the very old, like so many German towns where post-war reconstruction saved what it could, keeping to the old street patterns. A row of eighteenth-century baroque merchants' houses was interrupted half-way along by a steel and concrete structure. But much of the older Ingolstadt has survived, from the medieval town gates to the nineteenth-century Rathaus.

Having found a comfortable Gasthof in the suburb of Spitalhof,

I passed a few hours wandering the old town. A street market in the Rathausplatz selling everything from pottery to radios was too busy for comfort. Another market on the main shopping street, the Ludwigstrasse, was equally busy and there a number of the stalls were manned by Turks selling cheap jeans or asparagus or pots and kettles. On one corner a Turkish woman squatted with her child, hand extended in the age-old gesture of the beggar. Amid this busy prosperity it was curiously incongruous, unlike in Tunis or Cairo. At the eastern end of the Ludwigstrasse the street opened out into a small square below the towering walls of the Herzogschloss, a massive fortification dating from the fifteenth century and set back only a few yards from the Danube. Ingolstadt was for some centuries the principal seat of the Bavarian dukes when Munich was not much more than a village.

A platform had been raised in the square and, backed by a huge sound-system, half-a-dozen young people were giving a very energetic display of disco-dancing. Standing behind the platform was a group of bandsmen in traditional Bavarian costume, green cord breeches with white stockings and black shoes, white shirt and green cut-away waistcoat with red trim completed by green Loden jacket and soft hat.

The fortress, begun in 1418, is now the Bavarian military museum and its courtyard houses ten huge cannon and several smaller ones. The largest of them have lion mouths and a lion face on the base of the barrel; these were cast in 1599 in Munich for Duke Maximilian I. Each of them weighs 7,225 lbs. Even now, these black monstrosities look full of menace. As I was examining the cannon, the bandsmen began to play some Bavarian tune in a slow, swinging waltz time, all drums and brass and oompahing sentiment.

The main tower of the fortress is nine storeys high and even today looks forbidding. That and the enormous city walls – to judge by the surviving gates – made the town well-nigh impregnable and, indeed, it withstood several sieges. The most famous occurred in 1632 when the armies of Gustavus Adolphus besieged the forces of the dying Tilly. King Gustavus displayed his usual foolhardy courage and had a horse shot from under him. It was in his camp here that he was approached by a French envoy on behalf of Duke Maximilian of Bavaria, the same Maximilian who had been given the Palatine Electorate in 1623, with a view to saving his lands from the depredations of Gustavus. The envoy pleaded that there was much to be said for the Duke, to which Gustavus replied that there was much to be said for lice by those who cared for them.

Tilly and Gustavus had crossed swords several times, generally to Tilly's disadvantage. If Turenne and Gustavus were the leading soldiers on the Protestant side, then Tilly and Wallenstein were the leading figures in the armies of Ferdinand, who had himself been educated by the Jesuits at Ingolstadt. It was Tilly who crushed the Bohemians at the White Mountain and who established a terrible reputation for ferocity by his sack of Magdeburg. Out of thirty thousand inhabitants, only about five thousand survived and the city was left a burning wreck. Thereafter, whenever Ferdinand's armies asked for quarter, they were likely to receive 'Magdeburg quarter'. Now, aged seventy-three, he was dying of his wounds. Gustavus did not wait to reduce Ingolstadt but rode off to meet his own death at Lützen.

Back in the Rathausplatz a seven-piece jazz band of students dressed up in 1920s' costume was keeping a large crowd entertained. The top half of the square had been turned into a huge outdoor café with trestle tables. Vast quantities of beer and food were being consumed. It was still busy at eight in the evening. Street-stalls selling hamburgers and sausages were doing good business.

Food does seem to be a German, especially a South German (and Austrian) obsession. The food in the Gasthof Widman where I was staying was remarkable. The restaurant, pleasantly situated by a patio, looked out across farmland. It was plainly furnished with wood-panelling. The only oddity, from a Scottish point of view, being the large crucifix which decorated one wall. The table linen was fashionably pink, but the large octagonal black plates displayed the food wonderfully well and much attention had been given to presentation. Each meal began with a warm, two-inch, wholemeal roll and a little dish of Griebenschmaltz, a browned, salted pork-dripping. One thing I did appreciate in almost all the French and German restaurants I ate in, was the happy absence of Musak. For a first course at dinner I ordered a mixed starter, not sure what I would get. What turned up both looked and tasted extraordinary. The plate measured about twelve inches in diameter. Beautifully displayed on it were two twists of marinated salmon, sprigs of red and green lettuce and watercress, slices of passion fruit, two slices of filet of hare, a sprig of broccoli, two crumbed and fried mushrooms in a pale-gold sauce which I guessed to be pan-juices, reduced and bodied out with cream. A rosette of tomato garnished a slice of green and pink asparagus and smoked-salmon terrine topped with a teaspoonful of dill mayonnaise and a tiny crescent of puff pastry. Accompanied by an excellent dry Franconian wine, it was a delight to eat and very clever in its balance of colour, flavour and texture, something I do not always associate with German cuisine. For an unpretentious suburban Gasthof it was all rather a surprise. It was very much a family restaurant with children, teenagers and grandparents all eating together and was clearly somewhere to which the locals repaired for a weekend dinner. As I finished my meal an entire flotilla of portly Bavarians waddled out, having consumed vast quantities of beer with their enormous meal. I retired to the patio and listened to a blackbird. With no hills to diminish it, the sky was a great bowl of graduated blues and greens from the palest turquoise to deep indigo.

In two days' time (7th May), it would be the forty-fifth anniversary of the final German surrender in the Second World War though the cease-fire was not to take effect until midnight on 8th May. With the unification process underway (it happened at midnight on 2nd October, 1990), the anniversary of the European war's end had special significance in Germany. Back in my room I watched a devastatingly well-made history of European Jews from 1933-1945. It took as its title the poem by Paul Celan, *Death Comes as a Master from Germany*. A good deal of the historical footage I had already seen over the years and some of it, such as the dreadful footage of the Warsaw Ghetto, was only too familiar.

I suspect that for many young Germans it might be pretty meaningless, as it would be for their British or French contemporaries, who simply want to get on with their lives without having to attend to the doings of another generation. Perhaps prejudice now has other targets, but it has not gone away.

IT was a fine, warm Sunday morning and a sprinkling of elderly ladies were making their way to church. In the Rathausplatz the stallholders were setting-up for the day's business. Bicyclists were out in numbers and along the Danube, on the Parkstrasse, the air was heavy with the scent of lilac. Then the bells began their message. The Minster was first and the neighbouring churches replied like answering sea-monsters. The Minster had the gruffest basso but the others were undeterred and the whole tribe of them made a tremendous clangour. Without the traffic-free tranquility of the town centre, none of them would have been noticeable.

Next to the Kreuztor (1385) a shop specialised in devotional candles. Some of these were positively baroque in their splendid extravagance. One in particular, about a metre high, pale lemon in colour, was ornamented with neo-classical bandings in blue and gold. In its centre a hand-sculpted Virgin painted in blues, reds and flesh tones lifted the Christ-child heavenwards as she ascended through fragments of cloud.

One reason for visiting Ingolstadt is its several claims to religious fame, or notoriety. The Jesuit college here was the first in Germany (1555). But Ingolstadt was also the town where Dr Johann Eck spent most of his life. Eck was Luther's most unrelenting opponent and he is buried in the Minster. Patronised by the wealthy Fuggers of nearby Augsburg, he issued a defence of money-lending in 1514, although usury was condemned by the Church. Eck, in fact, became the leading theological defender of the establishment of his day. He accused Luther of being a Hussite and in 1519 at Leipzig debated Luther's *Ninety-Five Theses* with him. In the debate Eck relied on his considerable knowledge of patristic and conciliar learning, whereas Luther relied on the Scriptures. The arbitrators declined to issue a verdict. Eck, however, made his way to Rome and got himself appointed papal nuncio. Returning to Germany in 1520 with the papal bull *Exsurge Domine*, he sought to have the Emperor Charles V outlaw Luther and all his works. Eck's reputation was that of a sophist or dialectician rather than a profound thinker but in his day he exercised tremendous influence. He died at Ingolstadt in 1543, aged fifty-seven.

His patrons, the Fuggers, the Wall Street tycoons of the sixteenth century, were a similarly ruthless lot. Their fortunes were begun by Johann, a weaver, in the fourteenth century, but it was his great-great-grandson, Ulrich, who became banker to the Habsburgs, winning concessions for silver mines in the Tirol and copper mines in Hungary. They traded in spices, wool, silk and money at a time when Augsburg and Ingolstadt lay on the main trade route from the Mediterranean to the Baltic.

Like any shrewd businessmen, the Fuggers knew how to put their cash to political uses. In 1515 they bribed the Electors to vote in the Emperor Charles V and then farmed his silver mines at Guadalcanal and his mercury mines at Almaden. In 1534 they were granted the right to coin money. They farmed indulgences for the Popes which, naturally, led them to patronise Luther's opponents. In the early sixteenth century the family assets were estimated at more than sixty-three million florins. In effect, they funded the Empire. The ruin of the German economy which was completed by the Thirty Years War also brought the ruin of the Fuggers. Their finances were heavily embroiled with those of the Spanish Habsburgs and when their finances collapsed the Fuggers also went bust, in 1627.

The great French historian, Fernand Braudel, in his massive *Civilisation and Capitalism* traces, among much else, the gradual shift northwards and westwards of European banking from its beginnings in central Italy in the thirteenth century. When Edward I, Langshanks, waged his wars against Wales and Scotland, his armies were paid for by loans from Luccan bankers and when he reneged on the loans, the bankers went bust and Florence became the international financier of the day. Thence it goes via Venice to the great German families, the Welsers and Fuggers, westwards to Antwerp, Amsterdam and, eventually, London. Now London has to compete with New York and Tokyo. The reasons for the migration are hugely complex but the opening up of the New World and the Ottoman closure of Eastern Europe were crucial to it. One result was that Germany and Italy lost out because neither could achieve a strong centralised government. Neither became nation states until the nineteenth century. Both retained large peasant populations and in this century both tried to resolve their economic and social failures by resort to fascism. Even if that analysis is too simple, the threads that lead from the sixteenth to the twentieth centuries can still be followed.

THE next leg of my journey takes me the short drive to Regensburg and from there I follow a minor road to Cham, last stop before the German–Czech border post. The landscape becomes gradually more mountainous as you climb through the Bohemian Forest with its stands of tall, dark pines. Some of the scenery is very Scottish-looking with clumps of birch and hawthorn by the roadside and a scatter of tiny farming villages. The country women are wearing the sort of clothes my grandmother wore in the 1920s and 1930s, pinafores tied over mid-calf-length frocks, topped with cardigan and headscarf. In the little town of Roding an elderly woman is sweeping the streets with a birch-twig besom.

The border post formalities are quickly completed. A couple of boy-soldiers spend a few moments admiring Anastasia. Then, at once, everything seems different, no longer Western Europe. Passing through a tiny village called Babylon, the buildings are shabby and unkempt. There is a smell of dung from the fields, something I never encountered in West Germany. The village gardens are a mass of pink and white cherry blossom. The zebra crossings are faded to near invisibility and pedestrians look astonished to be allowed to cross by them. Every few metres along the Plzeň Road, is another cherry tree, which partly compensates for the immediate deterioration in the quality of the road surface.

But what is most extraordinary is that in all these little villages and towns there are Stars and Stripes displayed everywhere, usually in association with the red, white and blue of the Czech flag. One house had patterned United States and Czech flags alternately across each of its window-panes. Then, in the little village of Chotesov, all becomes clear. A banner strung across the road says, in English:

MANY THANKS TO THE AMERICAN ARMIES FOR THE LIBERATION OF CZECHOSLOVAKIA.

I felt I was in a time-warp. And where did they get so many Stars and Stripes, not, surely, a commodity much on sale in the socialist republic? And, of course, the American army did liberate this south-western corner of Bohemia, though it is only in recent weeks that the new government has permitted the fact to be acknowledged. I find it all rather spooky. On the car radio the BBC World Service announces that this morning (6th May), for the first time in forty years, the authorities in Soviet Moldavia have opened the Soviet-Romanian border across the river Pruth and that people on both sides of the border have launched millions of flowers into the waters, with thanksgiving services being held on both sides of the border. Strange times indeed.

On the outskirts of Plzeň I see that bizarre mixture of heavy industrial plant and allotments which is so characteristic of almost every major East European city. It is a revealing combination. No landscaping here of unsightly factories. Groups of soldiers on the streets of Plzeň, lounging or looking in shop windows. An air of ancient neglect about the town, making French raffishness look positively house-proud. It was this western part of Czechoslovakia that Hitler was so keen to get his hands on; not so much for the Pilsener lagers, but for the Skoda machine plants and the iron and coal resources of Western Bohemia. He let Slovakia go more or less its own way under the puppet regime of Father Tiso. Now that Czechoslovakia is stepping out of the Stalinist ice-box, nationalist voices in Slovakia are beginning to be heard again.

On the E12, the Plzeň-Prague highway, outside Plzeň, a queue of hitch-hikers, including a number of soldiers, is strung along the road. Having checked that they are heading for Prague, I give a lift to the two young men at the head of the queue. Neither speaks French or German but one has a few words of English, so he sits in the front. As Anastasia has a right-hand drive, overtaking safely can be difficult, and a passenger is an invaluable set of additional eyes. Conversation had to be minimal, but they did guide me through the maze of one-way streets, diversions and road-works which makes driving in Prague difficult even if there are no other cars on the streets. Alas, the streets *are* full of Czech drivers intent on displaying maximum aggression. The general standard of driving was only slightly above that of the average twelve-year-old at the dodgems. Amazingly, we arrived unscathed in Wenceslas Square and I set off to find the Čedok offices to arrange accommodation. Officially, all visitors have to book their accommodation and change currency through Čedok. As an organisation, it represents everything rotten about a Stalinist bureaucracy. Czechoslovakia still insists on an inflated hard currency exchange rate which reflects its closed economy.

The girl at the Čedok desk had clearly been chosen for her conventional good looks. Her charm rating was negligible. Having changed money in one office, I was directed to another office a few streets away to arrange accommodation. The town centre hotels which were suggested were fiendishly expensive and at first

I was told nothing else was available. Forewarned, and insisting on something cheaper, I was booked into The Hotel Olympik, a couple of miles from the centre, but still expensive. I explained that I was driving and asked for directions. These I was given, but, as I soon discovered, directions which would have taken me there in an almost straight line. No such route was possible or had probably ever been possible. It took over an hour to negotiate the couple of miles to the hotel and only then because, in exasperation, I ignored all rules of good driving not to mention half-a-dozen laws, and made my way blithely down a one-way street (the wrong way, of course) and down a (prohibited) tram-only lane. Half the streets have no name-plates.

My hotel room was everything I knew to expect from previous sojourns in socialist Europe. The view looked across a concrete courtyard from the thirteenth floor of a planning disaster, a delicious confection of grey concrete and dirty glass, to another, equally hideous architectural gem. The plastic-covered swivel chair had been torn. The brown carpet was cigarette-burned and none too clean, but at least it did not clash with the shabby beige of the walls. The bed was hard and absolutely spotless. Lighting consisted of a 40-watt bulb in the ceiling and a bedside lamp with another 40-watt bulb. After dark, reading or writing was a difficult operation. There was, of course, no plug for the shower or wash-hand basin, but I had brought my own. It was, all in all, a tourist factory, at once pretentious, shabby and expensive, and boasting levels of service unique to Eastern Europe, for no one in Western Europe would tolerate them for a moment. The clientele were mainly, it seemed, Germans and, to my surprise, bus parties of Russians.

Feeling pleased that I had at least negotiated the day's essentials, and the afternoon being well advanced, I thought it would be good to have a more leisurely look round Wenceslas Square and find somewhere to eat. As I refused so soon to repeat the horrors of the afternoon, the taxi ride from the Olympik to Nove Mesto (the New Town) was a real treat. The driver, a heavily built, mustachioed man in his fifties, elegant in sweat-sodden T-shirt, opened the conversation with (in German) 'You need here no seat belt'. My usual response to being addressed in German was to reply (in Russian) *'Ya nye Nyemyets'* ('I'm not a German') which confused them since I clearly was *not* Russian. My driver was under the impression that I had instructed him to break the world land-speed record. One would not have believed his grubby Lada capable of such manoeuvres as he coaxed from its grinding engine but, after a moment of horror, I sat back and enjoyed the ride. Prague pedestrians show a sage and absolute distrust of Prague drivers. As it turned out, he was the only taxi driver not to try to cheat me.

Wenceslas Square is a long, wide, gently sloping rectangle with the famous bronze statue of the equestrian warrior-king at its head. This is the heart of Prague's business and tourist quarter and the Square is lined with hotels and what are, by Prague standards, up-market shops. The Square was busy with window-shoppers. There were a couple of queues out into the street for toiletries. The sinking sun was just catching the gilding on the green dome of the buildings behind St Wenceslas. Most of the buildings were grey or black with age and pollution. There had been no refurbishment programmes here.

My associations with Wenceslas Square were not so much with the events of 1989, though it was here on the 18th November that the crowds gathered to protest about the police violence of the night before. From then on the snowball gathered momentum until on 24th November, the entire Politburo resigned, to be followed by the collapse of its still communist-dominated replacement government on 7th December. Rather, they were with the events of August 1968 and, in particular, with the self-immolation of the young philosophy student, Jan Palach, in January 1969. His suicide, in protest at the invasion of Czechoslovakia by the forces of the Warsaw Pact – only Romania declined to participate – seemed to catch at the Western conscience as somehow symbolic of those dreadful days, though it produced no result other than a further deepening of the Cold War. Apart from the Cuban missile crisis, it was the first political event really to break into my late adolescent consciousness. It was also, I suspect, together with the defeat of the 'radical unrest' in Paris and elsewhere in the spring of 1968, a final body-blow to any hopes of a revival in the fortunes of West European communist parties. Indeed, it led to the so-called Euro-communism of the 1970s, when communist parties with quite substantial support, as in Spain, Portugal and Italy, began to distance themselves from the policies of the Soviet Union and its satellites.

Wenceslas Square was laid out for one of Bohemia's most attractive rulers, King Charles IV, Holy Roman Emperor, who was born and died in Prague. Charles was the eldest son of John of

Luxemburg, King of Bohemia, one of those knights errant of late medieval history and cousin to Philip VI of France. When Edward III of England invaded France, John went to Philip's aid and fought at the battle of Crecy where, as R. W. Seton-Watson describes it: 'giving the reins of his horse to two of his companions, and shouting the battle-cry of "Prague", he charged into the thick of the fray and, blind as he was, soon went down fighting (26th August, 1346). His son Charles was also wounded in the battle and only escaped with difficulty.' Charles was thirty at the time. Three months later he was crowned German King at Bonn.

In the fourteenth century Prague was very much at the centre of European affairs. Charles married his second cousin, Blanche, sister of the French king, and it was on the Parisian model that he founded the University of Prague in 1348. Along with Bologna, Oxford and Paris, it became one of the great centres of medieval scholarship, attracting students from all over Europe. Charles set out to turn Prague into a city to rival any in Europe. He ordered the construction of the *Karlovy Most* (Charles Bridge) and began the rebuilding of the Hradčany Castle and St Vitus Cathedral which still dominate the Prague skyline. It was Charles also who, in the *Golden Bull* of 1356, regularised the constitution of the Empire and the rights of its seven electors. His daughter, Anne, married the unfortunate English king Richard II.

Having been turned away from two restaurants, rather to my surprise for it was still early evening, I finally secured a table at the *Restaurant Français* of the Hotel Ambassador in Wenceslas Square. The upstairs restaurant was a split-level affair which might once have been elegant. There were some pretty stained-glass windows in art-deco style and some painted porcelain chandeliers. Most of the bulbs in the chandeliers, however, did not work and the once-fine carpets were worn threadbare. I was lucky with the aperitif, a campari, which it is difficult to destroy. I began with what the menu described as *bouillon*. It was a lukewarm liquid on which floated a thin layer of fat and which contained in its suspicious-looking depths lumps of boiling beef, pieces of cauliflower and other assorted vegetables. It was dreadful. Unlike most of what was on the menu, two wines were actually available, a semi-sweet white and a semi-sweet red. The red was sharp and thin but drinkable, though one would not care for a second glass. The *pièce de resistance* (or *coup de grâce*) was the main course, imaginatively described as *Filet de Boeuf Madagascar*. It was, at

51

best, stewing steak from a very ill and elderly cow. Its elasticity would have made it the ideal candidate for a trampoline-cover. It was topped with a slice of ham, a layer of plastic cheese and served with pickled onions and chips, the latter being of the fifty-fifty variety, that is: fifty per cent potato and fifty per cent grease. Being exceedingly hungry, I ate the slice of ham. It was as disgusting a concoction as I have seen and not particularly cheap. The meal was accompanied by the tinklings of a white-jacketed and clearly talented pianist who was equally clearly bored. The whole place had the glamour and attractiveness of an elderly whore still on the game long after her teeth have gone.

During this trial by ordeal the restaurant was almost empty although people kept arriving and being turned away because: 'There are no tables.' Several groups of Americans were turned away despite protests that tables had been booked for them by Čedok or by their hotels. Most persistent was an aristocratic-looking Japanese boy who returned several times to his protest. The maître d'hôtel was not impressed and eventually the Japanese boy, like the others, had to admit defeat. The mystery of this curious behaviour intrigued me, but it was several days before I discovered its logic from a Prague friend. The tables were and would remain empty. They had been booked in advance on a quota basis by Čedok, so they would be paid for whether any one ate at them or not. As this met the requirements of the hotel, serving customers would merely have been a needless waste of effort and resources which could be profitably siphoned off elsewhere. If any of those who had been turned away chose to complain, they would meet the same bored lack of interest. No one is personally responsible for anything, so everyone gets away with it. It is a phenomenon one encounters continually in Eastern Europe, but most blatantly when one has to have any dealings with state-run organisations. If a market economy is introduced, an awful lot of people are going to have serious problems of adjustment. The best part of the meal was the coffee and slivović I nursed while I watched the charade unroll. By the end of the evening I had come to feel sorry for the waiters who had so debased themselves by their participation in the comedy; not because they were cheating the state, but because they never responded to anyone except as an object, a part of the system in which they were trapped.

It was a relief to be in the open air again but, lacking a street-map, I decided to take a taxi to the riverside and find my way about from there. The Vltava here is wide and the Charles Bridge by night was stunningly beautiful. An almost full, yellow moon hung above the Castle. The street-lamps lining the promenade on the right bank glittered in the waters below the bridge where a flotilla of ghostly swans floated in the current. The bridge was pedestrian-only and had been taken over by assorted buskers playing jazz or folk music. Little knots of people, mainly young, clustered round them. But not everyone; a young soldier and his girlfriend sat on the balustrade, dangling their legs over the water, oblivious of anyone else.

The Charles Bridge was Prague's only bridge until 1841. At the Castle end is a romanesque tower, the only remnant of the Judith Bridge which was swept away in 1342. Most of the bronze statues which line the present bridge were added in the seventeenth and eighteenth centuries. There is a story that the Charles Bridge was to be stronger than any other bridge so the mortar had to be mixed with wine and eggs. All the villages in Bohemia were asked to contribute but one village, afraid the eggs would get broken, hard-boiled them first. Not much of the bridge's history is as droll.

In 1393 Charles IV's son, Wenceslas IV, quarelled with archbishop Jenstein over a matter of monastic revenues. Wenceslas captured and imprisoned the archbishop and his vicar-general, John of Nepomuk. After having been broken by torture, the poor Nepomuk was bound and thrown into the Vltava from Charles Bridge. Much later, in 1729, at the behest of the Jesuits, John Nepomuk was canonised on the basis that, as the queen's confessor, he had been executed by a jealous king because he refused to reveal her confessional secrets. John Nepomuk never was the queen's confessor. The motive for Nepomuk's canonisation appears to have been an attempt by the Jesuits to set up an alternative national hero to the heretical Hus. Religious problems came back to haunt Wenceslas for, at the time of his death in 1419, the Hussite movement which prefigured the Reformation was already a cause of conflict throughout his kingdom.

When Ferdinand II attempted to impose Catholicism on largely Protestant Bohemia, the citizens of Prague rebelled, thereby opening the struggles of the Thirty Years War. After the defeat of the White Hill, Ferdinand sentenced the leaders of the revolt to public execution in front of the Rathaus in Prague. Twelve of their heads were impaled on the Charles Bridge *pour encourager les autres* and remained there for more than a decade. Ironically, when, at the very end of the war, Prague was again under siege, this time by the Protestant forces, the by-now Catholic citizens of Prague defended the bridge for three months with a zeal they had failed to show in 1620.

At every point in those historic struggles which founded the Protestant and radical traditions in Europe, and which severed radicalism from the body of the Catholic Church, the struggle was as much for personal gain or for political or economic dominance as it was for any pure-hearted vision of goodness. Untainted heroes are, with the rarest of exceptions, an invention of ideologues with something to sell.

From the Charles Bridge I gradually worked my way back to Wenceslas Square. By ten o'clock the town was only half-lit and many of the smaller back streets not at all. The almost complete absence of neon advertising signs from buildings and shop windows increased my sense of being in an ancient city. At the north end of Wenceslas Square, not far from where Palach immolated himself, a pop band and disco-dance group were doing their thing to an audience of enthusiastic youngsters. I encountered a lot of very drunk people in Prague, more than in any other city I have visited except perhaps Belfast. And a lot of aggressive drunks. For all that, it had the feel of a city wakening up after a long sleep and beginning to shake off decades of despair.

C ZECHOSLOVAKIA is an invention of the twentieth century and, in particular, of the Allied victories of 1918. The history of Austro-Hungary through the nineteenth century is one of alternation between repression and compromise in its effort to maintain the fabric of the empire against its increasingly centrifugal tendencies. It had never been a homogeneous state, more a collection of dynastic holdings, and its ruling caste never subscribed to the liberal notions of the Enlightenment or the French Revolution. They did, however, take up that romantic nationalism which went hand in hand with them. As the nineteenth century progressed, German nationalism became increasingly the blunt instrument with which Austro-Hungary attempted to bludgeon Bohemia and Moravia into quiescence, while in Slovakia the Hungarian ruling caste pursued a policy of Magyarisation. But nationalism is a treacherous weapon and may rebound on its user and, especially after the failure of the European radical movements in 1848, the Pan-Germanism and anti-semitism which Vienna adopted only served to stir the embers of Bohemian nationality.

The leader of the national movement in Bohemia and Moravia was T. G. Masaryk. Masaryk was an eminent liberal scholar who stood out against the Catholic-led anti-semitic hysteria of the 1890s. In particular, he denounced the accusations of child-murder and ritual abuse which became standard elements in Viennese demonology in that decade. Early in the First World War substantial numbers of Czech and Slovak troops went over to the Allied side. This was followed by the creation of a national committee in exile headed by Masaryk in London. By the end of the war there were independent Czechoslovak legions in France and in Russia. Once the Allied powers had recognised the creation of a Czechoslovak state as one of their war aims, it was not long until that state came into existence, which it did in October 1918. Masaryk was its first president. Significantly, when elections were held for the new parliament, the German politicians refused to participate. The new state comprised the historic provinces of Bohemia and Moravia together with Slovakia which, until 1918, had been part of Hungary, together with Ruthenia and a northern fringe of the Hungarian plain which, though it was Magyar-speaking, the new state claimed it needed on economic grounds.

From the very beginning the new state was founded on a contradiction: the basis of the post-war settlement was the self-determination of peoples, especially as proselytised by President Wilson of the United States. At the same time, economic and political realities had to be accommodated. The result was a fusion of Czechs and Slovaks with neither having much time for the other. In Slovakia the nationalists supported a clerical fascism. Any state founded on nationalist principles is going to find it difficult to accommodate more than one nationality. The census of 1930 revealed the true state of affairs when it showed that more than twenty-two per cent of the population were ethnic and linguistic Germans.

That alienation of the German Bohemians showed up in the

1935 elections when Konrad Henlein's pro-Nazi *Sudetendeutsche Partei* became the second largest parliamentary party. Hitler saw Czechoslovakia as the key to breaking Germany's encirclement while Neville Chamberlain excused his appeasement of Hitler with the excuse that he knew nothing about the Czechs. Hitler occupied Bohemia and Moravia in March 1939, Hungary swallowed Ruthenia, and Slovakia became a fascist, pro-Nazi state under the leadership of Father Tiso.

For many Czechs the failure of the Republic was deeply demoralising, for it was never contested in any serious way. Europe may have turned its back, but the Czechs also sold themselves out as the Poles did not. Although there was a resistance movement to the German occupation, it never developed on any scale and did not have the support of the mass of the people who were coddled by the occupying regime. The Jews and the intellectuals suffered most. After the liberation, elections were held in 1946 in which the Communists gained thirty-eight per cent of the national vote. The demoralisation generated by the occupation was taken full advantage of by the Communists to establish a socialist republic. Prague has a long history of defenestrations and in 1948 Jan Masaryk, the foreign minister, the founding president's son and one of only three non-communist ministers in the government, was found dead, having apparently exited from his office window.

By 1952, at the height of the Stalinist purges which swept the Eastern *bloc* as part of the anti-Titoist crusade, *Rude Pravo*, the Party newspaper, could write that 'Love of the Soviet Union does not tolerate the slightest reservation'. It was widely rumoured that when the party leader, Klement Gottwald, died, in March 1953, it was from grief at the death of Stalin a few weeks earlier. Amid economic recession, the purges continued through 1954. Joseph Rothschild sums up the effect of these events: 'Facts became taboo and suspicion pervasive. Politically, power drifted toward the security services . . . while the inner life of the Communist parties petrified. An orgy of denunciations and evasions of responsibility was unleashed throughout the upper and middle levels of the bureaucracy. As a consequence, the very idea of politics became degraded and execrated in the minds of the citizens, as it seemed to them synonymous with lawlessness, mendacity and opportunism.'

Gottwald was succeeded by the equally devout Antonin

Novotný. It was not until 1963 that a reformist element was able to make itself heard, with the election to the position of first secretary of the Slovak party of Alexander Dubček. The Soviets trusted Dubček. He had spent his childhood in the Soviet Union and had studied there. His reformist programme, partly economic, partly political, was aimed at creating a more open 'communism with a human face'. After the crushing of the Prague Spring in August 1968, Gustáv Husák's regime entered on a two-decade-long period of economic stagnation and social demoralisation. An underground, 'black' economy was allowed to flourish as a substitute for politically indigestible reforms, with the result that corruption became a way of life. What finally shook the edifice apart were not so much domestic events as Gorbachev's abandonment of the Brezhnev doctrine of interference in the affairs of the Soviet satellites. When a peaceful demonstration of some 50,000 people in Prague was suppressed with the usual police violence on 17th November 1989, rumour quickly created a martyrology of murdered saints. In fact, no one was killed, but the tinder had been lit and, bereft of foreign support, the regime crumbled in the space of three weeks.

I KNEW of Doctor Ladislav Mareda through British friends who had worked with him for the English-language section of Prague radio until the crushing of the Prague Spring in 1968. Having tried unsuccessfully to reach him through his office – he edits a weekly newspaper for veterans of the wartime resistance – I decided finally to drive out to the village of Roztoky where he spends much of his time.

Ladislav is seventy. He studied law before the war and during it worked with the resistance in Prague where he had been born. After the war he became a journalist and, eventually, head of the English section of Czech radio. Ladislav was a party member who supported Dubček's reforms and was partly responsible for organising a famous Party Congress during the Warsaw Pact invasion in 1968. The Congress, held in a factory, condemned the invasion. Thereafter Ladislav could not keep any post for long before the authorities hounded him out of it. For the next two decades he made a sort of living finding bits and pieces of editing and translation work. He is not a large man, but portly now and rather short of breath. Quiet-spoken and deeply read, he is an instructive and entertaining conversationalist with a sardonic sense of humour.

My first efforts to find Roztoky, which is only a few miles outside Prague, were a horror story of wrong turnings, lengthy detours and rush-hour traffic. Eventually, I did get to the village, which perches high on a hillside above the Vltava. Stopping to ask a local woman where I might find Dr Mareda, I discovered that I was speaking to his companion, Vera, and that I had stopped outside their front door. Ladislav was at a lecture in the philosophy department of the university but would be back in an hour or so.

Vera and Ladislav share a small upstairs flat in a detached house set in its own, rather over-grown garden in a quiet tree-lined avenue. Vera's mother occupies the downstairs apartment. There is a small sitting-room, a small bedroom and kitchen. The walls of the sitting-room are lined with Ladislav's paintings, mostly unframed. In the main they are brightly coloured works in the expressionist tradition. Books are much in evidence, in Russian, Czech, German and English, lining an old, elegant glass-fronted display cabinet. Another cabinet is filled with glass and china. On top of both, displayed like trophies, are reminders of gifts from Western visitors, a packet of Nairn's oatcakes, an empty bottle of Macallan whisky, a packet of Silk Cut cigarettes. Strangely, they do not look out of place or incongruous and in the context of Czech commodities, the sophistication of their design is immediately apparent. I am hot and sticky from my drive, but the scent of lilac drifts in from the garden with the sound of blackbirds, and within a few minutes I feel much at home. While Vera prepares something to eat, we chatter.

Vera is younger than Ladislav, slim, cheerful and vivacious. Her English is tentative, correct but rather old-fashioned and uncolloquial. She teaches history and Russian at the equivalent of a British junior secondary school. Since 1948 Russian has been a compulsory language in Czech schools, but as of next month, she will be able to switch to teaching English and German. Within a few minutes, I am presented with a plate of cold meats, cheeses, breads and a salad of cabbage and herring in a sour-cream dressing, bottles of soda-water and coffee. It was the best meal I had in Czechoslovakia. I feel mildly guilty about accepting such hospitality. Neither she nor Ladislav could be said to be well-off. Neither has a car and journeys into Prague have to be carefully planned. Both are heavy smokers.

Asked for her impressions of the events of the past six months, Vera admits to twinges of pessimism about the slow rate at which progress is being made. 'We still have no elected government. Only Havel has been elected, the rest are appointees. The interior minister for example, Mr Sacher, held office as a member of the People's Party under the Communists, although he was not a minister. But he is in control of the police and the security services. The bureaucracy, which is largely a Communist *nomenclatura*, is still in place and that is worrying. They talk, for example, about the continuing need for state secrets and Havel seems to go along with that. Until November, we still believed that the tanks might come back. I heard on the television yesterday that thirty-five people had been sacked from the interior ministry so that may be an encouraging sign. And there are other difficulties. After the revolution there was a general amnesty for prisoners and that included criminal elements. Was that a move by the police to undermine the new authorities? Who advised Havel to do that? Even here in Roztoky there have been burglaries.' Ladislav and Vera are careful to lock their door even when in the house. Ladislav said later that there had been a murder in Roztoky just a few weeks earlier.

Vera did not eat anything while we talked but sipped at some of her excellent black coffee and smoked endless cigarettes. Asked about the possibility of economic difficulties, she was concerned about how they would manage: 'The new government does not know where to begin with the economy, which is in a shambles. It is appalling to think that the prices of basics like meat and butter could double. The ministers claim we have to take a different approach from the Poles or Hungarians but they do not say in what way different. Certainly, we have less international debt than Poland or Hungary and we are owed money by the Soviet Union. But the Soviets refuse to give their tourists who come here any Czech currency. It is difficult to say what will happen. The elections are scheduled for mid-June, a month from now. But the campaigns have been very amateurish and low-key and many of the younger people are not interested. Too many parents have been too afraid ever to acknowledge the real state of our affairs to their children. So there is a lot of apathy. There is a real change though. People are no longer afraid to speak out – loudly – and that is wonderful. The rest will depend on what happens in the economy and that, as I say, is a mess.'

Asked about whether she thought nationalist tensions would resurface in any significant way, Vera explained: 'A few weeks ago Havel said that the word "socialist" would have to be removed from our country's name. As a result of that, the federal assembly spent two weeks squabbling over the issue. Everyone agreed that "socialist" should be removed but the debate exacerbated nationalist tensions between Czechs and Slovaks. There were even demonstrations in Slovakia for an independent republic. Finally the assembly agreed on "The Czech and Slovak Federal Republic". All the different interest groups have suddenly been allowed to come out into the open and in some cases it is a question of each for himself and damn the rest.'

Just then, Ladislav arrived and Vera's welcomes were repeated over again. He found it extraordinary that I had been able simply to get into a car in Britain and drive unhindered to Roztoky. 'It is a good omen,' he said.

Ladislav toasts us with *nadraži* and laughs. He explains that an Englishman he knew at Czech radio used always to get the usual toast *na zdrave* (health) wrong, confusing it with *nadraži*, meaning 'railway station'. So, we toast the railway station and I tell him the only Czech joke I know. It dates from 1968 and I have no memory of where I first heard it. An old man who has been living in exile returns to Prague in 1998. He goes up to a kiosk in Wenceslas Square and asks for a copy of *Rude Pravo* (Red Truth), the Party newspaper. The old woman behind the counter says, 'Where have you been? *Rude Pravo* hasn't been published for fifteen years.' He thanks her and goes away. Fifteen minutes later, he is back again, 'A copy of *Rude Pravo*, please.' She explains patiently, again, that *Rude Pravo* has not been published for fifteen years. He thanks her. Fifteen minutes later, same thing again, but by now she is very angry and starts shouting at him, 'Don't you bloody listen? I've told you, *Rude Pravo* hasn't been published for fifteen years.' The man smiles at her and says, 'Oh, I know. I know. I just love to hear you say it.'

I ask about his work with the veterans' organisation. He explains: 'There was a group of army officers who organised themselves as "Defence of the Nation". This began before the war, from the time of the Munich agreement in 1938, for it was then that the Communist Party was made illegal. Later, of course, the Molotov-Ribbentrop Pact divided the movement. This officers' group lasted for the duration of the occupation, which is to say, for six years, though most of its leaders were caught and executed in the course of the war. You have to bear in mind that the occupation did not apply to Slovakia. A different section of the resistance consisted of the political wing led by ex-President Beneš. He kept in touch with General Nečas, leader of the officers' group, by radio. But this is a small country and the Nazis were quite efficient and had a good network of informers so General Nečas was eventually executed. Prior to 1968 the veterans' organisation was called "Fighters for Freedom" which was really an umbrella organisation. After the events of 1968 it was renamed "The Union of Anti-Fascist Fighters" which was an attempt to make us restrict our goals. Now, since December of 1989, we have changed it to "The Union of Freedom Fighters".'

Asked whether he shared Vera's doubts about progress since the collapse of the communist regime, Ladislav lights another cigarette and settles himself at the table: 'A lot of the intellectuals are unhappy that the so-called "transition" is taking so long. And this unelected government should not be making so many new and fundamental laws, for some of these will be an embarrassment to an elected government and it will take time and trouble to repeal them. On the other hand, Havel is a figure who commands trust and respect, unlike Iliescu. He has a moral stature which comes from being wholly untainted by the previous regime. He has no history of political manoeuvring.'

Since the conversation was outpacing my efforts to note the salient points, I gave up trying and used the little tape-recorder I had brought with me. I dislike using them in conversation, for they can add a measure of artificiality to what should otherwise be casual. But Ladislav had no objections and we were already well launched. What follows is an edited version of some of that conversation:

WP   Why is it that Czechoslovakia in its moments of crisis turns to scholars and writers? I am thinking of Masaryk and, obviously, Havel?

LM   That will happen in any small country trying to establish itself or struggling to survive. In such cases cultural values acquire a new importance and can become decisive. I suspect that cultural matters here have a higher significance in the lives of ordinary people than is the case in the West.

WP   I suppose Scotland could be a case in point, with the status given to writers such as Burns and MacDiarmid who are national as much as literary figures. And Yeats in Ireland. It is difficult trying to imagine England according that kind of status to a writer. But in Britain, in any case, the issue is complicated by class. There is an underlying hostility to the arts in Britain on the part of the mass of people and that, I think, is a result of the way in which the arts have become associated in many people's minds with snobbery, with money and, in the case of Scotland, with anglicisation.

LM   But don't you think England is interesting inasmuch as its outstanding feature, as a political culture, is its traditionalism?

WP   I think you have to distinguish the appearance from the reality. English history has a tendency to assimilate developments into a mythic story, so that events which were a victory for some faction or interest group get retrospectively sanctioned as a sacred progress of democratic tradition. The outstanding example of that is the so-called Glorious Revolution. Universal suffrage in Britain dates only from after the Great War and the right for non-property holders to participate in local elections only dates back to 1949. But I'm more interested to hear your views on Czechoslovakia than my own on Britain. What do you think is going to happen next?

LM   There are two essentials which *should* happen next. The first thing is to get rid of the Soviet Union's presence here. The NKVD (security service) has a deep-rooted hold. It has cast its net right across Eastern Europe. The dismantling of that establishment is only just getting under way. What Havel recently referred to when he said that 'I cannot speak about everything I know' were secret treaties between Czechoslovakia and the USSR which cannot as yet be disclosed. The second essential is to try to get the economy into some kind of shape. Our present minister for finance, Mr Klaus, is widely known as The Playboy. He is something of a monetarist and, as such, the devaluation of wages, not to mention the debasement of people, doesn't seem to worry him.

WP   It will inevitably be confusing for those in Eastern Europe who mistake the rhetoric of Western ideology for the reality of economic life – just as it is for many in the West. Capitalism accompanies its development with a fanfare about freedom of choice, free markets, and all the rest of it. But it is a system of winners and losers and in periods of crisis there are far more losers than winners. The difference between the West now and the West in the nineteenth century, is that now the largest part of the price for development is paid by the invisible people of the so-called Third World, rather than by the pauperised urban proletariat of mills, mines and factories, though there are still some of them about too. There will be some serious disillusion to follow on the heels of the euphoria of freedom.

LM   True, but in domestic terms our debate is not so finely drawn. We are at the stage of trying to work with a broad brush without much understanding of the problems of detail. We have always in Czechoslovakia been proud of being Europeans, as we were before the First World War and between the wars. For us to be reduced to the level of a Balkan state is very hard. Soviet policy with regard to Eastern Europe was sloganised as 'development in groups', as though we had to wait for Mongolia to catch up before we could be allowed to develop. Bohemia, unlike Britain, was historically the crossroads of Europe. In the later Middle Ages, Prague was an important merchant city and cultural centre.

WP   Yes, but then the fringe moved, so to speak. I mean that

Britain, for example, became more central to the currents of world trade. When Prague lay near to the great trade routes between East and West and from the Mediterranean to the Baltic, then it was a valuable staging post for all of Europe, including the far West. But when the Cape route opened and the New World beckoned, the centrality of Prague diminished. The Thirty Years War was more a symptom than a cause of processes already well advanced. With the Turks at the gates of Vienna as late as the seventeenth century, it is not surprising that Bohemia came to be half-forgotten by Western Europe.

LM   It is very easy in the kind of society Czechoslovakia has been in the past twenty years to lose a more general perspective on events. And one of the distinctive features of life here has been a gradual loss of the ability to distinguish right from wrong. And that wears you down. You end up speaking the same jargon or formulae as the establishment without stopping to think. So, I have always to go back to the beginning if I want to sort something out. And for me the beginning was when I was young; before the Soviets, before the Nazis. It is like living in a low-level but persistent depression. It is hard to think *reasonably*, to keep your brain working, not to repeat the old slogans. I trained as a lawyer and I think that helps.

    I first came to distrust communist ideology with the concept of the 'new man', the idea that *after* social conditions have changed, *then* human nature will improve. I cannot believe that. People are bad and good, are primitive and clever, and so on.

WP   Certainly, people respond to whether they perceive the world as threatening or reassuring. But that doesn't rule out altruism.

LM   But natural beings are always living in the expectation or half-expectation of aggression.

WP   That's too simple. Socially, it is not too difficult to imagine getting rid of some of the provocations which produce aggression. Existentially, it is another question. Heidegger's *Geworfenheit*, the fact that we are thrown onto the dice-board, without choosing when or where or whether, that must always be a source of anxiety. The world abuses our rationality, as Pascal acknowledges. It treats us arbitrarily, as though we were mindless and could not care. But we do care and in that sense, yes, aggression is rooted in the world.

LM   And I suppose we have already eliminated many of the causes of aggression – in some measure. But even in sex we do not behave rationally!

(At which Ladislav chuckles.)

The evening was wearing on and I was nervous of finding my way through the maze of central Prague by night. We arranged to meet at the hotel the following morning. As I drove back towards town, a rich, yellow moon hung suspended between violet clouds and another glowed in the Vltava. I did lose my way in the network of Prague alleyways. There was almost no traffic on the roads, though it was only ten-thirty. A few staggering drunks near the centre were the only people about. Back at the Olympik, I looked up a passage in Pascal which had been in my mind earlier in the evening:

The whole visible world is only an imperceptible atom in the ample bosom of nature. No idea approaches it. We may enlarge our conceptions beyond all imaginable space; we only produce atoms in comparison with the reality of things. It is an infinite sphere, the centre of which is everywhere, the circumference nowhere . . .
   But to show him another prodigy equally astonishing, let him examine the most delicate things he knows . . . Perhaps he will think that here is the smallest point in nature. I will let him see therein a new abyss. I will paint for him not only the visible universe, but all that he can conceive of nature's immensity in the womb of this abridged atom. Let him see therein an infinity of universes, each of which has its firmament,

its planets, its earth, in the same proportion as in the visible
world . . .

For in fact what is man in nature? A Nothing in comparison
with the Infinite, an All in comparison with the Nothing, a mean
between nothing and everything. Since he is infinitely removed
from comprehending the extremes, the end of things and their
beginning are hopelessly hidden from him in an impenetrable
secret . . .

Let us then take our compass; we are something, and we are
not everything. The nature of our existence hides from us the
knowledge of first beginnings which are born of the Nothing;
and the littleness of our being conceals from us the sight of the
Infinite.

LADISLAV arrived at the Olympik, promptly at ten o'clock.
I offered a taxi into town but he preferred to walk to the
exhibition he wanted me to see in Na Příkopě, near the centre.
It used to be called *Am Graben* which is German for 'the moat'
because that was where the medieval city walls ran. As Ladislav
has a mild heart condition, we dawdled towards the Centre in the
morning sunlight. He conducts an imaginary interview: 'And what
are you doing here, Mr Perrie? Ah, so you are taking photographs.
I see. And you are taking notes. Yes. And you are speaking with
people and gathering information? So, you admit that you are here
as a spy. It will help if you confess all at the trial.

'When the Germans came, in March 1939, it all happened in
one night. People in Bohemia had been so full of self-confidence
that they were taken by surprise. There is a story that two
painters had been drinking until dawn and, on hearing the news
of the occupation on the radio, went out and found themselves
an inspector of police. They just said to him: "Come with us!"
And he did. They took him to their rooms and gave him a
glass of vodka or slivović and teased him. So it is in times of
confusion. Just as in Bulgaria you need only say *Derzhala sigurnost*
(state security) to make people very nervous.

'We say that the Slovaks are cousins to the Poles and the
Ukrainians whereas the Czechs are more like the Germans.

Moravia is not so much another nationality in the blend but, rather, a district. We say too that the Czechs drink beer, the Slovaks drink wine and the Moravians whatever they can get hold of.'

Walking with Ladislav, I became aware of just how noisy a city Prague is, with its trams and cars with broken or inadequate silencers. I asked him about the disrepair of the buildings. 'During the war,' he said, 'people had other things to think about. After the war most of the proprietors were dispossessed. The state here is only a collection of functionaries, so it does not care about the aesthetic condition of the buildings it administers. And people are demoralised. If Stalin came back tomorrow, most people would quite soon knuckle down.

'I grew up in what was, at least in principle, a model democracy. In school, we were taught by teachers who were conscientious and honest people. Some were Christians. Some were even good communists. Most, though, were liberals who instilled in us, or tried to, the values of decency, hard work, truthfulness and honesty. Then the war brought a climate of repression. The new generation has grown up in a continuation of that climate, one of falsity and evasion. One young man I used to teach said to me: "You don't need to teach me when to applaud and when to shut up. That I know already." Gorbachev must be facing a similar problem in the USSR, in the taciturnity of Soviet youth.'

We paused to watch a hawk hunting above one of the islands which splits the Vltava, and I asked Ladislav about the posters I kept seeing in windows. These were amateurish-looking election posters. One of them was for no particular party. It was just anti-communist. I asked whether the unification of Germany was an issue. He replied that the older Czechs were wary of the idea of a unified Germany but, for the young, West Germany was something of an ideal whereas they despised the DDR. 'Germany,' he said, 'has been the *spiritus agens* of the whole development of Middle-Europe – from Hitler to the collapse of the Berlin Wall, which encouraged and prompted our own transformation.

'I did not join the party until after the war and I was ignorant about its structure and discipline. I thought it was just like any other party. And as an overly individualistic sort of fellow, I was taken aback by what I found. Vera asks me: "Why did you stay a Communist for so long, even after your friend was executed in 1950?"' The friend in question had been a schoolmate and they had worked together in the resistance. He had told Ladislav when the Communists came to power: 'This is the beginnings of a police state.' 'He was right. Most people shut down when faced with repression. But passive resistance doesn't work. If you are alive, you have to fight. It has taken me a lifetime to learn that lesson. The real crime of the USSR is to have spoiled an opportunity for the whole world, they have so discredited socialism.'

On my visit to Wenceslas Square the evening before, I had seen no sign of the *corso*, that ritual evening promenade which is found all through the Mediterranean world and up into Northern Italy and Central Yugoslavia. It does not exist in Germany and I was curious as to how far into Central Europe the *corso* penetrated. Ladislav answered: 'When I was young, the *corso* was called *drafouš*, which is actually a corruption of *Trafalgar Square*. So, we would say: "I will meet you in *drafouš*" which, at that time, was the lower part of Wenceslas Square. How the association with Trafalgar Square developed I don't know. But the *corso* used also to exist in Austria.'

Over a glass of wine Ladislav told me the following story: 'There was a Bohemian landowner called Prince Paar. He owned a very large portion of Southern Bohemia, perhaps a hundred thousand hectares. He made a deal in 1948 with the communist authorities that, if he could get passports for himself and his entire family to leave the country, he would make over his lands to the state. I got the job of delivering the thick bundle of passports to him. At that time I was very young and very anti-aristo. When I arrived at the Big House, I was asked to stay to lunch. I debated with myself whether it was right to have lunch with an aristocrat but I was also very curious to see what lunch with him would be like and accepted the invitation. A maid was immediately summoned who took me down to the servants' quarters. A place had been set for one and I was given bread and a bowl of goulash.' Ladislav grinned.

The exhibition Ladislav wanted me to see and which he had not yet seen himself, was a series of documents and photographs relating to the events of 1968, none of which had been made public before. It was accompanied by a street exhibition on the political history of Czechoslovakia from its foundation in 1918 until the present, again using of lot of materials not seen before. On the way we passed a very old man, bent almost double, wearing the uniform of one who had fought with the Czechoslovak Legion in Russia.

Theirs is an extraordinary story. The Tsar had given permission for the formation of the Legion but, a couple of months later, the Tsarina rescinded the order. When the Bolsheviks came to power, Trotsky insisted that the Legion be disarmed. They resisted and defeated Red Army troops in several engagements. Then, led by Masaryk, they retreated right across Siberia to Japan, the United States and, eventually, back home.

Na Příkopě, which is a wide street lined with shops had been closed to traffic. The queue for the exhibition of 1968 stretched right out into the street and round a corner. I commented to Ladislav on the coincidence of eights in Czech history: 1618 when Ferdinand's deposition led to the Thirty Years War; 1918 when Czechoslovakia was founded; 1938 and Munich; 1968 and Dubček. We decided not to wait and to content ourselves instead with the street exhibition that day. The street was jammed with people. All along its length rotundas about ten feet high had been set up. Each rotunda was devoted to a different aspect of recent Czech history. There was one on the persecution of the Church, another on the post-war internment camps for dissidents, another on the collectivisation of the villages, still another on the show trials of the early 1950s. There must have been a dozen rotundas, each displaying blow-ups of contemporary newspaper clippings, photographs, posters, etc. The display windows of the shops had also been taken over and in some of them were displayed uniforms such as that of the Russian Legion which I had just seen.

People were crowding round the displays, reading the posters with great intensity and, by and large, in silence. At a rotunda devoted to the death of Stalin people were chuckling. The clippings said: 'Stalin will live for ever in the hearts of mankind' followed by the text of a funeral oration delivered by Gottwald. Then there were the obituaries for Gottwald a few weeks later. The heading stated: 'Gottwald is with us. We will transform that sorrow into strength.' Below that there were the texts of very bad but sincere poems published in newspapers of the time by worker poets in honour of Stalin and Gottwald. It was at these that the onlookers were chuckling. Most of the rotundas, however, provoked a sombre reaction, though Ladislav pointed out that many of the younger people would not have recognised the faces of Novotný and Gottwald even if they knew the names. The very existence of the internment camps had been a state secret and virtually all the materials on display would have been 'classified' before the recent revolution.

One schoolchild, Ladislav said, had recently asked him if he could remember Stalin and Beneš. And, when he said he could, went on to enquire whether he could also remember the Thirty Years War.

Halfway along Na Příkopě a set of cut-out figures of Czecho-slovakia's rulers since the war had been erected along the top of a wall, with the largest figure in the centre – Stalin. A little old woman, clearly upset, was going about tugging at people's sleeves and pointing to the figures. I asked Ladislav what she was saying. Having misunderstood the irony of the display, she was telling people: 'Don't believe them. They are all murderers. Every one of them.'

Ladislav himself was taken aback by the rotunda devoted to the show trials of the 1950s. The heading read: 'Trials of the Fighters in the Prague Uprising.' Just as we got to the rotunda, a jazz band further up the street started to play. One enlarged photograph showed a man in the dock. The figure was Major Jaromir Nechansky who had been a commander of a paratroop regiment, and who had played a prominent role in the anti-Nazi uprising of 1945. He and many others were charged with being American spies. Ladislav said, pointing: 'He was at school with me – and him – also executed.' This was the friend of whom Vera had spoken. Ladislav had not seen these photographs before. This was political education with a vengeance. He said: 'In 1968 I went on a visit to Mexico . . . I met an old Jew there who had left Prague thirty years before and he asked me if there were still whores in Wenceslas Square? "Oh yes," I said, "but now they all work for the Ministry of the Interior."'

Today is a public holiday to mark liberation day so the flags of the four powers are prominently displayed above the street. It is strange, seeing the Union Flag there.

I wanted to take Ladislav to lunch, and he suggested a restaurant near Wenceslas Square. As we poked away at the goulash soup with its lumps of pork and potato and which had been interestingly seasoned with caraway, Ladislav wanted to know my impressions of what I had seen and, in particular, my own attitudes to Marxism. Within the confines of lunch, I did my best to formulate what I thought.

I remarked on the truculence, boorishness and dishonesty which I had encountered, routinely, in the hotel and in restaurants; indeed, whenever I had had dealings with anyone in a public capacity. Attempts to excuse such a situation as 'the price of socialism', I said, is doing socialism no favours. On the other hand, a high moral tone may denounce but fails to understand the problem, which is more than simply one of human weakness. Certainly, individuals may behave badly in any system. But a system which institutionalises bad behaviour has something deeply wrong with it. Besides, socialism was, in my mind at least, associated with the sharing of resources and pleasures, rather than about Byzantine state bureaucracies. What I had seen of Czechoslovakia was a society which encouraged a miserable waste of human resources. I was reminded of the Brecht poem in which the politicians decide that they cannot trust the people and that they had better elect a new one.

To some extent, the demoralisation and poverty of spirit I had encountered could be attributed to the misfortunes of geography; to the fact that Czechoslovakia had such ruthless neighbours as Nazi Germany and the Soviet Union. But that still leaves unanswered the more basic issue as to whether the whole Marxist enterprise was so wrong-headed that the economic and human failures were not, in some sense, built into the ideology. Nor will it do to argue that state socialism is a perversion or corruption of some pure source, for the source has been so consistent in what it has given rise to, and so wrong in its predictions, that the suspicion of some intrinsic connection between theory and practice cannot be evaded.

The great strength of capitalism, I suggested, whatever its failings, is what we may call its psychology of opportunism, its offer of more. It has behind it a powerful cluster of motivating forces, accompanied by a theory of motivation which, however inadequate, works sufficiently to keep the system going. At its best, what it offers the individual is the possibility of personal material and/or educational improvement. The fact that there may be others in society who do not do so well need not even occur to the individual. In reality, the theory of wealth 'trickling down' does not work and the farce of a 'representative' rather than a delegated democracy means that a high price is extracted from society for the 'freedom' on offer, since social cohesion and environmental safeguards are no necessary part of the legislative framework which allows capital to keep on growing. All that admitted, you don't make omelettes by stopping people from eating steak. The governments of Eastern Europe have deprived individuals of both motive and freedom as the price of a supposed social planning. The West, in contrast, pretends that social planning is more central to its ideology than it really is and fails to support many of those who, for whatever reason, lose out on the benefits of the system.

My own interest in Marxism grew, I explained to Ladislav, in part at least, out of my readings of Hegel at university. Marx started out as a Young Hegelian in the early 1840s and never threw off the underlying presuppositions of Hegelian rationalism. He never developed a theory of individual motivation because he was not interested in the individual. Marx believes that the individual is socially constructed but never provides or even attempts to provide the theory of knowledge which could support his claims. Marx simply assumes that *how* we know things is not a problem. He is wrong. The Hegelian bias shows up again in the ambition of the Marxist enterprise. Hegel believed that a substance was exhausted by the sum of its predicates, which is another way of saying that he identified the categories of the German language with those of abstract thought, and those of abstract thought, in turn with those of Mind or *Geist*. Since the world was essentially *Geist*, the categories of language were ultimately those of reality, and reality was ultimately abstract. For a philosophical Idealist, this is a perfectly respectable approach, whatever one thinks of it.

Marx fancied that he could simply take over the Hegelian analysis and, in Engels' famous phrase, 'stand Hegel the right way up' with no reference to the fact that Hegel's whole analysis is rooted in an effort to resolve quite specific problems which he inherited in the theory of knowledge. Marx simply adopts the identity of linguistic categories with actualities as though there were no further difficulties and as though the Hegelian approach could be divorced from Absolute Idealism, which it cannot. The upshot is that Marx never even concerns himself with questions such as the relation between individual perceptions to objects or the texture of feelings, sensations and thoughts, which might have led him towards a theory of where individuality occurs. He forgets Aristotle's basic dictum: no thoughts but in things. Marx writes as though the world could dispense with particularity and there betrays the real depth of his borrowings from Hegel and, more crucially, the uncritical nature of those borrowings. His bias is to believe that the general carries greater weight than the particular, and that uniqueness is somehow accidental or incidental to the world. The loss to Marxist theorising of all those elements which stress human individuality and specificity as central to the nature of experienced reality, means that Marx cannot account for how we behave except as statistical averages. Translated into political terms, the result is a profound and consistent bias away both from individuality and from the libertarian element in the radical tradition. Marx, as a pupil of Hegel, always favours Law over uniqueness. It is therefore a theoretical structure flawed in some of its fundamental conceptions and all too readily adaptable to the needs of hierarchical bureaucracies. C. G. Jung points out that Christianity at least provides a powerful set of motives for the individual to conform to a social and moral code. Marxism attempts to replace that code without providing any serious motive to induce people to behave decently and for the common good.

All of which is not to deny that, in that hugely complex tradition which is Marxism, there are profound insights which need to be kept in sight. But, above all, the moral and radical impulse which lay behind the Marxist tradition needs to be preserved. Ladislav absorbed all this, nodding agreement from moment to moment. I had to leave Prague next day and was sorry to be losing his company so soon. He declined the offer of a lift home, wished me an interesting journey, and set off through a light Prague drizzle.

I LEFT Ladislav near to the Staroměstské náměsti (Old Town Square), to the north side of which stands the statue erected in 1915 on the five-hundredth anniversary of the burning for heresy of Jan Hus, one of the founders of the European radical tradition. Hus was rector of the University of Prague and in 1403 translated the *Trialogus* of the English reformer, John Wycliffe, in which he summarises his theology. Wycliffe denounced the abuses and corruption of the clergy and Papacy and insisted that the authority of the Scriptures was self-sufficient. English scholars went to Prague in the wake of Anne of Bohemia, Richard II's wife, and there introduced the works of Wycliffe. Hus quickly became a popular figure in Bohemia. It is easier to understand the attractiveness of his doctrines for the mass of people if we bear in mind that Wycliffe had claimed that property was sinful. Clerics in Bohemia were also landlords on a large scale and, very often, foreigners. As most of the higher ecclesiastical posts were held by Germans, there was also a nationalist element to the movement. By 1411 Hus had become so influential that Prague was laid under papal interdict. In 1415, Hus was summoned to defend himself at the Council of Constance, having been assured of a safe conduct by the emperor Sigismund. Sigismund betrayed his promise – he is supposed to have blushed when confronted with the fact – and, after a farcical trial, Hus was burned. At the same Council it was decreed that Wycliffe's remains should be exhumed and burned, which they were.

When news of Sigismund's treachery reached Prague, a rebellion broke out. Across the Old Town Square from the statue of Hus, the Old Town Hall still stands. From its windows a crowd, led by John Žižka, threw the anti-Hus councillors to the crowd below, who promptly lynched them. When the Bohemian king, Wenceslas IV, heard of the revolt, he was seized by an epileptic fit and died a few days later. Žižka went on successfully to defend Bohemia from the crusades which were preached against the Hussites who, by this time, had acquired a thoroughly democratic and Protestant cast. The Hussites held out successfully until, in 1436, an agreement was reached which allowed them to consolidate their achievements. From then until the Battle of the White Hill in 1620, Bohemia was effectively Europe's first Protestant state.

Prague's second famous defenestration took place at the Hradčany Castle when Bohemian Protestants again thought themselves threatened in 1618. On this occasion the officials thrown from the window managed to survive, since they landed in deep piles of castle refuse. That event is usually seen as the beginning of the Thirty Years War. It was in front of the Old Town Hall that the leaders of the revolt were executed after the defeat at The White Hill.

After completing a tour of the baroque wonders of Prague, I decided that my detour from the Danube had lasted long enough, and that it was time to head south again. But the last word on

Czechoslovak politics should be Ladislav's: 'The Czechs want freedom as a child wants a balloon. But, having gained it, they do not know what to do with it – yet.'

ONCE out of Prague the road began to rise through pine-woods into the southern Bohemian uplands. Strands of early morning mist still clung to the hollows as the sun tried to break through the patchy cloudscape. The villages on the road for Tabor looked less dilapidated than Prague. The road surfaces tend to be worse in the towns than in the country. Ladislav explained that the constantly changing maze of roadworks and diversions in Prague was the result not of ambitious renewal programmes, but of bureaucracy gone mad. The state bank which provides the cash for roadworks does not pay out money until a project or part of it, is completed. Therefore, on any given project, a manageable chunk will be completed to secure enough cash for wages. That project will then be abandoned in favour of some other quickly completable component elsewhere, so that even relatively minor works can take years to finish. The result is chaotic. More alarmingly, driving in Czechoslovakia puts one's lungs at risk, as the quantity of black fumes spewed out by cars and lorries is, on occasion, quite unbelievable. One would find oneself driving along in a pall of black poison. Pollution simply does not figure on the list of governmental priorities.

On the outskirts of Tabor there were long rows of multi-storey apartment blocks of an extraordinary ugliness; many flats looked empty. Every East European town of any size seems to be disfig-ured by these viciously utilitarian structures and several suburbs of Prague consist of nothing else, as though the provision of other amenities were no concern of the planners. Even when allowance is made for meagre resources, there seemed often to be a wilful and needless callousness to many of these suburban barracks.

As the Tabor primary schoolchildren were making their way to their classes, it was hard not to think of a scene from 1950s Britain, the children all in their uniforms and carrying satchels.

Tabor, named from a hill a few miles from Bethlehem, was

founded in 1420 by the Taborites, the radical wing of the Hussite movement. It was chosen partly because it was a defendable site, raised above the surrounding landscape. The countryside south of Tabor is mainly cereal-growing, dotted here and there with little lakes. Much of the road is lined by beeches and limes. Aiming to cross into Austria at Gmünd, I came on the border post sooner than I had expected and, misreading the signs, drove past the guard-post to the frontier barrier. Waved back by a Kalashnikov-wielding, spotty boy-soldier, I was subject to a ten-minute harangue by two bad-tempered border guards. Since I refused to acknowledge that I understood a word of Czech or German, I just shrugged my shoulders as they droned on. They gave up in disgust and I was waved through, saluted by the spotty boy.

The Austrian officials were quite another matter; middle-aged, self-confident, well dressed and courteous, they enquired how long I intended to stay, glanced in the boot, and waved me on with the hope that I would enjoy my stay. The immediate transformation in the road surface, its increased width, signalled my return to Western Europe. In the space of a few moments one crossed a cultural divide now generations deep. Even the sun, as if to mark my sudden sense of relief at being out of Czechoslovakia, chose to put in an appearance. I had not realised until that moment how tense the past few days had made me. From Gmünd eastwards to Horn and south to Krems was only a matter of a couple of hours through some lovely, fertile valleys, brilliantly green in their spring foliage. Suddenly, too, I was back in wine country with terraced hillsides stretching up on both sides of the road.

KREMS, at the eastern end of the Wachau valley in Lower Austria, is a handsome little town and somehow gives the impression that it is not large enough to house its thirty-two-thousand souls. I entered the old town on foot, having left Anastasia outside the Steiner Tor (1480) which guards Krems' western entrance. Within a few moments I had been directed to the Gasthof zur Alte Post and installed myself in a tiny room which was to cost about £12 for the night, including breakfast. When the girl at the reception desk discovered that I would be leaving early in the morning, she insisted on refunding £2, since I would be on the road before she arrived to cook breakfast.

By now the day was hot and bright and my first need was for lunch and a glass of wine. The Alte Post is old, parts of it dating from the mid-sixteenth century. Lunch could be had in the inn's cobbled courtyard. Lilacs had been twined about the balcony which ran round two sides of the courtyard and over the deep, ancient arches of the north and west walls. Since it was all in bloom, the yard was a riot of colour and scent. Pots of roses decorated the corners of the yard. Most of the tables supported big red-and-white parasols beneath which an assortment of elderly ladies were chatting away.

I was directed to a table set under one of the deep arches and which already had one occupant. The service was brisk but I was struggling to understand the drawn-out diphthongs of a heavy accent which gave *Ja* at least two syllables. Opposite me, sat a small, thin man with yellowed teeth who ate in a great hurry. He greeted me politely and we quickly got into conversation. He was a bookseller who knew London slightly and Prague well. He had, however, an appointment to keep, and a few minutes later I had the table to myself.

Looking about me, almost all the other tables seemed to be occupied by ladies of Habsburg vintage who sipped away at their camparis or white wine or, in two cases, glasses of beer. In the meantime, a sudden cloud had appeared, and a few large drops of rain spattered the courtyard. Something resembling panic broke out among the ladies. At once, the waiters began to reorganise the tables so that as many as possible could sit under the parasols and to hurry away the unused cushions and linen so as not to let them be soaked. I later witnessed exactly the same procedure carried out in a Budapest café with such leisurely incompetence, that everything was completely waterlogged before they *began*. Some of the ladies were being helped indoors to the restaurant by the waiters. It was only then I began to grasp that several of these old dears, whose daily habit to foregather here it clearly was, were as drunk as lords and were being helped not because of their age, but because otherwise they would fall down. It was very difficult to keep a straight face. It was as well that I did, however, for one most distinguished-looking lady of very advanced years moved to my table from the group of her friends who had been assisted indoors. The shower failed to materialise.

She had the translucent skin of the very ancient and I would have guessed her age at not far from ninety. She sat bolt upright, hands folded in front of her, a shock of thin, frizzy, snow-white hair atop her high-cheekboned face. Her eyes were a piercing, watery blue. When my food was brought, she nodded and pronounced *Mahlzeit* over it.

I had ordered a consommé to begin and, by the end of my first course, she was clearly growing restless. Crooking an index finger, she summoned a waiter and proceeded to inform him that she had been waiting fully half an hour for her pancakes and that it would not do. The waiters, who were obviously well accustomed to their elderly clientèle moved at a brisk trot. They could hardly have been more different from the swaggering louts of the Hotel Olympik who would chatter among themselves for ten minutes and then saunter towards one as much out of boredom as anything else. When, a few minutes later, madam's pancakes were brought, she ate her way through a plateful of stodge with brisk fortitude which would not have disgraced a squad of Irish navvies. I decided that I liked Krems, and suddenly understood what it was had attracted W. H. Auden to live in rural Austria – its high camp!

OLD Krems is built on the slope of the Danube's left bank just where the little river Krems joins its greater sister. The river is broad here, about two hundred yards, and from its banks one looks up to the baroque turrets of the Benedictine monastery of Stift Göttweig, perched high on its wooded hill. Above Krems, the slope is terraced to its summit with vines. Upstream, through the gorge known as the Wachau, runs one of the prettiest stretches of the river and I sat for a pleasant hour on its embankment watching the swallows skim its waters.

In the Stadtpark just behind the swimming pool, the cars parked under the chestnut trees were half an inch deep in confetti-like blossom. The main axis of the old town runs east-west along the Landstrasse, which is also a fashionable shopping street with cafés, ice-cream shops and every kind of boutique from one selling Armani jackets to one specialising in religious accessories. Like so much of Austria, Krems is up to its neck in churches. The parish church (Pfarrkirche S. Veit) is one of the oldest examples of Austrian baroque, built during the first decade of the Thirty Years War, although the interior fittings and paintings are largely work of the eighteenth-century high baroque. To someone brought up in the relative austerities of the Church of Scotland, all this gilt and marble, colourful painting and painted statuary seems rather extraordinary and, somehow, secular. Just a few yards along the road in the Piaristenkirche, there are further reminders that Austria was the home of the Counter-Reformation with paintings and statues of Saints Francis Xavier, Ignatius de Loyola and John Nepomuk of Prague.

As you go in by the west end of the nave of the parish church, two black memorial plaques have been set into little side chapels on the north and south walls. The one on the north wall is for the men of the cavalry regiments from the Krems area who fell in the First World War. In front of it a number of candles were burning. On the south wall the memorial was for the infantry regiments. It had no candles. I could find no memorial at all for 1939-45, though there is one elsewhere in the town.

Back at the Alte Post, I settled myself into an archway fringed with lilac blossom. Earlier in the day, while looking for the swimming-pool, I had found myself in a park containing the largest number of fire-engines I had ever seen. An exhibition and conference on fire-fighting involving companies and brigades from all over Austria was in full swing. The central section of the courtyard of the Alte Post had been set with a three-sided arrangement of trestle tables for a party of thirty and now they began to arrive. Some were in business suits, others in uniforms which had clearly been designed by a Gilbert and Sullivan enthusiast. As each couple or small group arrived, everyone was introduced to everyone else, the gentlemen bowing and shaking hands all round. The blue and yellow uniforms lent the scene a colourfulness not to be found in Britain, save perhaps in military ceremonial, and I could not but wonder why in our churches and social life colour has become so taboo.

79

Only the Austrians seem able to outdo Germans in the quantities of food one is expected to eat in restaurants. It must have something to do with the way the language heaps noun upon noun. The title of my main course was: *Alt-Wiener Tafelspitz mit Berner Rösti dazu Schnittlauchsause und Apfelkrem.* That particular mouthful amounted to thick slices of boiled sirloin accompanied by a pancake. The pancake, so far as I could tell, was a mixture of potato, cabbage, onion and seasonings. The two sauces on the side were apple and sour cream with chives. When I was unable to finish the heaped plateful, the waitress expressed concern that I had not enjoyed one of their local specialties; two, I felt, would have killed me.

VIENNA is the home of grandiose monumentalism. You can walk most of the Ringstrasse in a couple of hours but exploring this exercise in mass intimidation is a tedious business. The front section of the vast *Rathaus* has been restored to its original pale sand colour. It was flag bedecked and in front of it a brass band were parading in breeches, green-Loden jackets and cocked hats. They, or it, looked ridiculous. The Ringstrasse offers an architecture of desperation, of the assertion of coherence by fiat and, as such, it accurately reflects the state of the empire when it was built. The empire was the monarchy, and the monarchy was an administrative bureaucracy of extraordinary inflexibility supported by an officer-class recruited from the same social strata. The bourgeoisie were not admitted to the court or to the *nomenklatura.* They were, therefore, the most appalling snobs, trampling on whichever subsection of the bourgeoisie or proletariat lay immediately below them.

As the nineteenth century progressed, Austro-Hungary took refuge in reaction at home and adventurism abroad in an effort to contain the centrifugal forces which eventually blew it, and much of Europe, apart. Austria, and Vienna in particular, was the real home of Central-European anti-semitism. Jews were bottom of the pile. No matter how low you sank, the Jews were still below you, along with the gypsies. At the tail end of the nineteenth century, the Viennese politician Karl Lueger founded his power base on an anti-semitic platform. Stories of ritual murder by evil Jewish cabals figured regularly in the Viennese gutter press. It is no accident that Schickelgruber, the failed artist who became Hitler, should have been the son of a petty official and have spent his ambitions at the butt end of Viennese snobbery.

The peculiar cast of Austrian Catholicism must play some part in that story. In *The Thirty Years War*, C. V. Wedgewood suggests that Austria was ruined as the potential leader of a German-speaking *Mittel-Europa* by the dynastic linkage of the Spanish and Austrian Habsburgs. It is certainly true that for a few crucial generations in the late sixteenth and seventeenth centuries, the influence of Spanish Jesuits on the never-very-alert minds of the Habsburg emperors was decisive. The Spanish court, with its rigid protocols, religious austerity and fanaticism, planted the seeds of the Counter-Reformation in the rulers of Austro-Hungary. The ferocity of the Counter-Reformation was the *coup de grâce* to a Central Europe already suffering economic recession and the loss of its outlets to the east. But, if history is anything, it is an infinite series of 'if onlys . . .'. As Pascal observes: 'Cleopatra's nose: had it been shorter, the whole aspect of the world would have been altered.'

In Vienna not even the Danube runs free, for it has been channelled into a neat canal. In the town centre, in the upmarket shopping precincts near St Stephen's Cathedral, the old buildings have been elegantly restored and the new ones are all polish and price. There is no trace of litter, despite the hundreds of affluent shoppers who ebb and flow along these consumerist highways. The cathedral itself is a mob of tightly packed tourists. It is impossible to see or sense anything here *except* tourism. So why do most people come to the cathedral? Certainly not because they are historians, however amateur. They are, I suspect, fulfilling some obscure sense of obligation that this is 'what one does' in Vienna. In the Middle Ages they would have gone on pilgrimages to the knee-cap of Saint Whoever, to the great profit of the Church.

What irritates me about Vienna is a certain not-quite-definable smugness, a feeling that somehow this place feels itself to be *the centre*. In Scotland, by contrast, one felt oneself to be on a periphery and, in some way, helpless.

GETTING lost in Budapest is easy if you do not speak Hungarian. For the first and only time on the journey, posters, shop signs and street names meant nothing to me. In Romanian, Serbo-Croat or Czech, I can make a guess at meanings based on my bits and pieces of Italian, Latin, German or Russian. But not in Hungary, where the language does not belong to the Indo-European group at all, being related to Finnish and, ultimately, to some of the languages of the Asian steppe. I should have known I would have problems when I crossed the border of a place whose name I could hardly pronounce – Mosonmagyaróvár. From there to Budapest via Györ (pronounced Dyir) and Tatabánya, both rather unattractive towns, was a three-hour drive across unbroken plain on a swelteringly hot morning. On the outskirts of Budapest, however, the sign 'Centrum' began to appear. So once I had passed through the obligatory outskirts of post-war, multi-storey housing estates and entered a labyrinth of blackened buildings in canyon-like streets with traffic jammed solid, I knew I had to be somewhere near the town centre.

In a fortunate moment I noticed a sign reading 'Jardin de Paris – Restaurant Français', and abandoning Anastasia on a pavement, a procedure to which East Europeans do not seem to take exception, I ventured in to discover whether anyone spoke French. One young waiter did, but very (very) badly, and after several efforts asked whether I could speak English. He suggested an hotel nearby where his wife, who could speak German, worked as a receptionist. The Hotel Orion was only half a mile away. Unfortunately to get there I had to negotiate an amazingly convoluted one-way system. At the third attempt I gave up and hailed a taxi. Taxi drivers in any East European city are likely to speak some German and, having grasped the problem, he suggested I follow along behind him. In a few moments I was installed in a comfortable room about as near to the centre of Buda as it is possible to be. By happy chance, I had found a private hotel only fifty yards from the Danube and which, unlike its skyscraper neighbours immediately across the river, such as the fashionable

Intercontinental, did not cost vast sums of hard currency. The receptionist was polite, the room pleasantly furnished and clean. Could this be Eastern Europe?

It would have been boorish not to return to the Jardin de Paris for lunch, a short walk which took me along the right bank of the Duna to the famous Széchenyi Bridge and Clark Adam tér. Hungarians put their surname before their christian names. Adam Clark was the Scotsman who designed the Széchenyi Bridge. The tér is in fact a busy roundabout from behind which a cable car takes you up on to Castle Hill and the ancient fortress area of Buda. From the tér it was only a short walk along Fö utca (Clan Chief Street) to the Jardin. The menu was an exercise in school French, but the food was good, even if it bore no relation to anything I knew as French cuisine.

By Budapest standards, the Jardin de Paris was upmarket and expensive. The restaurant was little more than an intelligently decorated semi-basement with space enough for a bar and a half dozen tables. Clever lighting made it seem airy even though there was little light from the street. The walls were hung with posters and drawings with a Parisian flavour. At the next table a German couple were talking loudly and beyond them a middle-aged man on his own occupied a table for three. Ten minutes later he was joined by the couple for whom he had been waiting. He stood, and with a great sweep of his hand, bowed, said 'servus', and drew out a chair for his lady guest. However over-the-top he may have seemed, it was a vignette I could not have envisaged in Prague. If first impressions mean anything, I was getting a sense of a city more amiable and self-confident. The drivers seemed less aggressive, even stopping to let you into a stream of traffic. The taxi-driver, the waiters, the receptionist, had all shown a willingness to be pleasant. I looked forward to my time in Budapest.

FOR reasons that go deep into its past, Hungary has not done well out of the twentieth century. It was the main loser in both territory and population from the First World War.

It had suited Austria and Hungary's aristocratic rulers in the nineteenth century to keep Hungary largely rural and feudal. Hungary was the bread-basket of the Empire. The great pre-war estates were among the largest in Europe. With the defeat of 1918, the traditional 'lands of St Stephen' were decimated. Romania was given Transylvania, of which the north-eastern parts were mainly Magyar-speaking. Czechoslovakia was substantially carved out of what had been Hungary, at least in its eastern and southern parts. Yugoslavia was given the Vojvodina, that section of plain to the north of Belgrade. In all, Hungary lost a third of its territory and two-fifths of its population. It is not surprising then, that in the inter-war period, the principal aim of Hungarian foreign policy was to recover as much as possible of *Hungaria irridenta*.

Between the wars Hungary had no large industrial working class. The people running the country were the great landowners and bureaucrats of the old empire, who were themselves a class mainly created by the large-scale bankruptcies of the lesser gentry in the first half of the nineteenth century. There was no large, autonomous middle class apart from the state apparatus. Social change, therefore, was unlikely to come from the top and the peasantry were badly educated and impoverished smallholders. Joseph Rothschild points out that in the inter-war period, the whole of Eastern Europe, excluding Russia, produced only eight per cent of European industrial production and that a third of that came from Czechoslovakia.

After Bela Kun's failed attempt to establish a socialist republic on the Soviet model in 1919, an administration was established in March 1920 with Admiral Horthy as regent. Hungary's economic dependence on grain exports, mainly wheat, meant that she was badly affected by the economic crises of the early 1930s, when the average price of agricultural produce fell sharply while that for industrial goods rose. In 1927, in an effort to diminish her international isolation, Hungary signed a treaty of friendship with Mussolini's Italy. Now in the economic crisis, Italy and Nazi Germany found it politic to buy Hungarian grain. Economic difficulty and political dissatisfaction were inextricable, and from 1932 to 1936 Hungary's prime minister was the fascist Gyula Gömbös. Gömbös supported a German-Hungarian-Italian axis and by 1938 a Hungarian Nazi party, the Arrow Cross, had been formed and was agitating for land reform and a restoration of the old frontiers. Hitler cemented the German-Hungarian alliance by allowing Hungary to annex Ruthenia and a strip of Southern Slovakia when he carved up Czechoslovakia in 1939.

By a strange irony of history, the prime minister in 1939, as a result of deaths and resignations, was Count Pál Teleki who had already served briefly as prime minister from 1920 to 1921. He was one of the old, feudal aristocracy and fundamentally anti-German. But it was too late in the day to get Hungary out of its Axis alliances and it was he who annexed Ruthenia and negotiated the Vienna Award of August 1940, by which Hitler gave back to Hungary half of Transylvania, including the old regional capital of Kolozsvár (Cluj). Hitler's policy was clever: to keep Romania and Hungary in competition with each other to see which could make the greater territorial gains. In 1940 Teleki signed a non-aggression pact with Yugoslavia. In 1941 Hitler sought to use Hungarian territory for his attack on Yugoslavia. Teleki, aristocrat as he was, felt obliged to fall on his sword. As a reward for its co-operation, Hungary was given back to Vojvodina. As soon as the war was over, Hungary had to revert to its 1918 frontiers. Towards the end, Horthy tried to extricate the country from the impending shambles, but the Germans occupied it in March 1944 and, in any case, the Allies were no longer sympathetic.

Nor was Hungary's post-war history much happier. At first, Stalin did not insist on a communist regime and in the 1945 elections, the communists only obtained seventeen per cent of the vote. By 1949, however, as a result of Soviet pressure, the communists were able to submit a 'government list' for national approval. It was approved by ninety-five per cent! The communist leader was Mátyás Rákosi. It was he who carried out the Stalinist purges which lasted from 1949 to 1953. The most notorious of the show trials was that of László Rajk in 1949. Rajk was secretary-general of the party but his internationalism branded him as dangerously Titoist and he was hanged as a fascist spy and traitor. About two thousand other veteran communists were also executed, while hundreds of thousands were imprisoned or expelled from the party. The reality, of course, was that Rákosi intended to hang on to power. As Rothschild says: 'In effect, Rákosi killed more communists in five years than Horthy had in twenty-five, and the entire society was cowed into a condition of bewilderment and terror.' Rajk was eventually rehabilitated in 1956.

My own memories of the uprising of 1956 are hazy, though

I think I remember recordings of the appeal by prime minister Imre Nagy to the Western Powers for help. I certainly heard it in later years.

Nagy had already been prime minister from 1953 to 1955 but had fallen from favour and Rákosi returned to power. As with Dubček in the 1960s, the Soviets endorsed the new Hungarian leaders of 1956, János Kádár and Imre Nagy, who replaced Rákosi on the latter's death. Their reformist programme, however, quickly got out of hand when workers in Györ began to demand free elections. Since the communists were widely seen as an anti-national party, free elections would have been a disaster.

The tanks moved in on 4th November and Kádár took over. Nagy was hanged in June 1958. In the following years Kádár eliminated all opposition and reinstated forced collectivisation in the villages. In 1962, however, he began to shift his policies away from outright repression and towards a gradual reformism, summed up in the slogan, *Those who are not against us are with us*. This effort at reconciliation, combined with gradual economic improvement, allowed Kádár to steer Hungary through the 1960s and 1970s towards increasingly liberal, economic and social measures. The price was a tacit understanding that certain assumptions could not be questioned, in particular the leading role of the Communist Party and Hungary's commitment to the Warsaw Pact alliance. By the time Kádár resigned in 1988, he had come to be thought of as a kind of benign pragmatist, who had done what he could in difficult circumstances.

Kádár was succeeded by Károlyi Grósz in May 1988. Eight months later it was announced that Nagy and his colleagues were to be rehabilitated. Next month the party's Central Committee announced that it would institute a multi-party democracy. Foreign companies were to be encouraged to invest. In June 1989 Nagy was reburied, his body being extracted from the common grave into which it had been thrown. The occasion became one of national self-assertion and two months later the whole edifice of Eastern European solidarity was undermined when Hungary allowed East German citizens to exit to Austria via its territory. In the following month, October 1989, a new republic was declared, but by that time Soviet troops were already committed to leaving. The first genuinely free elections since 1945 were held in March 1990. They were won by the Hungarian Democratic Forum which went on to form a coalition government of right-of-centre parties.

MIKLÓS Vajda is literary editor of *New Hungarian Quarterly*. I had been given his address by friends in Britain and now took a taxi to his flat, a couple of miles from the hotel but still in the older part of the city of Buda. Miklós, in his middle fifties, is a tall, quietly spoken but imposing figure, very self-possessed.

The temporary flat in which I found him was littered with books. He was hard at work on the translation of a play which had to be ready two days later. Translation is a form of hack work among East European intellectuals. It is usually paid for via state-funded organisations and can at least be relied on even if it can be at times both economically and spiritually unrewarding. With the destruction of state socialism in Hungary, the old and relatively comfortable set-up in which officially approved writers could have access to funds, however limited, via the Writers' Union, will come to an end, since the Union itself will no longer have any official funding. The arrival of a fresh-faced entrepreneurial capitalism intent on whole new empires may not be entirely comfortable for writers.

Miklós made coffee while we chatted about Prague. My dismay at much of what I had found there disappointed him. As with many intellectuals in Hungary and Romania, Czechoslovakia had become for Miklós a token of what East European civilisation might be. It had been a democratic country and had ancient traditions of learning and libertarianism. It was a beautiful and cultivated city. But these ideas of his were of a Prague long gone, a Prague idealised out of my recognition. It was a Prague generations old, if it had ever existed.

Miklós is a native of Budapest, as was his father. His mother came from an aristocratic background in Transylvania and had quit Hungary in 1956 for the United States. During the show trials at the end of the 1940s she had been imprisoned *pour encourager les autres*, though she had no political associations. After serving two years of her sentence, she was released on probation. But when the justice minister who had agreed to her release himself fell from favour, she was reimprisoned and had to serve a further ten months before being rereleased. Miklós spoke of these matters dispassionately, any hint of feeling only emerging as scorn for the communist establishment. Like Ladislav, he smokes relentlessly.

'The key problems for Hungary now,' he said, 'are the economic and the national questions. Hungary owes something in the order of twenty billion dollars in international debt. Our national tensions are, in a sense, externalised. There are two and a half million ethnic Hungarians in Transylvania and almost one million in Slovakia, both minorities being a result of the punishment and reward system adopted in the treaties of Versailles and Trianon and substantially confirmed at Yalta. The only possible solution to those problems is to build a Europe in which national boundaries no longer have the political and economic significance they now possess.'

Only a few weeks earlier, there had been serious disturbances in the Tirgu-Mureş area of Transylvania with fighting between rival groups of Romanian and Hungarian nationalists. Historically, there is solid ground for the idea of a common European homeland. That stew of Celt and Teuton, Magyar, Slav, Latin and Scandinavian which comprises contemporary Europe has a good deal of experience in common, not just of wars, but in terms of underlying social and intellectual structures. The common experience of Christianity, of similar concepts of family, together with the more recent experience of urbanisation and industrialisation, all mark Europe out as fundamentally different from the Arab world or from India. I commented to Miklós that I had little hope of the New World solving the problems of the Old when it could not face up to its own difficulties. I would like to believe that Europe can develop into an association of humane societies which people can believe in. Sadly, we agreed, such prospects lie a long way off.

The remarks which follow are extracted from our subsequent conversation:

Miklós Vajda: Here in Hungary it would be very difficult for us to be integrated quickly into a structure like that of the European Community. The kind of industrialisation we have developed, together with the quality of the commodities we produce, would have to change with dramatic painfulness. I daresay it can be done if you think of the kind of economic growth rates produced by places like South Korea . . .

WP   Yes, but South Korea started from a nil base so far as industrialisation was concerned and with labour costs not much above peasant-subsistence level.

MV   We don't have any shortage of cheap labour here.

WP   True, it may be cheap by European standards but not by those of the Far East. To have to compete with Third World labour costs would produce massive unrest in a population already urbanised and used to the standards of a Western industrial society.

MV   And South Korea could count on a peculiarly nasty dictatorship to help quicken the pace of its capitalist development.

WP   How do you think Hungary will adapt to having a real parliamentary democracy?

MV   It will, and so will Czechoslovakia. We have been a nation state for a very long time. That gives us a foundation and a coherence to work from. What it is difficult for those from the West fully to grasp, is just how surreal life under state socialism has been, especially in the early fifties when the system reached a kind of apogee of dementia. Sometimes I wonder now whether I dreamed some of it, so much was just unbelievable, so grotesque.

WP   Can you give me an example of what you mean?

MV   I spent four years at university, from 1949 until 1953. Those years were the high points of the Stalinist repression in Hungary. I began by reading English and French and, after my mother's trial, I was allowed to continue my studies by the personal intervention of Rákosi – by his special grace – because my godmother, my father's first wife, was an extremely popular actress on the national stage, a great star. She went to see Rákosi on my behalf. The upshot was that I was summoned by the university authorities and told that I was to be allowed to continue my studies but only under certain stringent conditions. First, I was never to mention these events. Second, I had to pass all my examinations with top grades. Last, I had to help the peasant and working-class boys who had been forced to go to university with no background education whatsoever. Hundreds of these youngsters were hearing French or English for the first time at, for example, a lecture on the Lake Poets. Of course, within a couple of years the standards simply plummeted because they simply could not cope. At the end of the first year I was summoned to the Dean's office. 'Comrade Vajda,' he said, 'you cannot go on studying two imperialistic languages. One is already too many. You must choose one or the other.' So, I abandoned French and in its place took up Hungarian studies. That kind of farce was just the tip of the iceberg.

If it sounds funny now, it was not so at the time. Sometimes it would happen that during a lecture – at that time the secret police were very active – there would be a knock at the door and two men would enter. One would say: 'Comrade so and so,' and their poor victim would turn white and he would have to go with them and perhaps we never saw him again.

WP Has much been written as yet about that period?

MV Yes, in memoirs but not imaginatively assimilated as it should be as, for example, in fiction. Kádár was fairly liberal in that respect, so long as a few taboos were respected, especially the role of the Soviet Union. But, of course, if you wanted to write seriously, then the taboos were difficult to avoid. That kind of self-censorship is very dispiriting.

WP Have you been able to travel much?

MV Yes, first of all because my mother was in the United States and, after the early 1960s, we were relatively free to travel. The real problem was hard currency. I was able to visit her several times and then, in my capacity as literary editor of

New Hungarian Quarterly, I was often sent to make contact with poets in America and so on. That in turn would generate further invitations.

WP   Have you always done the kind of work you do now?

MV   Yes. I graduated in 1953. That was still a time when serious writing was impossible, so I began to translate, mainly English, American and German novels and short story collections. Then, at a certain moment, I just could not go on with that any longer. It is so tedious and tame. I felt stifled, so one day, right in the middle of a huge novel by Theodore Dreiser, I stood up and said: 'No, I can't go on.' I was right in the middle of a sentence.
(Miklós was chuckling to himself at this.)
    I got in touch with the publishers and told them they would have to find another translator. Since then, I have only translated for the stage.

WP   Why drama?

MV   Oh, because I love it, I love the theatre. I grew up close to my godmother so as a child I was inoculated with the theatre.

WP   What do you think of the notion that much of the poetry produced in Eastern Europe as 'dissident' poetry has had a kind of easy ride because of its political context? In the West, poetry in translation from Eastern Europe has been widely disseminated in the past couple of decades. East European poets have had a relatively straightforward relation to their society. The obvious stupidities and brutalities of some East European regimes provided a soft target as well as a social role for dissident poets. Under a capitalist system of parliamentary democracy, do you think that poets will find themselves in a more difficult and ambiguous situation in which their previous models are no longer appropriate?

MV   The poet here has acquired a political status because of our peculiar history. In the long tale of Hungarian literature, not since the sixteenth century has the poet been able to

91

avoid political issues; they so dominated life. Hungary was for centuries the frontier state between the Ottomans and Europe. Secondly, in times of censorship or foreign occupation, the *only* available political expression may be a cultural one and then you have to develop idioms suited to that situation.

WP   And do you think that will change now?

MV   Yes. And I hope so. Now Hungarian poetry may begin to change towards a poetry which is more autonomous, more self-subsistent with its own themes and materials, not necessarily so directly structured by our political situation. And not only poetry but other forms of literature also. One must too make the qualification that where a major talent is at work, even in a politically committed situation, then something more universal may result. Dante is a political poet but he is also a great deal more than that.

WP   Clearly there will be difficulties in turning the country round from state socialism to capitalism. What do you think the transitional problems will be?

MV   In the main, economic ones. As you know, the post-election negotiations are still in progress and ministers have not yet been named. The issue will be whether the new government will have the courage to face the problems and introduce the harsh measures which will perhaps be required, at the price, it may be, of its own popularity. What must happen, and rather quickly, is the privatisation of the economy. Hitherto there have been no real owners. We already have an inflation rate of about five per cent and it is projected to go higher yet this year. We also have some unemployment now but not yet on a significant scale. Perhaps in two or three years we will have a convertible currency. I worry that the necessary measures may radicalise the working class which is, of course, the sector most prone to unemployment.

WP   Do you think we could see a reversion to the kind of right-wing authoritarianism which characterised Hungary between the wars?

MV That is not a problem at the moment, but this part of the world has always been unpredictable.

WP What about the sleazier aspects of capitalism? I am thinking of prostitution, pornography, the commercialisation of cultural values.

MV Oh, pornography can already be bought at the news stands. It is terrible. It has recently become an issue because it is so visible and entirely unregulated.

WP When East Berlin opened up a few months ago, there were mobile porn shops visiting different quarters of the city. They have, it seems, been doing a brisk trade. One entrepreneur described it as: 'The return of the pioneering days'. Do you not agree that you writers have had an easier time of it than we in the West, in a closed society where your cultural values are protected, albeit at a price? You have no open commercialism to compete with. The gutter press and the entertainment industry do not yet exist here in the way they do in Britain or in the United States.

MV Well, we do have a gutter press here but, of course, it is new, and in a while these things which are, for the moment, sensational, will go back to their proper place.

WP That is very optimistic.

MV I am optimistic overall.

WP So you do not think that Hungary will become one more cog in the greedy progress of capitalism?

MV Yes, but that will still be so much better than a so-called communist or socialist society, and I don't think people here have too many illusions about capitalism. What might be more dangerous is that forty years of so-called socialism have made people accustomed to a kind of egalitarianism, so that they will not readily tolerate great differences in income or lifestyle. I hope they will get used to that because it is indispensable that some people should make more money.

WP   Whatever else can be said about the East European regimes, they clearly failed to motivate their populations.

MV   That is true and, of course, it wasn't really any kind of socialism. It was more a sort of colonial system with the great difference that, whereas in typical colonial systems there is a highly developed mother-country and underdeveloped colonies, here we have an underdeveloped colonial power and more developed colonies. The ideological claim was that the Soviet Union was, by definition, more advanced since it had a deeper experience of socialism, but that of course is nonsense. Then too, there is no such thing as Soviet culture, whereas with the British Empire there was English culture, which is still a feature in many of your former colonies, together with the language. But here people could not hate Russian more. The language was compulsory but no one understands it, not a word, nothing. It has left no trace.

WP   Even I can confirm that. I gave a young army captain a lift into Budapest from Györ. He had neither French nor German nor English, as one would expect. But after what I understand would have been several years of compulsory Russian, he could barely manage *da* and *nyet*. Either he had genuinely repressed what he knew or he refused to acknowledge it.

I left Miklós to his translation, having arranged with him that we should meet for lunch two days later. He came to his front door to say goodbye, which he did with a handshake and a slight bow.

I CROSS the Széchenyi (Chain) Bridge several times a day, passing the gaze of its guardian lions. Even if not as ancient or beautiful as the Charles Bridge, it is a lovely artefact from which one commands splendid views of the Parliament Building and of the skylines of Buda and Pest. Designed by Adam and W. T. Clark and constructed between 1842 and 1849, it was the first bridge between Buda and Pest. Adam Clark also designed the tunnel which runs under Buda hill connecting the western parts of Buda with the waterfront. The bridge was the project of Count István Széchenyi, one of the most talented and unhappy of Hungarian patriots. He should have been a character in a Balzac novel.

The young count belonged to one of the wealthiest land-owning families of Hungary. His father founded the Hungarian National Museum. After serving in the army during the Napoleonic wars, Széchenyi turned to the management of his estates. He was an anglophile and an enthusiast of the works of Jeremy Bentham. He first came to public notice in 1825. Chancellor Metternich, the reactionary old fox who did so much to determine the shape of Europe's political alliances after the downfall of Napoleon, did not like parliaments and, so far as possible, did without them. In 1825, however, he badly needed money to finance his Italian armies and had few options left but to convene the long-neglected Hungarian parliament. During the first half of the nineteenth century Hungary was still a feudal state. Serfs were tied to the land and the great landowners did largely as they pleased. They could not, however, raise money on their estates, since, under a medieval law of entailment, their lands could not be seized to recover bad debts. No one, therefore, would lend them money and the estates went undeveloped. The 1825 parliament became a forum for the discussion of national grievances and Count István offered a year's income from his estates for the foundation of an Academy of Sciences. In 1830 he produced a book on the state of the Hungarian economy entitled *Credit*, arguing for the abolition of entailment and other progressive measures. It was his declared intention to 'rouse Hungary from its Asiatic slumbers'. At the same time, another young man was managing the estates of one of Hungary's other great landowners, the Countess Andrássy. The young man was Lajos Kossuth. In the following years Kossuth turned to journalism with a keen sense that his mission was to reawaken Hungarian nationality.

Széchenyi sponsored a great variety of projects, from the regulation of the Danube to the building of the Chain Bridge, and a general reform of the Hungarian economy. But reform could not be separated from the rising tide of political nationalism and Kossuth's and Széchenyi's fates became entwined.

In March 1848 Europe witnessed a surge of revolutionary activity which quickly spread from France to Italy and Vienna and, of course, Pest. By 1848 the Count had become an important figure in the administration of Hungary but the prospects of civil war and revolution led to his nervous collapse and he spent the next decade in an asylum. In 1857 Széchenyi, now recovered, was appalled by the effects of the decade of repressive absolutism which had followed on the collapse of the national movement in 1848–49. He published a pamphlet condemning its effects, only to be harassed by the police. In despair, he committed suicide in April 1860. His antagonist, Kossuth, called him 'the greatest of the Magyars'.

Kossuth was an extreme nationalist who did much to seal the fate of the Hungarian revolution of 1848 by his refusal to allow any of the subject nations within Hungary, such as the Serbs and Croats, any degree of cultural or political autonomy. By early 1849 Kossuth's popularity in the face of armed intervention by Croat and Austrian armies made him virtual dictator of Hungary. As the armies of general Windischgrätz approached, parliament retired to the eastern town of Debrecen where Kossuth made the declaration of Hungarian independence, having taken with him the regalia of St Stephen, founder of the Hungarian state. Despite early successes, the rebel armies could not withstand the intervention of Russian forces, for Francis Joseph had appealed to the Tsar for help.

Kossuth fled to the protection of Hungary's ancient enemies, the Turks. He crossed the frontier at Orsova, now in Romania, but, before doing so, buried on the Hungarian shore of the Danube the crown, orb and sceptre of St Stephen. Kossuth's tragedy was that the very fervour of his nationalism made him so intolerant of other ethnic groups within Hungary, that he damaged the cause he sought to promote.

SUNDAY is a working day in Hungary, for the time being at least. Because the communist authorities tried to discourage Christian worship, Monday is a closing day. As I cross the Elizabeth Bridge on my way to the National Museum, three optimistic fishermen are casting lines from a small sandbank. I would be chary of anything caught in these murky waters. A noisy crew of black-headed gulls is wheeling below the bridge,

Great Uncle Nathaniel Blackley 1896-1916

Prague *Vladislav Mareda*

Prague *The Charles Bridge*

Political education in the streets of Prague

Budapest *László Kunos at Gerbeaud's*

Budapest *Miklós Vajda*

Belgrade *Doko Stojičić*

Romania *The tent city in Bucharest – later attacked by Jiu valley miners*

Romania *The seafront promenade at Constanţa*

Carmen Sylva's Pavillion at Constanţa

Romania *Wild horses in the Danube Delta*

Wallachia *Stork and sparrows*

Petreşti *The Rotars' kitchen from the side*

Romania *Mr and Mrs Rotar in Petreşti*

feeding on the river's detritus. The bridge, named after Francis Joseph's empress, was blown up by the retreating Germans in 1944 and the present structure dates from the early 1960s. The riverside section of Pest opposite Castle Hill is the city's main shopping district. A few neon signs are beginning to appear on the larger buildings advertising the usual Western wares such as Levi jeans. The other neon sign which surmounted the Parliament building, a huge red star, has recently been removed. The great blocks of nineteenth-century neoclassical building which characterise this part of Pest give it a rather grand manner, though a century of knocks has rather frayed its hauteur.

The collections of the National Museum are divided into pre- and post-Magyar sections, both labelled in Hungarian. My main objective, however, was to see the regalia of St Stephen which have played so large a part, albeit symbolic, in Hungarian history and which have gone on such varied walkabout. It was only under President Carter's administration that they were returned to Hungary, having been removed from the potential clutches of Germans and Russians in 1945.

These objects – a crown, an orb and a sceptre – are not, for Hungarians, mere relics. In some mystical way they actually *are* Hungarian nationhood, its authority, its manna. Before you are allowed into the room in which the regalia are kept, you have to put on felt overshoes, as though the treasures were subject to being disturbed by excessive scuffling of feet. A party of schoolchildren are shushed by their teacher before they enter what is more a sanctum than a room in a museum. The room is dimly lit and the regalia are mounted in a centrally placed glass case. Armed guards stand watch. The crown consists of two circlet crowns welded together and into which has been set a cloth-covered headpiece. Round the rim of the broader circlet, which is about a foot in diameter, are a series of Byzantine portraits worked in enamel and separated by large rubies and sapphires. The whole object looks more Byzantine than I would have guessed, an effect heightened by the pendants which hang from each side. It is a curious blend of delicacy and crudity and has something rough and barbarian about it. But why should the crown possess this mystic attribute of being able to contain and confer sovereignty? The answer goes back to the origins of the Hungarian nation and tells us something about its individuality.

The Magyars were a nomad people of the steppes, claiming

kinship with those Huns who briefly occupied the Danubian basin in the fifth century and who helped finally to bring down the edifice of Roman power in the West. Győr was a Hunnish settlement, as was Buda, the latter, according to legend, named after a brother of Attila. By the ninth century the Magyars had settled around the river Dnepr, north of the Crimean Peninsula, having been expelled outwards by that movement of Asian tribes which rolled peoples westwards for a thousand years. The lands around the Dnepr proved insecure from raids by another Asian tribe, the Pechenegs, and so the Magyars, under their chieftain, Duke Árpad, set out to find fresh territories. Árpad's father was offered as a human sacrifice before the trek began. The relation of all this to the regalia is that, before setting out, the assembled tribes are supposed to have made a sacred 'Blood Agreement' by which the new lands would be governed.

The terms of the agreement were that the sovereign would be elected, initially but not necessarily, from the house of Árpad. The nation bestows that sovereignty by conferring the princely cap, later the crown. The Hungarian monarchy is not therefore held by divine right, but by election by the whole nation. The further conditions were that the assembly of the people constituted that national will, and that land was held in common right by the nation. However historically authentic (or not) this account may be, what is clear is that Hungarians adhered to it for a thousand years after their arrival in the Danubian plain at the beginning of the tenth century. Through all the vicissitudes of history, the crown came to embody Hungarian nationality and the Kingship remained elective, so that it was still possible for Hungarians in 1860 to deny Francis Joseph sovereignty because he had not been crowned with the crown of St Stephen. The historian Otto Zarek writes:

> The golden circle and the golden cap which form the basis of Stephen's Crown became for Hungary something more than the mere symbol of royalty. Kings and royal houses may disappear, but the crown remains; it incarnates National Power; it is the legal source and bearer of all rights, while the temporal wearer shall be its executive.

The Magyars behaved at first as Asiatic nomads are supposed to, by ravaging across Germany. Crushed, however, at the Lechfeld near Augsburg in 955 by Otto I, they were forced to turn inwards to the settlement of the Danubian plain. Christian missionaries were sent at the request of Duke Géza, and his son, Prince Vajk, was christened as Stephen. On coming to power in 997, Stephen brought the nation fully into the Catholic Church, decisively turning Hungary's face towards Rome rather than Byzantium. In recognition of that, Pope Sylvester II sent him a crown in the year 1000 and, so it is claimed, apostolic rights over the Church in Hungary. Stephen reorganised the state on a non-tribal basis and encouraged German knights to settle in its lands, very much as Malcolm III in Scotland invited Norman knights to settle in his country.

The waves of Asiatic invaders did not, however, end with the Magyars. The Pechenegs were sent against Hungary at the instigation of the Byzantine Emperor Michael Dukas as a means of checking Hungary's southward expansion. They were defeated by King Solomon of Hungary in 1073, but as a means of stirring up further trouble, Michael sent the victor, Duke Géza, Solomon's brother, a Byzantine crown. Géza, in fact, succeeded Solomon the following year and later the two crowns, those of Rome and Byzantium, were welded together.

When the house of Árpad became extinct in 1301, the crown itself became the object of civil war which continued for a decade until Charles Robert of Anjou finally secured both throne and crown.

Nearly six hundred years later, the reforming emperor Joseph II attempted to assimilate Hungary fully into the hereditary Habsburg dominions. As part of his attempts to Germanise and, as he thought, civilise Hungary, he had the crown brought to Vienna, having refused to be crowned, thereby avoiding the traditional oath to uphold the rights and privileges of the Hungarian nobility who, by this time, had become exclusively identified as 'the Nation'. Joseph's reforms led to peasant risings, which he put down with extreme brutality, and to conspiracies among the nobility. The upshot was that Hungarian nationalism was stimulated and Joseph was forced to rescind most of his reforms in 1790. After Joseph's death that year: '. . . the journey of the Holy Crown from Vienna to Buda in February 1790 was almost a triumphal procession. The Crown was escorted by the private armies of the Hungarian nobility with the soldiers arrayed in Hungarian national dress. Entire villages turned out for the spectacle and in Györ, the

Bishop himself headed the assembled burghers. In Pest-Buda, the cannons thundered and the whole city celebrated.'*

THE collections in the National Museum are impressive: an entire Roman mosaic floor from the time of Marcus Aurelian and a beautiful stele of Orpheus playing to the animals. The most astonishing item, however, is a piece of peasant work. It is the base of a tree with its root projections intact. It is rough, black, about four feet high and three feet wide, and huge iron spikes have been hammered in a ring around the top. It takes a moment to realise that it is not some pagan idol, but a head of Christ on the cross, that the spikes represent the crown of thorns and that in the wreckage of the ancient trunk a face has been carved. It is a savage and immensely powerful piece of sculpture, reminding one that Christianity is *not* a religion of sweetness and light and that much of its appeal must have lain in its very primitivism. There are many other beautiful things there but I cannot resist quoting a caption – for once, given in English – in the room set aside for the revolution of 1848. It is an extract from Act no. 18 of the parliament of 1848 and reads: 'Censorship having been abolished forever, freedom of the press re-established, each may freely convey and express his thoughts through the press.'

MONDAY morning, and it had been arranged that I would meet Miklós for lunch and then have the chance to talk with some writers from Hungarian PEN. First though I wanted a break from downtown Budapest and took a cab out to Margit-sziget (Margaret Island). When István Széchenyi proposed the regulation of Hungary's rivers, he probably did not realise that his suggestion

Concise History of Hungary, Corvina, p. 91.

would eventually lead, later in the century, to the three little islands in the Danube, just a couple of miles upstream from central Budapest, being girdled together by a retaining wall. The result is a beautiful leisure park, one and a half miles long and nearly a mile wide, in the middle of the Danube.

Before the war it was reserved for Budapest's more prosperous citizens. Now it is free, and very agreeable it was on a spring morning to walk through its coppices and gardens of oak and maple, white roses and birches and every kind of shrub. Mothers with toddlers and courting couples abounded, drawn here, as I was, by the quiet. A number of monastic orders had churches here in the middle ages. The island is named after a daughter of King Bela IV who pledged to build a Dominican convent for her on the island if the Mongols could be defeated. The park is dotted with the busts of notable Hungarians such as Kodály, Bartók, Ady and Atilla Jószef and assorted ruins. One church which has been restored in the present century, belonged to the Augustinian order of white canons. Originally a twelfth-century building, it was destroyed during the Turkish occupation. During its restoration, a storm blew down a huge walnut tree in the roots of which was found the church's bell, one of the oldest in Hungary.

I had taken with me my copy of Pascal's *Pensées* and by a nice irony came upon a passage which echoed the motto for the 'new thinking' of János Kádár:

> So there is open war among men, in which each must take a part, and side either with dogmatism or scepticism. For he who thinks to remain neutral is above all a sceptic. This neutrality is the essence of the sect; *he who is not against them is essentially for them* . . .
>
> What then shall man do in this state? Shall he doubt whether he is awake, whether he is being pinched, or whether he is being burned? Shall he doubt whether he doubts? Shall he doubt whether he exists? We cannot go so far as that; and I lay it down as fact that there never has been a real complete sceptic. Nature sustains our feeble reason, and prevents it raving to this extent.

Pascal's target here is Descartes and, in trying to think oneself back into the overwhelming urgency of their debate, it has to be remembered that their lives were overshadowed by the struggles of the Counter-Reformation. Descartes, indeed, was with the

101

armies of Maximilian of Bavaria in 1619 at the very beginning of the Thirty Years War when, at Neuberg on the Danube, he had that sequence of dreams which convinced him that his mission was to seek out truth by means of reason. Descartes could not avoid being a product of the Counter-Reformation, having been educated at the Jesuit College of La Flèche. In the midst of religious and political wars of startling insanity, the idea that God at least must have created a rational, knowable order must have acquired immense attraction in a world where religion and politics were still inseparable. The mission to certain knowledge in those circumstances also gains a political weight, for undeniable truth will surely diminish the grounds for conflict. Descartes' need for certainty was part of his religious sense. Pascal, quarter of a century younger, was also tensed by a religious vision; in his case confirmed by a mystic experience of great emotional intensity. But Pascal, under the influence of Jansenism, was fundamentally hostile to the Jesuits and their notorious sophistries.

What marks out Pascal is his refusal of the illusion that we can be *merely* rational, while yet insisting that reasoning be pushed to its limits. With an emotional frankness almost unique in pre-twentieth century philosophy, Pascal insists on his unhappiness and anxiety: 'We desire truth, and find within ourselves only uncertainty. We seek happiness, and find only misery and death. We cannot but desire truth and happiness, and are incapable of certainty or happiness.'

His sally at Descartes when he remarks that there has never been a complete sceptic goes to the heart of the issue and it was David Hume, arch sceptic, who wondered aloud why it was that his scepticism vanished whenever he left his study. To many, scepticism has seemed a blind alley and yet, somehow, unavoidable, and much of the literature of the twentieth century has paraded its nihilism as being intellectually justified by the power of the sceptical position. Nevertheless, as both Hume and Pascal recognised, a rigorous scepticism does not square with how we go about our daily business.

The English philosopher G. E. Moore returned to the problem in a famous paper, *A Defence of Common Sense* which, in its turn, forms a background for Wittgenstein's effort to demystify the issue in *Über Gewissheit* which, along with the *Philosophical Investigations* and, of course, the *Tractatus*, are the only texts he ever actually prepared for publication. The whole fantastic assortment is dealt with at length in Stanley Cavell's *Claim of Reason*. If I understand him aright, it ought to be possible to show that Descartes' stripping away of the 'accidental' qualities of objects is illegitimate, because based on a series of elisions of meaning between one use of an expression and another *where the two expressions look the same but have different meanings*. The process, however, is a subtle one and its analysis hinges on the kind of view of meaning which underlies Wittgenstein's later work.

The essence of the argument is that linguistic expressions derive their meanings and legitimate usages from the range of activities and contexts in which they have evolved – meanings, therefore, derive from what Wittgenstein calls 'forms of life'. Underlying such forms are the facts of the existence of other people and of their movement through time as well as space. The presumption is not a logical postulate but is, rather, an empirical condition for the development of particular language games. The kind of language game in which we talk about 'the back of' something is one in which that expression has meaning because it has evolved out of all kinds of activity in which 'backs' exist and can be shown to exist, because verified either by our own movement through space-time or by that of other persons, or both. The kind of testimony which makes sense of and verifies 'backs' is one involving its related activities. If, however, we wish to prove the existence of 'the back of' something using quite different criteria of testimony and disallowing all those activities which gave rise to the concept in the first place, then perhaps our proof of the uncertainty of the existence of backs will be less powerful than has been imagined. This, Cavell suggests, relying heavily on Wittgenstein, is what Descartes does in his famous *reduction* of the material world to a mass of uncertain epiphenomena. The central point is that Descartes conducts his philosophising alone and immobile in his study, arguing as though that frozen quality characterised all language use. In brief, the Cartesian *reduction* may rest on a set of difficulties which are linguistically generated by treating language as a less complicated thing than it in fact is. And it is a sense of the forced quality of those arguments which leads Hume to worry about why his arguments lack conviction when he leaves his study. Pascal goes some way towards this recognition when he observes: 'I

103

see, in truth, that the same words are applied on the same occasions, and that every time two men see a body change its place, they both express their view of this same fact by the same word, both saying that it has moved; and from this conformity of application we derive a strong conviction of a conformity of ideas. But this is not absolutely or finally convincing . . .'

The morass of such reasonings is very treacherous and many have disappeared into it, suffocating in its mud. And yet the problems reason hopes to resolve will not go away and we are little wiser in that respect than when Pascal wrote so perceptively: 'Man is neither angel nor brute, and the unfortunate thing is that he who would act the angel acts the brute.' Religious faith has become largely the province of the unreflective and the anti-rational. We say 'everyone is entitled to his beliefs', recognising the nastiness of a world which will not tolerate alternative beliefs, but over-looking the fact that some beliefs *are* nonsense and deserve to be called prejudice, bigotry or superstition rather than merely belief. But as Pascal also knew, our prejudices do not respond to reason alone. It is as though all the proofs and evidences of philosophy had mistaken *their* rationality for how people actually think.

MIKLÓS arrived just before one o'clock in an elderly red Skoda. We lunched in Pest, ten minutes walk from the PEN and Writers' Union offices near Heroes' Square. At the PEN office were Imre Szász of PEN, Ottó Orbán, a poet whose work I had admired in translation, László Kunos, translator and an editor with Corvina, the national publishing house, and Maria Körösy, translator and secretary of Hungarian PEN.

The conversation turned to the nature of class accents. I suggested that people in Britain were acutely aware of the relation between accent and class. Imre Szász, a large, solid-framed man, pointed out to me that in Hungary the Budapest accent was, for a long time, held to be inferior because it had been debased by non-Magyar and, in particular, Jewish elements, whereas the country accents were all perfectly acceptable. Miklós wanted to know why the Scots seemed more at ease as British than the Irish. Scotland, I suggested, had entered into a voluntary association, whatever questions have been raised about it since. Ireland was simply conquered. Only with the plantation of Scottish settlers to Ulster did any profound cultural division grow up in Ireland which remained ideologically Catholic and Gaelic. Scotland, in contrast, was already self-divided at the time of the Treaty of Union with two mutually hostile cultures in place – Gaelic and Lowland. Irish resistance never quite died away, while Culloden and the Clearances between them broke the back of Scottish Gaelic life. Burns became a cult figure because he was on the winning side, but appeared late enough on the scene to be able to sentimentalise the vanquished, thereby creating the illusion at least of being a national poet.

Imre Szász commented: 'We have the same kind of cult with Petöfi. He was killed in Transylvania at the Battle of Segesvár in 1849, fighting with Kossuth's armies under general Bem. He was only twenty-six. English-language poets compare him with Burns and the idealistic side of Shelley. But you are fortunate to be writing in English. In Hungarian PEN we have an uphill struggle to try to promote those Hungarian writers who are worth promoting, but so many of them travel badly in translation. A few have become internationally known, but it often seems a hopeless task. Our usual joke is that for a Hungarian novelist to get published and widely read, he has first to be sent to prison. I think our new government may make a tremendous mistake here by not realising this and failing to send any writers to prison. The result will be that Hungarian writers will get forgotten outside Hungary.'

I said that was a risk most East European writers were going to have to run: 'Several have already become important figures in the political establishment, Dinescu in Romania and, most obviously, Havel. With the loss of that easy, oppositional role, how will they survive?'

Szász laughed and said: 'Yes, now it is a totally different situation to be writing in. Hitherto, if you wanted to say something, you took a risk. You tried to hide it and not to hide it. Now you can open your big mouth as much as you want which, in many ways, is a much less interesting situation. It certainly makes very different demands on the writer.'

I ADJOURNED with László Kunos to Gerbeaud's for coffee and buns. In Budapest Gerbeaud's is *de rigueur*. The café, which dates back to the last century, has been maintained intact, at least in its decor. It was, and is, the haunt of fashionable intellectuals. Gilt ceilings and old silver certainly make it different from the usual run of East European cafés and on a warm early evening it is pleasant to sit outside and watch and chatter. Its pastries and ice-creams are excellent, though I have no taste for such things.

László is a lugubrious-looking, pale-complexioned, big-eyed, Budapest Jew with a sly sense of humour and an enormous fund of kindness. As we sat over our coffee, László explained how one of Pest's main streets, Pest's answer to the Champs Elysées, had had five changes of name since 1948. His parents had known it as Andrássy after the Count who had been prime minister when that part of Pest was laid out. After the communists came to power, the name was changed to the Stalin Allee. After Stalin's fall it became the Road of the Heroes and then was changed to the Road of Youth. Now it is back to Andrássy, which is how László has always known it.

In return, I described my discovery of Weimar's system for naming streets when I had visited it a few years earlier. The central section is named after Marx and just outside that is the Engels Strasse. Next in the expanding network is Lenin Strasse with assorted communist theoreticians and luminaries awarded a street closer to or further from the centre, depending on how high their star stood at the time. Gramsci was well into the outskirts.

I asked László about the *corso*: 'Yes, it did exist here before the war and now, gradually, it is coming back, along the embankment by the international hotels.'

As we wandered across the Széchenyi Bridge towards my hotel, László pointed out that in the last days of the Nazi occupation, Admiral Horthy had protected the Budapest Jews. The Jews in the countryside had been rounded up, with the active and sometimes enthusiastic support of the Hungarian authorities, and most had been sent to Auschwitz. The Budapest Jews, however, had been harassed but allowed to live. In the last days, with the Red Army approaching, groups of Budapest Jews had been rounded up, more or less at random, and taken to the embankment of the Danube where they were shot. It was convenient simply to have the bodies fall into the river. A few brave or lucky people had jumped and somehow survived, but very few. Looking into the Danube here, where it flows fast, deep and immensely powerful, it was difficult to imagine anyone surviving.

NEXT day I took the advice I had been given by my friends at the Union and went to see the exhibition of the Bibliotheca Corviniana in the National Library on Castle Hill, partly because Matthias I, or Matthias Hunyadi, known as Corvinus because of the crow motif on his banners, was one of the most striking and decisive characters in East European history, straddling the histories of Transylvania, Hungary, Bohemia and Austria. He was the Napoleon of Central Europe, though without Napoleon's greed and vindictiveness. Partly too, because I just like looking at beautiful books.

Matthias' father, János Hunyadi was voivode of Transylvania and devoted his considerable talents to halting the Turkish advance into Europe. He could not, however, prevent the fall of Constantinople in 1453 and, with it, the final demise of the eastern empire and the complete subjugation of Serbia. János Hunyadi was regent of Hungary during the minority of King Ladislas V, but had to step down at the very moment of the fall of Constantinople when Ladislas came of age. His last victory, by relieving the Turkish siege of Belgrade in 1456, held up the Turkish advance for several generations. On his death the same year, the king had the elder of János's sons beheaded and the other, Matthias, imprisoned in Prague by the Bohemian ruler, George Podiebrad. In 1457, however, Ladislas died and Matthias was elected king of Hungary (1458). Matthias' aim, apart from regulating the internal affairs of Hungary by subduing the powers of chronically feuding magnates, was to create a Danubian empire strong enough to withstand the Turkish assault. In 1476 he married Beatrice of

Aragon, a daughter of the king of Naples. It was she who introduced renaissance culture to the Hungarian court. Matthias did not reign long enough to consolidate his achievements for he died in 1490 at the age of fifty.

His library, the Bibliotheca Corviniana, was one of the most renowned in Europe and the exhibition had brought together some of its scattered codexes from Paris and London, Tokyo, Rome, New York. The library had been housed in the castle at Buda and was begun in the 1460s. Matthias was not too fussy about how he went about his book-collecting. Mainly, of course, he bought books and arranged for others to be copied, but whenever any of the magnates fell foul of him, he would confiscate his library. His marriage to Beatrice of Aragon gave new impetus to the collection, for she brought with her humanist scholars from Italy. To one of those, Taddeo Ugoleto, Matthias gave the care and control of the library: 'Ugoleto sought out Greek codexes for the library and copying was carried out on a far greater scale than ever before. When the king died in 1490 there were 150 codexes in the copyists' workshops.' It was here that the corvina binding was developed. It consisted of wooden boards covered with leather, usually elaborately gilded. In the closing decades of the fifteenth century, Florence and Venice in particular supported a large industry of book-copying when the art was at its height. All that vanished with the invention of the printing press a few years later, but many of the books in the Corviniana were made in Italy at that time.

The books themselves were stunningly beautiful, each one an example of several renaissance arts but, most strikingly, of painting and calligraphy. Among them was a splendid *Book VIII* of Ptolemy's *Geography*, made in Florence from 1485–90. The Mediterranean was accurate enough, but India was shown as an island and northern waters had been left blank. There was a Bede, *Natura Rerum*, in which the blues seemed still as intense as they must have been when first painted. But among the loveliest exhibits was a two-inch by three-inch *Horae Beatae Mariae Virginis*. It had been made in Naples in the fifteenth century, presumably at the court of Beatrice's father, for it had belonged to her and she had left it behind in the castle at Esztergom when she left Hungary in 1500. It was found there in 1595 when the castle was recaptured from the Turks. It was easy to imagine how the tiny volume might have been overlooked, more difficult to conceive that it was half a millenium old. However impractical, I like the idea that books should be physically beautiful. It encourages a proper attentiveness.

JUST along from the Corviniana was a quite different exhibition entitled *Sztá-lin! Rá-ko-si!* It was a reworking of the same materials apropos Hungary as I had already seen in Prague apropos Czechoslovakia. The displays covered the events of the first decade after the war. The introductory leaflet did not mince its words: 'It was a period when words contradicted deeds, propaganda realities, and when everyday life was full of fear, hypocrisy, and people felt helpless, having been at the mercy of those in power.'

The exhibition presented in stark contrast a series of ideological pronouncements on the wonders of life in the 'people's democracy', together with images and reconstructions of the realities: 'fake elections, the forced exploitation of workers in the form of "work competitions", the ruining of peasants, the servile imitation of Soviet methods, the ridiculous praises given to domestic and Soviet conditions, the unscrupulous abuse of everything in the capitalist system, the unlawfulness which had been part of the system from the very beginning, persecutions, the drabness of life, of the immediate surrounding, of the work-place, of the living quarters, of the clothing, the false and forced propaganda inundating everything . . . The exhibition ends with the remnants of the statue of Stalin which was destroyed on the night of October 23, 1956, to show the collapse of a main feature of that sad era – that of the cult of personality.' The exhibition was crowded and I felt that, really, this was for Hungarians, as though I were intruding on a private grief.

JUST a few hundred yards from the palace area of Castle Hill stands the Matthias Church. Begun in the 1250s, it was several

109

times remodelled and in the 1470s King Matthias added a fine tower which still stands and for which the Church has been named since. It was here that the kings of Hungary were presented to the people. It was, for a time, a mosque, during the Turkish occupation. It was damaged and partly rebuilt several times until, in the nineteenth century, it was restored in neo-Gothic style. In 1867, nearly twenty years after coming to the throne of Austria, Francis Joseph was crowned here by that same Count Andrássy who, in the aftermath of 1848, he had sentenced to death. A delicate building, it is so intricately decorated that it is difficult to tell which parts are original and which later modifications. Though flanked by what ought to be a couple of monstrosities of incongruence – the Hilton Hotel and the nineteenth-century Fisherman's Bastion – all seem quite compatible. The Hilton is absolutely undecorated, consisting of great columns and slabs of reflective glass which return images of sky and church. The Bastion is a fake-medieval construction, designed by the architect who restored the Matthias Church, and represents a turreted chunk of city wall. It houses an elegant restaurant from which the views across the Danube to the parliament building and much of Pest are magnificent. None of these structures competes with the others which is perhaps why they work as a trio.

ALTHOUGH the Hungarian restaurants in which I ate did achieve a far higher standard than anything I encountered in Prague, almost all had in common a poor sense of presentation and good ingredients were often spoiled by ignorance and negligence. A piece of venison, for example, had not been properly trimmed of its silverskin so that in cooking, the silverskin contracted, warping the meat which therefore cooked unevenly. Where high-quality cuisine is regarded as a wicked, capitalist indulgence for the rich, it is, I suppose, inevitable, that the necessary skills should have decayed and lapsed. The lack of opportunity for people to travel and study abroad would have hastened that decline. But the brutalisation of culinary skills to a level where even basic techniques have been lost, seems to me not an achievement but an indictment of a fundamentally wrong-headed approach to human values.

The symptoms may seem trivial: dirty buildings or badly prepared and unimaginatively-presented food, but Hungary or Czechoslovakia are not inherently poor countries and their peoples are merely insulted by such decay. I was reminded of stories about some immigrant Irish who arrived in America in the aftermath of the Great Hunger, bereft of even the basic skills of domestic cookery. Their lives had been so impoverished that even those elementary things had been taken from them.

DINNER in the restaurant of the Fisherman's Bastion was a treat for three reasons: the fairy-tale view of the Danube lit by the reflections from the lights strung along the Chain Bridge and the neo-Gothic parliament building, the fact that the food is as good as is to be had in Budapest, and the conversational delights of my friend, László Kunos. Over our pre-dinner drinks I asked him to tell me about his own background. It is a tale which, in some respects, typifies what I think of as Middle Europe.

László's family were Ashkenazim Jews. His mother's people came from Munkács in Ruthenia – now Mukacevo in the USSR. His father's father Ignatz Kunos, was a well-known intellectual, who studied at the Calvinist university in Debrecen. Jews could live there but not give birth within the city boundary: when László's great-grandmother was pregnant, she had to leave the city to give birth. László's grandfather became a scholar of oriental lan-. guages. For Magyars, László explained, the Orient is the locus of a 'roots' fantasy. Ignatz learned Turkish and went on an expedition to track down Hungarian tribes in Moldavia. These people, called the Csángó, still live there. Between 1895 and 1900, he travelled on horseback in Turkey collecting folk tales and folklore and, in due course, became one of the leading intellectuals of his day. Two of those collections of Turkish folk-tales were published in English.

In 1938 and in the early years of the war, the laws restricting Jews in Hungary became tougher. Ignatz, who died in 1945, was exempt from those restrictions as a member of the Hungarian

Academy, of whom only a tiny number were Jews. He did not, therefore, have to move into the ghetto. László thinks of himself, he said, as a Jew first and a Hungarian second. His mother's father had a small business in Munkács selling industrial lubricants. They were half-peasants. László's father was a doctor. As a Jew, he was barred from military service and was eventually sent to Mauthausen, the Austrian concentration camp. When Mauthausen was liberated, his father weighed just under eighty pounds. He tells the story of lying on the ground, watching a jeep drive straight at him and believing that, finally, he was going to be killed. The jeep stopped in its tracks and American soldiers got out. Because he could not keep solid food down, they fed him spoonfuls of a kind of Advocaat, a bottle of which is now the family's annual gift to him.

Until March 1944 Hungary was relatively free of first-hand experience of the war. Admiral Horthy was trying to manoeuvre Hungary out of the war, which led to a Nazi-inspired putsch and a German occupation. Until then, Hungary's one million Jews had not been in immediate danger. Now, with Eichmann in charge of the 'Jewish question', they were. Through the summer of 1944 the Jews in the countryside were rounded up, the majority of them being sent to Auschwitz. Most of László's mother's family disappeared during that time. Finally, in August of 1944, Horthy ordered that the 'export' of Hungary's Jews should stop and, surprisingly, it did. In October he declared Hungary's neutrality. László's mother was blonde and blue-eyed. She went to the police claiming to be a refugee from Transylvania and asked for fresh papers. Whether the police guessed the truth or not, they issued her with another set of papers and she acquired a new identity.

László thinks of himself, he says, as a teacher and translator rather than a writer: 'Perhaps dealing with other people's work results from a kind of fear, a Jewish retreat from putting one's head too far above the parapet. My real audience is my circle of intimate friends, ten or a dozen, not all of whom are Jews.'

There is, he says, no Magyar or Hungarian race. The exterminations and mass movements long since made that absurd. Language, however, *is* the race, in the sense that it has assimilated all the incomers, so that if Magyar is your mother tongue, you are a Hungarian. But just as Hungary is seen by many as an island of Magyars in a sea of potentially hostile peoples, Slavs and

Latins and Teutons, so László sees the intellectual life of central, cosmopolitan Budapest as an island.

SETTING out at quarter past five, I get lost in the one-way system and by ten to six have crossed the Danube three times by the same bridge. Still, it is a pretty morning, the sun hanging as a great red disk just above the buildings of Pest. Now, heading south, low strands of mist are burning off as the sun changes to gold. The mist stops at treetop height and the landscape looks like something from a children's story book. It is flat, agricultural landscape, broken only by occasional trees. Lots of old farm buildings but not much livestock; a few sheep and cattle, but the verges are often aflame with poppies. It is also orchard and vineyard country with many cherry and plum orchards; a countryside varied enough to be interesting and something of a paradise for birds. The farmhouses are creamy white and the peasants in the fields or by the roadside do not look like products of the twentieth century. Horses and carts jog along every couple of miles and occasionally a man or a couple appears pushing a hand-cart.

Many of the greens in the fields already have a sun-bleached look, but tourism must be making some impact, for *Zimmer frei* signs are frequent in the towns and villages. I had intended to follow the river south so as to be able to visit Mohács, the scene of the Hungarian Flodden at the hands of the Turks in 1526. But, too late, I realise I am on the wrong road and decide to head for Belgrade via Kecskemét, avoiding the main road and passing through Kiskunhalas and into Yugoslavia at Subotica.

At Tompa, a tiny village a couple of miles from the frontier, I find a shop selling mineral water and fruit and vegetables. It is busy and full of the smells of freshly picked produce. There are heaps of pale green peppers, trays of strawberries and tomatoes, bundles of carrots with their tops still on, clumps of green-stemmed garlic, cucumbers, grapefruit, lemons and, strangely, coconuts. The locals seem to buy everything in huge quantities – four kilos of tomatoes or half a dozen cucumbers. I buy what I want by pointing and letting the old woman who serves me rake through the handful of change I hold out. The fruit tastes wonderful and costs pennies, though what I really want is mineral water, since it is now getting into the seventies outside, and eighties inside the car.

Passing through the frontiers is a matter of ten minutes and as soon as I approach Subotica, there is the first red star adorning a building. Only a few months earlier Czechoslovakia and Hungary would have been littered with them. Gone as though they had been a dream. And, in a sense, they were, for the people never wanted them and, so far as they could, ignored them. They were, if anything, a negative reminder of their subjection and the miseries of geography.

A truck driving along in front of me throws up huge clouds of pale brown dust which hang in the roadside trees like mist. Again, everything changes at once. The women wear a peasant dress much more like that I am used to from the Mediterranean, from Italy and Greece, with their black, ankle-length frocks and black headsquares with a grey pinafore worn on top of the frock. On the outskirts of Subotica a middle-aged man with a vast beer-belly, wearing sweatshirt and shorts and no crash helmet rides a scooter down the middle of the bumpy road, smoking a cigarette.

The general level of prosperity does not seem as high as in Tompa. A half-dozen brown pigs are browsing and rooting in an orchard, and in the next field two young men, stripped to the waist, are tying corn-sheaves by hand. Their bicycles lie by the roadside. Their lives suddenly seem very remote from anything I can truly imagine.

This is the Vojvodina, one of Yugoslavia's two autonomous provinces, the other being Kosovo. Together with the six republics they make up the federation of Yugoslavia. It is also the sub-region known as the Bačka which was heavily settled by Germans until the last war and was part of Hungary until 1918. Many of the people here still speak Hungarian and there are no Cyrillic signs to be seen on the shops or roadsigns until you get further south. The Bačka is almost wholly agricultural, with large tracts devoted to cattle-rearing. The roads are lined with maples and wild, pink dog-rose. After Subotica I join the *autoput* for Belgrade but there are so many insects shattering on to the windscreen that the wipers cannot cope with their accumulated goo and I have to get out at regular intervals and clean it off by hand.

DECIPHERING the runes of Yugoslav politics is rather like trying to fill in a crossword puzzle without the clues. Since the key to the problem is Serbia, it is not a bad idea to begin there. Serbia has existed as a coherent kingdom since the twelfth century. By the early fourteenth, the Serbian tsar, Stephen Dushan, was aiming to expel the Turks from Europe from his base of Serbia, Macedonia, Albania and Thessaly. The Turks had crossed the Hellespont in 1301. After Stephen, however, there was a short period of chaos until King Lazar, who came to power in 1374, tried to form a Christian League to expel the Turks. His armies were smashed at Kosovo Polje (the blackbird's field) in 1389. As Flodden was to Scotland, Mohács to Hungary, so was Kosovo to Serbia. The aristocracy were all but extinguished and from then until 1459 Serbia was a kingdom unoccupied by, but paying tribute to, the Turk. It was during this period that the Serbian King George Branković, together with János Hunyadi, defeated the Turkish forces at the battle of Kunovitsa in 1444 but the respite was temporary. In 1456, the same year as Hunyadi, Branković died and the Sultan Muhammed II occupied Serbia. For the next three hundred and forty-five years, Serbia was a Turkish pashalik.

At the tail end of the eighteenth century, Belgrade changed hands between the Austrians and Turks on two occasions. But it was not until 1804 that a native-led rebellion under Karageorge had any substantial success. In 1806 he captured Belgrade and by the Treaty of Bucharest in 1812 Serbia gained a measure of recognition. The Treaty also gave Russia the right to interfere on behalf of the Serbs. The next year saw a reconquest carried out with customary Balkan ferocity when a few hundred of the leading notables were impaled or beheaded. In 1815 Miloš Obrenović arranged for the assassination of Karageorge and established a rival dynasty of Serb chieftains. In 1842 the Obrenović dynasty was ousted in favour of Alexander Karageorgević, only to return in 1858. A decade later Michael Obrenović assassinated his Karageorgević rival. Serbia gained a further measure of international recognition by the Congress of Berlin in 1878 and was declared a kingdom in 1882. In 1903 Alexander Obrenović and his queen, Draga, were assassinated in their palace in Belgrade and replaced by Peter Karageorgević.

The trouble really got under way in 1908 when Austria-Hungary annexed Bosnia-Hercegovina on which Serbia had its own designs. By 1912 Turkey was in a state of chaos, and Serbia, Bulgaria and Greece in alliance took the opportunity of driving Turkish forces from most of the Balkans. Austria-Hungary was not amused and sought to provoke Serbia, which meantime had gone to war with Bulgaria in 1913 over the Macedonian spoils. The peace settlement by the Treaty of Bucharest that same year gave Serbia much of Macedonia but left Turkey and Bulgaria feeling put out, with the consequence that they entered the Great War against Serbia's sponsors (Britain, France and Russia).

Serbia's next contribution to world peace was the assassination of the heir to the Austro-Hungarian throne, the Archduke Franz-Ferdinand at Sarajevo. Austria was still keen to humiliate Serbia and so Europe was drawn into one of the most fruitless wars in history.

By the end of the war much of the territory which became Yugoslavia was in ruins and the most cohesive force around was the Serbian army. In December 1918 the kingdom of the Serbs, Croats and Slovenes was proclaimed, but from the very beginning it was a nest of feuds. The Croat political party wanted a federal system. The Serbs wanted a strong, centrist, Serb-dominated state, and by 1928 the whole caboodle had lapsed into its customary anarchy and King Alexander took over as royal dictator, proclaiming the Kingdom of Yugoslavia in October 1929. But Alexander was no better at placating the Croats than the politicians had been, and his resort to traditional methods of police and military terror, especially as carried out by the largely Serb gendarmerie in Croatia, only deepened the hatreds. Even today Yugoslavia is about forty per cent Roman Catholic (Croatia) and fifty per cent Orthodox (mainly Serbs) with no affection between the two strands of the Christian faith.

True to family tradition, Alexander had been himself assassinated, along with the French foreign minister, at Marseilles in 1934 and his nephew Paul became regent on behalf of the young king, Peter. Yugoslavia was surrounded by enemies. Italy had its eyes on the west and Hungary on the north.

When Germany and her allies, Bulgaria, Hungary and Italy,

invaded in April 1941, the Yugoslav armies, with no defensible frontiers to the north, collapsed within a week. Italy and Germany carved up Slovenia between them. Italy also took the Dalmatian coast and an independent Croatia was established under the puppet pro-Nazi regime of the Ustaša. Hungary took the Bačka and a puppet state was established in Serbia. Bulgaria took part of Macedonia, and Kosovo went to Albania under an Italian protectorate. The Hungarians attempted to re-Magyarise the Bačka and there was a massacre of Serbs and Jews. The Croat Ustaše gangs, after the fashion of South American death-squads, massacred those Serbs who would not become Catholics. In the eastern part of the Vojvodina, the Banat, local German populations of many generations' standing collaborated in administering the new regime. Yugoslavia was decimated.

The resistance movements in Yugoslavia were largely Serb-based, under the rival leaderships of the right-wing Mihajlović and the communist Tito. It was not just an anti-German struggle, but an inter-ethnic and inter-religious conflict of great complexity and bitterness. So much so, indeed, that much of the country was destroyed and one and three-quarter millions were killed, about eleven per cent of the population.

With Tito's dominance at the end of the war and the fact that the Serbs regarded their liberation as largely their own doing, the Soviet Union never exercised the authority in Yugoslavia that it exercised elsewhere by virtue of the feats of the Red Army. Nor, as in the other East European states, was there a party of communists in exile who had sat out the war in Moscow waiting to return and do Moscow's bidding. Tito had made the wartime party and had consolidated his position sufficiently to follow his own line without the risk of a rival from within the party gaining Moscow's support.

As Stalin was intent on creating a conformist block, Tito's wayward nationalism led to a breach in relations in 1948 which in turn led Stalin to institute that series of pre-emptive purges which terrorised much of Eastern Europe between 1948 and his death in 1953. Although there were further reconciliations and quarrels after Stalin's death, Yugoslavia never again really fell under Soviet influence, and by the 1960s was pursuing its own policies both at home and abroad. Yugoslavia never joined the Warsaw Pact and during the Cold War played an influential role as one of the leaders of the non-aligned movement.

Tito introduced several packages of economic and constitutional reform, but was unable to dissolve the underlying ethnic tensions. In 1971 he had to squash a Croat surge for autonomy and had several times to rein back the Serbs. Yugoslavia held together partly because Tito was powerful and cautious enough to hold it together. When he died in 1980 (at the age of 88) the package began to unravel. Only a year after his death, there were outbreaks of large-scale violence by Kosovo's Albanian population resulting in almost a thousand deaths. Since then, the problem of Kosovo has simmered until Slobodan Milosevič, Serbia's nationalistic prime minister, brought it back to the boil by his efforts to incorporate Kosovo into his fiefdom by depriving the great bulk of the population, the Albanians in Kosovo, of their political, civil and, in some instances, human rights. Serbia's communist party is the only one in Eastern Europe to have retained popular support; a trick pulled off by Milosevič by his astute identification of the party with the most aggressive elements of Serbian chauvinism, encouraging the Serbs in Croatia to agitate for incorporation into a greater Serbia. Milosevič seems to be reckoning that by pushing Serbian claims, even to the extent of breaking up Yugoslavia, he will be able to dominate a larger and more coherent Serbia, which can in turn pick off its less populous neighbours. However, since Croatia and Slovenia will not submit to Serbian hegemony, and since Albanians hugely outnumber Serbs in Kosovo, he is setting the stage not just for the fragmentation of Yugoslavia, but for a civil war of potentially crippling savagery.

I HAD first come to Belgrade eight years earlier to attend the annual writers' conference organised by the Serbian Writers' Union. An English friend, Richard Burns, who now lives in Belgrade, had booked me into the Park Hotel in the town centre. The Park was shabby and not particularly cheap; pasteboard furnishings and no plug in the sink. The corridors reeked of Turkish tobacco and the carpets were dotted with cigarette burns. This was the Belgrade I remembered from my previous visit.

On that visit I had been a guest at a dinner given by a man who was then a professor of French at the University of Belgrade. He seemed an intelligent and cultivated fellow. In the course of the meal the question of Kosovo had come up and the professor engaged in an anti-Albanian tirade which would have disgraced a hard-line Afrikaaner. When I asked him to explain why he so detested the Albanians, he replied in all seriousness that they were Asiatics, just down from the trees and not quite human. Many Serbs share that extreme view of their Albanian neighbours and it is that bigotry which Milosevič has exploited.

I never felt in Belgrade that I was entirely in Europe, though I found it hard to say why. In part, at least, I think I was just encountering a society in which there has been no history of liberalism, either in politics or in society in general. I certainly found people more strident and self-dramatising than anything I was accustomed to.

Belgrade is substantially a modern city, having been sacked and rebuilt so many times that few buildings date back beyond the present century. The reason for it being here at all, is that the old fortress of Kalemegdan, from which the modern city radiates, sits at the confluence of the Sava and Danube rivers and near to the Danube's reception of the Tisa and Tamiš rivers. The fortress had to be taken before any northward advance could be secure. After falling to the Turks in 1521, it changed hands several times, going to Austria (1688), back to Turkey (1690), Austria (1717), Turkey (1739). Its most recent destruction was by the Luftwaffe in 1941. Apart from the low hill on which the fortress stands, the town is relatively flat and so presents few landmarks. This makes it difficult to grasp its structure in the way that one can easily do with Prague or Edinburgh. Much of the post-war rebuilding was done with low quality materials, poor workmanship and poor design, so that some sections of the city are really quite ugly and could be loved only by a devoted urbanite.

It was a relief, therefore, when Richard was able to arrange for me to stay at the flat of a colleague in one of the older and more attractive eastern fringes of the town. I had had enough of hotels for a while and was not looking forward to the brusque manners and poor food in the depressing Hotel Park. My host, Steve, rented the upper floor of a two-storey detached house. The garden sported a huge cherry tree, heavy with ripe fruit and the street was a profusion of climbing roses. Many of the houses were solidly built middle-class homes from the earlier part of the century with decent-sized rooms and, often, a balcony. As Steve was going to be away for part of my time there, I would have the flat to myself. He was a quiet-spoken, easy-going Englishman who had been in Belgrade for a year and who, after initial dislike, had come to enjoy the city, finding its hassles less exacting than those of Cairo where he had worked for several years with the British Council. I took to heart his early advice: 'Relax, you're in the Balkans.'

Over coffee we chatted about the new economic measures which had been introduced a few weeks earlier. In 1989 the annual rate of inflation had been running at just under two thousand per cent and, in an effort to deal with that, the dinar had just been revalued and made convertible. Prices, Steve said, were beginning to fall and it was clear even from window-shopping, that whatever the economic problems, they had less to do with the supply side of the economy than with other weaknesses. The root problem, Steve and Richard both maintained, was that the federal structures did not have the necessary pull with the individual republics. Every republic had to agree to any federal proposal and every measure had to proceed through each parliament. The consequent shambles is not difficult to imagine in a country with so many ethnic and religious feuds.

Richard explained that much of the country ran on the basis of the *veza* system. In effect, the bureaucracy was sidestepped by a system of mutual favours so that corruption became endemic. Thus, pressure might be put on a teacher to pass a particular student, with the understanding that some reciprocal favour would emerge at a later moment. Richard's wife, Jasna, worked as a kind of economic inspector, checking on trade frauds. The mechanic who serviced their car hoped to open his own business. He would not charge for his services, despite Richard's insistence, in the expectation that when he came to get his business permits through the bureaucracy, Jasna would somehow be able to expedite matters for him. The result, of course, is a massive black economy and a kind of ontological gap between what actually happens and what officially happens. To some extent, this system derives from Yugoslavia's Byzantine and Turkish background in which rigid administrative hierarchies and endemic corruption went hand in hand. I was told later by a friend in Romania that he knew the term *veza* as a Macedonian expression referring to that network of reciprocal obligations for revenge imposed by tribal *vendetta*.

Private business has always been possible in Yugoslavia but,

Steve explained, only on a very small scale. It was possible to run a business provided you employed no more than five persons. But your wife or cousin was also entitled to employ five people. Yugoslavia is anxious to attract foreign investment capital and the rules governing private business ventures are changing. There is, for example, a proposal to have a free-trade zone using hard currencies along a stretch of the Danube at Belgrade. There can be little prospect of economic improvement, however, unless some reconciliation can be achieved between the states. Recent elections in Slovenia and Croatia had produced substantial anti-communist votes and in Croatia the right-wing nationalist, Franjo Tujdman became prime minister. Richard blames this divisiveness partly on the fact that each republic has its own television network. Zagreb TV, he said, had stopped showing any programmes from Serbian TV, with the result that there was a consistent bias in the news reporting of each republic. There is no national network.

Richard and Jasna wanted to take me to a fish restaurant by the Danube that evening. It was busy and, with considerable libations of local wine, cheerful. My memories of Serb cuisine were not very enthusiastic – grilled meats followed by more grilled meats. Basically, it is a peasant cuisine, but is often debased in commercial contexts, where quantity takes precedence over quality. Jasna had just bought herself a Bible. Her father had been a convinced member of the Communist Party, an army officer, and she had never been allowed to know anything about religion except that it was subversive. Now she wanted to find out for herself. I think she found it rather innocuous.

THE Writers' Union offices in Belgrade are to be found in a rather ramshackle building just off Trg Republike, one of Belgrade's main squares, housing the National Theatre and the National Museum. Its basement restaurant is one of the best in Belgrade and a fashionable place to be seen. At one time it must have been an impressive town house, but is now a series of offices and conference rooms housing both the Union and the Serbian PEN offices. I went there with Richard to meet some writers

121

who, I hoped, might be able to put me in touch with writers in Romania. Instead, I met Ivana Milankova, a petite, vivacious brunette in her early thirties who was about to set off for a cousin's wedding in Timişoara. She was not certain whether she would be able to get there, since a variety of stories were in circulation about the frontier crossing. But the wedding was not until the next day and there was no reason why I should not drive her there. Ratko Adamović, secretary of the Writers' Union, a pale, bearded, Dostoyevskian-looking character, knew that some Serbs had recently run into difficulty in Romania, having been accused of being 'rich communists' and 'spectators'. Nevertheless, he assured us, it would be better to try to get in now rather than later, before a dictatorship could be re-established, as he expected would happen. I had heard so many conflicting reports about conditions in Romania that it was impossible to make any sensible decision. Friends in Hungary had assured me that food was unavailable and that petrol was impossible to obtain.

Since Ivana no longer needed to rush off to catch a bus for Timişoara, I offered her lunch and we adjourned to the Archiv restaurant of the Hotel Metropol. The Archiv had been a library, badly bombed in the last war. A new library had been built across the road and the Archiv's terrace, looking out over Kalemegdan park, made an attractive setting for lunch. The food was less bad than usual. Ivana ate only a salad, but I had a spicy bean soup and then a piece of pork in a cream sauce. Ivana explained that Kalemegdan was a Turkish word; *kale* meaning fortified town and *megdan* meaning field or park. Ivana was a lively conversationalist, her large chestnut-coloured eyes fixing on some invisible object in the middle distance as she held forth. All I had to do was to provide the appropriate prompts: 'People may be more or less well educated, but real ethics derive from feeling, from emotion. If their education is one-dimensional, as it so often is in Eastern Europe, *that* is immoral. It is that narrowness of vision which created fascism and communism and all the rest of it.'

Ivana's English was excellent. Her husband was Polish, an archaeologist, who had been killed in an accident while on a dig in Egypt. She made a living as a translator in addition to her work as a primary-school teacher: 'Yugoslavia, Bulgaria, Romania, down into Turkey, this is what a friend of mine calls the "witchcraft zone". It really is. In everyday life superstition and witchcraft still exist here. For instance, if a woman wants to get married, she knows how to set about it. People here would know how to insert a thread in your clothes so that you would fall downstairs or so that a woman might be made barren. It is widespread here and not just among the country people.' After Ivana's remarks, I began to notice over the next few days that people *were* superstitious. Wreaths of herbs and wild flowers decorated doors on their owner's saint's day, for example, as a good luck offering, though it was impossible to know whether it was taken seriously or was merely a residual habit.

Ivana was a dictionary of Middle-European races and religions and explained: 'I am a mixture of many bloods so I am expected to know several languages. My father's mother is German. Part of their village in the Banat was German and part Serb. The German influence dated from the Austro-Hungarian period. They were Bavarians, known as *pauri*. It means people who work in the fields. In the village there were also Spaniards, Hungarians, Frenchmen, Romanians, Slovaks, Ruthenes and Turks. The Austro-Hungarian empire was transnational and the authorities induced people to go where their skills were wanted. So the Spaniards were brought in to look after the vineyards. The Spanish community has vanished now, but you can still see the tombstones. Similarly, there are three religions in the village; Roman Catholic, Jewish and Orthodox.'

'On my grandfather's side, we are Russian, hence the name, Milankov. My grandmother, from a German Catholic family, lived in the same village as my grandfather and they ran away together. He was Orthodox. My father's grandmother was a Romanian from a village near Timişoara. She was a kind of witch. And my mother's mother was a Jew from Thessaloniki and her husband was a Serb, from Kruševac in Southern Serbia. He was a tradesman.'

As Ivana spoke, she sipped at her wine, drinking little. She is petite, not much over five feet, and sits very upright. She makes a point of being well groomed with unobtrusive make-up and carefully manicured hands. She had asked about my own family and I had told her about my visit to the memorial at Thiepval: 'It is said in the Bible that the graves will open again. In communist Yugoslavia we have had nearly forty years of ideology. Our history has suffered a gap, a breach. In our education system, 1914 and the years before that hardly existed. All that counted was after 1941 and the patriotic struggle led by the communists – apart, of course, from a few references to the early days of the

Serb Empire in the Middle Ages! Quite recently, only a few years ago, we began to reopen memorials to those who had fought in the First World War. So, "the graves are opening". Our memory is being restored.' Her fine fingers were often at her throat and, if hesitant in conversation, she would toy with the blue necklace and black, Spanish crucifix which hung there.

'I spent a year in the United States and six months of that time travelling. I could not find any equivalent to my European world and especially between people. There was some depth simply absent. Now perhaps I could live there, being more certain of my own values. In Europe I grew up in a world of suspicion. In the United States everything was surface and I could not stand it.

'Now I teach a hundred and fifty children a day through several classes. It is really only a factory where they are packed in like sardines rather than treated as people. I dislike having to do it, but it is a living.

'I was born in 1952 and lived an Eastern European life. By that I mean that we were presented with one kind of reality as the official version. But everyone knew that something else was the case. So, all my generation began to lead a kind of schizophrenic life: "My body is here. Do what you like to it. But my soul is elsewhere and you cannot punish my soul." Among my friends' favourite books was Bulgakov's *The Master and Margarita*, in which he presents a writer tortured by the regime.

'It is multi-dimensional in the ways it can be read. I suppose our first choice would really have to be Kafka, then Dostoyevsky, especially the confrontation between Christ and the Grand Inquisitor. And, of course, the poets; Osip Mandelstam, Anna Akhmatova, Marina Tsvetayeva and Joseph Brodsky. Brodsky really is "ours" because he is contemporary, a living witness.'

I was able to tell Ivana a couple of Brodsky anecdotes, having arranged a reading for him in Edinburgh. I read the English versions of his poems while he read in Russian. But as he only revealed his choice of texts at the very last moment, they had to be read cold, at sight. Not an easy task. The sponsor of that series of readings was a mean-spirited Church of Scotland minister who failed to pay proper expenses. While having a drink before the reading with Brodsky and Peter Jay, who was to read some poems by János Pilinzsky, we decided to disrupt the proceedings in a mild sort of way by interrupting the programme to recite our favourite W. H. Auden poems, having discovered a common enthusiasm.

Brodsky, despite the fact that he would only read his own poems in Russian – and made them sound like a liturgical chant – read Auden's *In Praise of Limestone,* a complex and demanding work, which he performed with great sensitivity.

Ivana continued: 'Because of my diverse origins, I think, I do not belong to any one place or role. That seems best to me. Writers here at the Union are president of this or general secretary of that. They are all official position and little gift. They are perfectly easy to talk to, affable and welcoming. But too concerned to be public figures to have anything very interesting to say. These writers, so-called, lead merely social lives. It is as though Christ had been asked down from the cross to give a lecture on miracles. It is all part of the way things happen here, this continual showing off and jockeying for status.'

Ivana summed up much of what had been bothering me about my contacts with the writers' unions in Eastern Europe. 'They have an official status and people *are* helpful,' I said, 'but they seem to have very little to do with what I understand as serious writing.'

'I think,' Ivana replied 'it is because people have become cut off from religion. The churches were turned into stables and some essential component in the people's lives was lost, for this was a religiously-minded society, not a wholly secular one. Something was incomplete so that missing element had to be found wherever it might be. Consequently any kind of flicker of miracle attracts attention and writers can figure in that charade. It is all surface, a kind of seven-day wonder. But now, of course, religion is back on the agenda in Yugoslavia.

'Now people can go to church quite freely and this year we will be able to celebrate Christmas properly for the first time in many years. When I was ten years old, my father said to me: You live in Christian surroundings but your mother was a Jew. It is up to you to choose. So I became Orthodox. As a schoolteacher, which is an official position, I could only wear my crucifix inside my blouse and not let it be seen. Until very recently I concealed the fact that I went to church and celebrated Christmas or Easter or my patron saint's day. Each family here has its patron saint. Mine is St George. On each 6th May we take a cake to church and in the evening have people in to light the candle and to cut the cake. [These are the origins of the west European birthday cake.]

'This year on 6th May, my headmaster, though he knew it was now permitted, just stared and stared at my crucifix as though he could not believe it. That there is no censorship now is really a major reform. You can speak your mind even though we still have photographs of Tito on the walls. We are not sure what to do with all these pictures. In school the children in the third grade were scheduled to read a whole book about Tito's life: his childhood struggles, his days as a partisan leader, his gifts as a writer and law-maker, and so on. Now all that has been removed from the syllabus. But nothing is clear yet. We have grown up in a scrapbook. Take a rose and press it. We *know* everything is changing – as a matter of simple fact – but we are fascinated by the book and keep turning back to the rose. Budapest is different. It is not Slav.

'I spent January in Warsaw and in Cracow. The Poles are Slavs, but eccentric Slavs. Give them their crowned eagle and even if they have no milk, no potatoes, they are still happy. In Budapest though, they can be rational in a way that is not possible in Warsaw or Cracow. But in Prague I felt the same kind of anxiety as I feel here.

'Mentally we are still suffering from the Turkish occupation. As an individual, I can feel perfectly ordinary or normal. I belong to the world. But when I have to show my passport, or am asked my nationality, I feel inferior and I think many people feel that way. Some of the Hungarians in Yugoslavia, in the Bačka for example, call us Serbs "Byzantines". Maybe we are. Our Orthodox liturgy is wholly Byzantine.'

By now we were the only people left on the terrace and the restaurant was closing for the afternoon. I arranged to collect Ivana from her home, only a five-minute drive from Steve's house, on the following morning.

AFTER several days of intense, sultry heat, the morning broke to a steady rain. Steve had decided to accompany us for the ride. By the time we crossed a slate-grey Danube on the way north-east into the Banat, the rain had slackened and mist was curling from the fields. Our first target was Ivana's home village of Srp Crnja (it means Black Earth) on the Yugoslav-Romanian border. The road ran in long straight stretches lined by acacias, some already in flower, limes, willows and, where the trees gave out, scrub dog-rose, elder and a great variety of flowers, yellow and purple and white. The Banat has a high population of gypsies and occasionally we passed their carts and wagons, or a peasant woman grazing her cow on a rope by the roadside. If this was Europe, it was certainly not the industrial world of North Germany or England. Our road headed north between the rivers Tisa and Tameş. Ivana said there was one theory which suggested that Celtic tribes had followed the course of the Tameş southwards, and that the name was that of one of their river-gods, hence Timişoara (the town on the Tameş) and London's Thames. Names in this part of the world can be a problem, for some towns have been known historically by several names so that Timişoara (Romanian) is also known as Temesvár (Hungarian). Less obviously, Bratislava in Czech becomes Pressburg in German and Pozsony in Hungarian.

The Banat is a more or less unbroken plain, very fertile with a lot of vineyards and orchards, often separated by stretches of marshland, the road fringed then by clumps of tall bullrushes. I find it oppressive, as though one might drive through it for ever without arriving anywhere. But, unlike the Canadian prairies, there are a sufficient number of trees in the Banat to break your line of sight so that the flatness is not compensated by endless horizon. One's sense of distance is constricted and there are none of those great canopies of sky. Perhaps one of the gifts of travel is that one learns something about what makes one uneasy. In the village of Žitište a fair was in progress and a banner slung across the road said 'welcome to our town'. The roadside was lined with alternating Serb and Yugoslav flags, both having the same red, white and blue colours, but in different sequence and the Serbian flag lacking the central red star. Žitište, which means 'place where you bring the corn', used to be called St George, but the communists did not approve of places being named after saints. A few kilometres down the road and we were at Srp Crnja where Ivana wanted to visit her relations, especially her grandmother.

Most of these little villages have the same kind of structure, generally lining a single road with scattered buildings set further back. Typically, the house will be one storey and set back about five yards from the road, with a ditch and tree-lined verge between, the ditches crossed by a short boardwalk. Many of the houses are fenced or walled round and are gable-end on to the road so that driving through, you really see very little of them.

Ivana's grandmother was Maria Feldbab, meaning fieldkeeper, her name a mixture of Turkish and German components. She was delighted to see Ivana but shy of these strangers because, Ivana explained, she was not wearing good clothes. She was dressed in a black headsquare, dark grey dress of rough material with a maroon over-jacket, black stockings and sandals. She is eighty-six and very bent, walking with the help of a stick though still active. She had been washing potatoes when we arrived and when she had dried her hands and came over to shake hands, her toothless, walnut-coloured face creased almost in two in a wide smile.

What from the road looked like a small house, turned out to be a long, substantially built cottage with the connecting corridor being a wooden verandah running along the outside of the building. The substantial courtyard had been divided into a flower garden, a vegetable garden and a hen-run, all meticulously maintained and heavy with the scent of roses and peonies. In the vegetable garden there was a section for peppers and a couple of vines. The exterior walls had been coloured with a beige wash which had obviously been put on with a roller cut in a floral pattern. The same pattern reappeared inside in pale green on the white-washed walls. The house, Ivana told me, dated from the 1850s. Maria insisted we should have coffee, which she served in tiny, thimble-sized cups. As we chatted, through Ivana, I noticed a large coloured print of the family patron saint (St George) among the old photographs of Maria's parents and husband. The rooms were low-ceilinged and sparsely furnished: a dresser, a table and chairs and a television in a corner. We were offered her home-made *rakia*, a distilled spirit usually made from plums but in this case from grapes. It was sharp, tangy, potent and delicious. Maria, once she had overcome her initial shyness, was pleased to show us her house. Her bed must have been very old. It was a high, step-up affair such as I later saw in a museum. Once, she explained, the bedroom had also had a Russian stove or range which was broad enough to lie on. The bed was covered with a heavily embroidered, deep-maroon, velvet bedspread, worked with gold thread and hung with tassels. The verandah she said was called a Gong which she thought was a German word, but I can find no trace of it. In the richer houses, the Gong would be closed in with glass of many different colours. Ivana's father had been a well-known novelist and critic and on the outside wall there was a plaque commemorating him.

From Maria's house Ivana then took us a few yards along the road to her cousin's house. Three young men were sitting on the verandah. These were her cousins and we were invited in to the sitting-room. This was very different from Maria's, though the houses were structurally identical. It was furnished in the modern way, with carpeting and a settee. *Rakia* appeared at once, again home-made, but this time from plums. No one except Ivana spoke anything other than Serb. As we sat sipping the *rakia*, the two women of the house appeared, one at a time, to be introduced and then, one at a time, three more young men and then, together, two little girls. A plate of tiny sweetmeats was produced. They were cakes made with eggs, cheese, flour and seasonings. Ivana explained that her 'brothers', actually cousins, but in Serb cousins are brothers, were not farmers but were small contractors who hired out their machinery to the local farmers. They were very much country people, rather shy and very courteous and hospitable. After the war a lot of the farm-workers, who were German, had been expelled and replaced by landless people from Montenegro and Bosnia. The Montenegrins are immensely tall, broad-shouldered people and anyone so built gets the name of 'the Montenegrin'.

The conversation quickly turned to Kosovo and, warned by a glance from Steve, I answered very carefully their questions as to why the British were hostile to Serbian aspirations in Kosovo. I noticed that stuck to one corner of the television screen was a little Serbian flag with the motto – God Save Serbia. I answered that people in Britain really hardly knew of the existence of Kosovo and that it was not an issue which figured much in the press and only then in the papers read by intellectuals. In fact, Serb policies in Kosovo seem to me thuggish in the extreme but my evasion satisfied these good people that I was not anti-Serb. The *rakia* continued to flow, though I was allowed to refuse since I was driving, but Steve looked as though he could be acquiring a taste for this dangerously palatable fire-water.

From somewhere an accordion was produced and our host's wife began to play. Soon everyone was singing as she moved from tune to tune, the songs being immediately known by their opening phrases. The songs, Ivana said, were local. I noticed that it was a Soviet-made accordion. At first the tunes sounded South German, but slower. Then the style changed, and I could easily have been listening to Russian folk songs. The *rakia* continued to flow and it became clear that we *had* to leave, or stay for the day. Our host, Ivana's eldest cousin, asked, 'Will you stay in my house and eat?' But Ivana explained that we would try to cross into Romania and really had to leave. After much hand-shaking all round, we left them to their ceilidh for which our arrival had provided an excuse. We learned later in the day that, the *rakia* running low, two of the cousins had repaired to Ivana's uncle to acquire further supplies. The ceilidh, it seemed, continued for the rest of the day.

Against the ills and vulgarities of urban boorishness, it was an object lesson in the continuities of what, for me, are the civilising qualities of village life, whether in Scotland or Serbia. When you have to face your neighbours every day, you learn that villages can exercise a network of constraints and kindnesses which can help humanise people. Where a quarrel or a friendship is a fragment of the life of the village, everyone has a stake in it, Whatever the discomforts of such a public world, they are preferable, I believe, to the atomising effects of city life.

We did then go on to the frontier post a few kilometres up the road. Ivana liked to say that the only way to deal with East European officials such as border guards, was to unsettle them; 'But are you quite certain that these regulations are entirely up to date? I heard that such and such a rule had been changed, are you sure?' Ivana's comedy routine was no help, however, for the Romanian authorities had imposed a two-hundred-dollar fee for any Yugoslav wanting to cross into Romania and which had to be paid in hard currency. Such a sum was out of the question for Ivana. Steve, as a Yugoslav resident, would also have required an exit visa, and regretfully, we had to abandon our project.

Just down the road from the border-post was a restaurant called the Kaštel (castle), a state-run place, which Ivana suggested for lunch. It was a big nineteenth-century villa set in its own grounds and had belonged until the end of the war to a German count. It was a handsome building and agreeably cool. The dining-room was in semi-darkness, with heavy lace curtains drawn against the blazing light outside. There were huge, arching oak doors and on the high ceiling heavy oak beams cross-hatched with rosewood struts, all highly polished. The food was good. We started with cold, sliced, smoked goose and ham, served in generous quantities, followed by a simple fillet of pork with salad. The local wine was a cool and tangy Banat riesling. By the time we left, a couple of hours later, some of the heat had gone from the day and promised a fine, cloudless evening.

As there was no particular urgency to get back to Belgrade, we passed an hour visiting the Orthodox church in Srp Crnja. It was a small church with room for perhaps fifty people if crowded. The walls were painted with crude frescoes in the Byzantine style, illustrating events in the lives of saints. We also visited the local cemetery so that Ivana could call at family graves. Swifts were skimming the dusty road, then veering upwards like tremendously versatile acrobats.

We called again on Maria to say our goodbyes. She was no longer shy and much regretted having only half a world left. I asked her what she meant, and she explained that old age did not allow her to get about as she used to, so the outside half had been lost. Nor, she said, could she keep up with the demands of the garden. She depended on the help of a local Hungarian man to whom she paid a little money, but he was usually drunk. And, besides, he had recently got divorced, so he had promptly become the local romeo. He was getting less reliable! She clearly thought it was rather funny.

By the time we left, the crickets were chirping away at full blast and the sky had turned a lovely pale, duck-egg blue. At regular intervals along the road magpies would flutter from the verges and away across the fields. The sunset was so spectacular, a purple globe sinking into the plain, that we stopped to watch the last ten minutes of its descent.

BY way of thanks, I offered Steve and Ivana dinner in a private restaurant Steve had discovered. It was called Rass and had not been open very long. Rass was the name of a monastery in the ancient kingdom of Serbia, and the restaurant kept to the monastic theme in its décor and menu. The setting and service were in the most marked contrast to any state-run restaurant I had ever been in. It had only a few tables and a small terrace in a corner of a new shopping complex, just behind the massive and not-yet-complete new Orthodox cathedral. The table-cloths were bordered with Old Church Slavonic lettering (glagolitic) and the chairs were heavy and hand-carved. Examples of traditional weaving decorated the walls and, although it was modern and thematic in a way I usually dislike, it had been done with restraint and good taste. The menu featured a number of traditional Serbian dishes and we stuck to those, beginning with a mixed starter of air-dried ham, *ajvar*, a kind of chopped paprika seasoning, *kajmak*, which is seasoned curds, a spicy bean mixture and a sort of *dolmades* of goat cheese wrapped in paprika skins. The main course was river-trout, white-fleshed and stuffed with a mushroom and cheese mixture. It tasted smoky and was very rich and good, accompanied by another of the Banat rieslings. There were also generous quantities of a traditional maize-meal bread called *proja*, coarse and yellowish, but tasty.

TO make *ajvar*, you need a couple of fresh paprikas. First roast and then skin them. Chop them *very* finely, having removed the seeds. Season the peppers with a little salt, lemon juice and, if wished, garlic. It is served in small quantities to spread as a seasoning on meats or fish. Served on a piece of lettuce or cucumber it also looks good. I have always found that ground paprika has to be used in quantities which require a lot of cooking-out to remove its gritty texture. One of my Hungarian friends put me right on what I had been doing wrong. If using the paprika for a soup or stew, such as a goulash, melt the fat for the roux and, before adding the flour, put in the paprika and cook it thoroughly in the very hot fat for several minutes and it will do it no harm even if it burns slightly. *Then* add the flour for the roux in the usual way. The difference in the effectiveness of the paprika is quite startling. A few caraway seeds are sometimes also added to goulash soups.

The paprika was in fact brought to Europe by the Spaniards, probably from Southern Mexico or Peru. The first shipment was apparently sent by a colleague of Columbus in 1494. It seems to have arrived in Hungary sometime in the sixteenth century, brought by people fleeing from the Turks, for the plant had found its way from Spain to the Balkans and was known in Hungary as 'heathen' or 'Turkish' pepper. Since then it has become the characteristic spice of Hungarian cuisine.

DOKO Stojičić is the director-general of the department of Serbia's government which has responsibility for foreign cultural and scientific relations, rather like a cross between the British Council, the Arts Council and the Highlands and Islands Development Board in Scotland. Richard Burns had had some dealings with him in his time in Yugoslavia and arranged for us to meet. His office was a comfortable modern affair with a small conference table and a scattering of armchairs, the walls decorated with reprints of famous advertising posters.

Stojičić is a heavy-framed man in his forties, heavy too in his movements, but a fast speaker. He greeted us with handshakes and a slight bow and sent for coffee and fruit juice. He had the manner of a man habitually bustling and wary of public statements. He really wanted to talk about cultural matters. I wanted to talk more generally economics and politics.

WP   Now that the Warsaw Pact is breaking up, will that strengthen Yugoslavia's relations with its neighbours, Romania, Bulgaria, Hungary?

DS   Well, you will know that we have never been part of the Warsaw Pact and have identified ourselves for many years now with the non-aligned movement in international politics. But, above all, now we want to play a full part in Europe. For example, we are at the moment engaged in a project to upgrade the road from Belgrade to Budapest and, eventually, Vienna, to motorway standard. Private capital will also be involved because it will ensure a much faster flow of goods and people into the heart of Europe, so it will have political as well as economic consequences.

(Croat politicians have complained that this project is an attempt to bypass Zagreb as a route into Europe.)

WP   What do you think of the suggestion that, following on the collapse of the East European *bloc*, that Eastern Europe will become a cheap-labour market for the West?

DK   At the moment we regulate joint ventures so that only forty-nine per cent of any business in Yugoslavia can be owned by foreign capital.

WP   It has recently become possible in Hungary for businesses to be one hundred per cent private and/or foreign-owned, so why should capital come to a restrictive context when it can go elsewhere and when there is fierce competition for that investment?

DK   I think we will introduce hundred per cent foreign investment very soon now. There is a Chinese proverb which says: Things will get worse before they get better. With regard to the ways in which the West will exploit Eastern Europe, I think that will be true, and we may well end up with high unemployment.

WP   Why are the Croats so hostile to Markovic? (It was Ante Markovic, the equivalent of a federal prime minister, who introduced the measures to revalue the dinar.)

DK   I don't know. (Whenever DK is hesitant about an answer, he tightens his red necktie, which is already tightly knotted.) I think he will stay in place because the other republics like him. And his is a voice for realism. He is introducing a more market-oriented economy and he does not agree with printing money. Control of the money supply is quite a new policy for us here.

WP   Do you think communism will survive in Serbia; it has already been heavily defeated in Slovenia and in Croatia?

DK   I suppose that depends on what you mean by communism. The Cuban and North Korean patterns of socialism have no connection with our style in Yugoslavia. Sweden has a socialist component in its society, with pensions and social security. I think we will try to create our own blend of socialism and capitalism within a market-oriented economy. My own view is that in future each country will need to develop its own forms. What we will end up with is a particular Yugoslav way of life.

WP   Do you not agree that capital is now wholly internationalised?

DK   Yes, but that is a different issue. For example, what is going to happen in Germany, or in Bulgaria? Each will regulate the activities of capital in its own way. At the moment things are changing every day, so prediction has become very difficult. We have just watched on television a revolution in Romania. Five years ago that would have been impossible to imagine here.

WP   Do you believe that the social tensions which must accompany the economic changes which are in progress can be contained?

DK   It is a complicated situation. As yet, because of our previous policies, international capital has no very strong foothold here. In six months' time there will be an election. We already have twenty-five different parties, but in Serbia the Communist Party will do well, partly because Milosevič is such a powerful figure and our policies are different from those pursued by the party in Croatia. We did have a multi-party democracy, seventy years ago and we have never been Bolsheviks in the Soviet style.

WP   (That is not quite true, since there was a brief period before Tito and Stalin fell out when the Yugoslavs acted as Stalin's hatchet-men in the international communist community.)

Do you think Yugoslavia will survive the nationalist tensions which now seem to be building up?

DK   Yes. We are all Slavs and every country has problems. Slovenia will stay because no other option would work. They cannot join up with Austria or Italy; they would just lose their identity. I think that realism will prevail.

WP   So this may simply be a transitional phase in which we are seeing exaggerated demands.

DK   Yes. Twenty years ago too we had problems, but they were kept secret. Party and parliament were a closed world. Now everything is in the newspapers. One foreign correspondent recently remarked: just read the papers, it's all there. And we do have a very open and democratic press. Yes, Yugoslavia will survive – with crises, but there are no better solutions. And we can improve conditions within Yugoslavia, for example, between the republics and in our educational system. We very much want to be Europeans. Our history and traditions and culture are European and Europe does not stop at Italy. If Greece is European, so too is Yugoslavia. There is much that can be said now which could not have been said ten years ago, and that is a fundamental change. I think we are adapting very fast. You would not recognise Yugoslavia now with how it was ten years ago. It is like another country.

WP   Though on the surface things do not look so different.

DK   But the basics are changing. You can go to a bank and buy pounds sterling or American dollars. There is a deep paradox here. You observed earlier that communism had failed to motivate its people. Now we have a deep crisis, but people are motivated and optimistic. They can see possibilities; for jobs, for education, for culture, for private business, so they see that improvement and progress are possible.

WP   It would be nice to believe so.

I T was my habit when leaving Anastasia for any length of time to park her, if possible, outside a British Embassy. In Eastern Europe there is often a police or military presence outside the embassy, and the sight of GB number plates deters them from questioning one's business parking there. The embassy in Belgrade is a large, handsome, yellow palazzo in the Austro-Hungarian style, set behind high, cast-iron railings and a small garden.

It had been proving impossible to get reliable information about what was going on in Romania. The international telephone lines were permanently down and the Serbs I spoke to were full of rumour about the dangers there. Our consul was able to tell me that they had had no reports of any trouble for Britons, but that official advice was to avoid the Tirgumureş area since the people there seemed sometimes to attack anything that moved. Television reports centred around angry claims by the opposition parties that the election results, which had just been announced, were the result of fraud and intimidation. British and American observers, however, thought that while there had been some questionable practices by Iliescu and his supporters, the results reflected, more or less, what people had voted for.

A T the Writers' Union there were about a dozen writers, not all of whom I knew. The discussion was chaired by Ratko Adamović, with Ivana translating. Adamović looked entirely the part of the late-nineteenth century, East European writer, with his straggly beard, white face and foot-long, curving cigarette-holder which he used as a kind of over-sized worry-toy. He introduced me at great length and then I read a recent poem on which I had spent a couple of hours with Ivana the evening before, trying to help with its translation. The poem is one of a series of alternating gift and loss poems:

Return

The small rain settles in to Creag nan Gabhar
drawing the skies down, stirring the ember
moss to brightness, hitching the faded haar
    more tightly to her shoulders.
    Then from the cloud and drowsing boulders
    nine regal does come trotting
down, indian-file, to their peat-black pool
and wait, alert, immobile, undrinking.
Unmoving I wait breathing slowly, wait
    crouched in the heather, sodden
chilled. The curlews are silenced, the spate
of the earth-brown burn inaudible.
What are we waiting for? But still they
    wait till the hillside shivers
numbly and forgetting to exhale.
    Then I see, half-see him through the haar
albino stag, almost invisible.

It is difficult to tell anything about how native speakers perceive a poem in a language you know something of, far less in one of which you know almost nothing. How an evocation of Scottish landscape strikes Serbs may well have nothing at all to do with the text of the original (untranslated) poem. There is a story told somewhere by W. H. Auden of a poem he very much admired by Paul Valery. Auden's French was anything but shabby and he had known the poem well for many years and had translated it. It was only years later that he came to understand that the language register in which Valery had written the poem was a send-up, a burlesque of a style of writing which Auden, not being a native speaker, had simply failed to hear. Translation is inevitable and perhaps often valuable, but to be treated with immense caution.

I was asked whether *Return* was a religious poem and the discussion quickly became lively as between the role of the sacred versus the secular in writing. I declined to identify it as in any sense a religious poem, while wanting to claim that it recorded an experience of something numinous. Interestingly, the drift of the interventions was anti-political and anti-secular, with one or two speakers wanting to insist that there was no room in poetry for the *merely* profane. While I disagreed strongly with that extreme view, I was fascinated to be hearing almost exactly the opposite of the sentiments I had heard in that same building eight years earlier. Some of the speakers wanted to know about conditions for Scottish writers, and especially how it was possible to make a living. There may have been some underlying anxiety that they might be thrust sooner than they wished into the cold, where they would have to survive without the protection of state support. In fact, Serbian writers are not funded directly by the state, but once they have had a book accepted by the Writers' Union and have become members, they are likely to be able to have their work published and become eligible for pension rights and other benefits. Those rights increase *pro rata* for each book published, so there is economic pressure to produce, though it is not directly commercial.

I DO not much care for most cities and certainly not for Belgrade. Driving in it is a test of nerves as drivers cut across your bows at amazing speeds and seem to ignore every possible traffic regulation. At many of the busy intersections in downtown Belgrade, young gypsies will dart among the cars, offering to wash the windscreens for a few dinar. As the traffic was revving up at the lights, as in the seconds before the flag falls for the start of a *grand prix*, it always astonished me that they were not killed or injured. Some of the gypsy boys must have been very young, no more than nine or ten years old, and most were very persistent, refusing to take no for an answer. One young man in his early twenties was standing by the kerb at a busy intersection, gesturing his minions towards whichever cars he had selected for attention. Anastasia, of course, being very obvious among the Ladas, Skodas and Trabants, was invariably selected. I waved the children away several times, but he gestured them back. They were hanging over the bonnet as the lights changed. Whether the strain of Belgrade driving had got to me or not, my temper snapped, for the first and only time on the journey. I switched off the engine, despite the shouts and blaring horns of the drivers behind, got out and shouted some abusive advice to the fellow on the kerb, the performance of which would have led to grave physical discomfort on his part. No one was more surprised than I when he and his entire entourage turned and fled the scene. I felt that I was not behaving as one is expected to in the Balkans.

BEFORE leaving Belgrade I stocked up with food and wine since I was repeatedly told that nothing much would be available in Romania. I had decided to cross the border at Vršać, once capital of the Vojvodina which ends there, for the hills which rise behind the town are really the beginnings of the Carpathian ranges. Crossing the Danube on the road for Pančevo, the river for once looked blue. Pančevo itself was unkempt, the verges overgrown, a flock of goats grazing the central reservation of its main street. It was a very hot day and the hills were no more than a blue-grey shimmer.

Vršać was once shared by Magyars, Germans, Serbs and Romanians, but seems now to have been largely Serbianised. The Germans have gone or been assimilated, as have the Hungarians. In 1848 the pro-Austrian Serbs were defeated here by the Hungarians, who were in turn beaten the following year by Austrian forces. Like the rest of this section of the Banat, the town was controlled by Hungary again between 1941 and 1945. It seemed rather a sleepy place set among huge tracts of vineyard.

I was still hoping to make contact with the people I wanted to meet in Bucharest but, in the aftermath of the elections, it proved impossible to get through by telephone. Much of the day went on endlessly frustrating efforts to get a line.

Just outside the town on Vršać Hill there perches a fourteenth-century tower built as a fortress against the Turks. Reached by a winding track, it looks completely uncared for, though supposedly a national monument. About sixteen yards square, you can climb to its summit, a hundred or so feet up, first by an outside stair with a rusty guard rail, and then by an open internal stair. It is a faintly disconcerting experience – even for one accustomed to climbing – with its shaky railings and missing steps. The view from the summit, however, was worth the effort and I could look across into Romania on one side, and across the plain of the Banat on the other, the latter heavily planted, the former an apparent wilderness. Local legend has it that a terrible demon lives in the tunnels supposed to exist below the tower. If so, there was no sign of him, though it was a wild enough spot in the windy twilight.

AT seven o'clock on an overcast morning I arrived at the Yugoslav-Romanian border. There was a queue of about a dozen cars on the Yugoslav side and, from what I could see, a longer queue on the other. A bedraggled-looking woman with a birch besom was rearranging the dust in desultory fashion, but, apart from that, nothing was happening and happening very slowly. The border guards stood in a little knot chatting among themselves. After more than an hour had gone by with no sign of movement, I decided instead to follow the Danube on the Bulgarian side and cross at the main border post at Ruse, by which time conditions in Romania might have settled somewhat.

In order to reach Vidin in Bulgaria from Vršac it is necessary to return to Belgrade or detour via Bela Crkva and cross the Danube at Kovin, for there are no other bridges. From Kovin a minor road follows the river along the Romanian-Yugoslav border, while the main road cuts through the Homoljske hills to Negotin. Since it was to be a drive of well over a hundred miles and with two borders to negotiate, it seemed sensible to take the main road.

As soon as I left the Banat plain at Požarevać, my spirits began to lift and the pale-blue silhouette of the hills on the horizon seemed to promise more than the plodding monotony of the plain. I had brought with me a number of cassette tapes: some Mozart piano concertos; Beethoven's last three string quartets; a miscellany of operatic arias by outstanding singers and a selection of tunes performed by Pipe Major Angus MacDonald. It was definitely a morning for the pipes and his magnificent performance of *Mrs*

MacPherson of Inveran with its marvellously disciplined energy quite restored me.

Between Požarevać and Negotin there are no towns of any size and much of the countryside is forest, completely shrouding the hills in an impenetrable, green tangle. What agriculture there is, is largely confined to the immediate valley of the narrow river Pek which cuts its way through the hills. For most of the way, the road also follows the river. It has to, for the hills rise steeply on either side. Farming here is still a primitive affair, a matter of a few pigs and goats and fields won from the wooded hillside, hoed and planted or ploughed with a pair of oxen. By the roadside a boy with a pair of pigs on leashes waved as I passed. A little further on, a couple of mud and wattle huts stood behind a long row of beehives, all painted blue. Winding and twisting its way along the riverbank, the road could have been through Perthshire were it not for the fact that there was no tree-line on the hills. The faces of the peasants who stared after the car seemed darker here, more weather-beaten.

As I ate my lunch of olives and bread and cherries, by the roadside, a pair of distant eagles circled the hilltops in front of me. The variety of trees around the riverside was very great with several I could not recognise in addition to the oaks, acacias and elders. The woods sheltered a barrage of bird-noise, some of it unrecognisable. Further down the valley I could see two children playing by the roadside, having been left in charge of the goats tethered beside them.

The best moments of a journey are for me those when the illusion of going somewhere is temporarily broken. Driving a car is like a kind of specious ambition. In fact, the car drives the person, confining it to manageable roadways, very much as the ego confines us, most of the time, to socially acceptable behaviours. And, like the ego, it has a hard-to-escape, mesmeric intensity, as though the soul looked out through the eyes in the way a driver looks through the windscreen. Most of the time, the road is tolerable enough. Its confinement enables us to perform the rituals that allow us to make a living, lead a life, without paying too drastic a price. Travel, with its attendant strains and anxieties to reach entirely fictitious goals exaggerates the whole process. It is a way of keeping-on-doing and its pauses become all the more intense moments of not-doing, of simply being. Bereft of such interludes and of the gratitude they engender, the journey would all too soon become intolerable and the traveller a victim of his own ego-driven ambitions.

At Maidanpek (Fortress on the Pek) a huge quarrying project has sliced away the side of the mountain to a depth of several hundred feet. The town seems almost wholly new, built to house the hundreds of workmen and their families. Much of the most recent building in Belgrade – as here – attempts something more imaginative than the absolutely functional austerity of the 1950s' and 1960s' developments. Unfortunately, the style which seems to find official favour is just as ugly, albeit more inventive. The trappings of modernism have replaced no trappings at all but without regard to context, so that a futuristic-style sports complex will be set down in the middle of a nineteenth-century suburb. Even so, it is an improvement on the shabby nastiness of much of East Europe's post-war building. The modernist decoration of the housing blocks here though, was designed to please the planners rather than the inhabitants.

Peasant dress varied from village to village. In Štubik the women wore very dark blue instead of black and the over-jacket was a deep magenta. Outside one house an old granny in peasant dress was talking to a girl in her early teens dressed in jeans and denim jacket. A frequent sight is a group of two or three women making their way to the fields with a small back-pack of food and water and a mattock-like hoe carried over a shoulder.

At Negotin the landscape changes from the predominantly conifer-growing hills to a more open pasture-land, articulated by clumps of woodland, mainly oak. The scattered cottages often have two or three haystacks beside the house, with the hay piled round a central pole in beehive shape to a height of twelve or fifteen feet. Some of the agricultural practices in these rural areas have probably not changed much in centuries, except where collectivisation has introduced machines. But in the poorer and hillier areas, that was never a practicable project and was never enforced with the same universal and theoretical ruthlessness as it was in the Soviet Union or in Hungary, at least after the very early days of communist enthusiasm.

Crossing the border at Bregovo was again accomplished without trouble or delay. There is so much junk in the boot that no one ever seems to want to examine it, their only curiosity being the boxes of books. Once they grasp that they are mainly guides, dictionaries and histories, they lose interest.

Bulgaria – and within a few minutes everything feels different, though it is difficult to pinpoint why. No two countries ever feel the same though it may be only a mile or less from one village to the next. For all the evident poverty of rural Serbia, this seems poorer still, nearer to subsistence. The carts now are not horse-drawn, but donkey-drawn. In one such tiny cart, driven by an old man, there is just enough room for his wife to sit in it, her legs dangling over the back and in her hand a leash for the pair of goats trotting along behind. In a nearby field I see a man ploughing with a donkey-drawn plough and in the neighbouring field a new-looking tractor.

At the border post I have to change dollars into leva. The woman who fills in the currency forms speaks reasonable French and directs me to the ferry terminal at the Vidin-Calafat crossing to buy petrol coupons; she is gap-toothed and cheerful, which is more than can be said for the doll-like creature who staffs the tourist shop at the ferry terminal. Made-up in what she doubtless thinks fashionable in the West – she in fact looked like the stereotype of a tart in a bad 1950s' film – she does not want to be bothered with anything other than attending to her crimson-painted nails. 'The coupon office is closed,' she said. Does it re-open? 'Yes.' When? 'Wait, you must wait.' Half-an-hour later a more helpful colleague arrived and sold me the coupons I needed.

Next I had to find petrol. There were two stations, one on either side of the road just outside Vidin. My heart sank when I saw the half-mile-long queues. After about forty minutes and no progress, I walked to the head of the queue where the attendants were chatting in their office. One of them spoke some German and indicated that I should bring the car up. There was no ordinary petrol: 'We are waiting for a delivery,' he said, a tale I was to hear often. There was, however, lead-free petrol for tourists with coupons. Whether the petrol was lead-free or not, I never discovered, but Anastasia ran on it perfectly well and if it was lead-free it would certainly have been useless to the Ladas, Moskvitchs and other motorised *dreck* which made up the queue, though I did feel slight guilt pangs at being able to queue-jump in this way.

Having gone through the essentials of getting money and petrol, the next thing was to find an hotel. Since there seemed only to be two in Vidin, that was easy and within half an hour I was settled in the Hotel Bononia. My room on the third floor looked out towards the Danube less than a hundred yards away. Fittings and furnishings were poorer than anything I had seen hitherto, though perfectly clean. The curtains were little better than thin calico and the ancient carpeting would have been gracefully retired anywhere else. There seemed to be no hot water and, of course, no plugs. But, by comparison with the Hotel Park in Belgrade, it was a haven of friendly courtesy.

Vidin was for centuries both fortress and trading centre. Surrounded by marsh, it made a highly defensible site. There was a Celtic settlement called *Dunonia* here and the Romans named it *Bononia* when it became part of the province of Moesia Superior. The great medieval fortress of Baba Vida on the waterfront was built over a Roman predecessor. In the later Middle Ages the pretty Tsardom of Ivan Stratsimir had its capital at Vidin and when the Turks conquered it in 1396, it became the administrative centre for the pashalik of Vidin.

When Europe began to panic about the encroachments of the Turks in the fourteenth century, a papal crusade was preached and taken up by Louis the Great, king of Poland and Hungary. His army wiped out a superior Turkish force of some eighty thousand men just by Vidin and he captured the fortress in 1365. Louis then made an alliance with the Byzantine emperor, John V Palaeologus, against the Ottomans, but it was already too late.

Ottoman is a western misreading for the *Osmanli* dynasty of Turkish rulers, named after Osman I (1281-1325). The Osmanlis held their lands from the Seljuk sultan but gradually extended their territories under a series of brilliant political and military leaders. They were still essentially a nomad culture with a powerful military tradition so their interest lay in tribute and plunder as much as in settlement, much like the Mongol tribes who had driven them westward in the first place two hundred years earlier. By 1340 they had reduced the holdings of Byzantium in Asia Minor virtually to the city itself, and when the Byzantine usurper, John Cantacuzene, appealed to them for help against the Emperor, John V, in 1345, they took the opportunity to occupy Gallipoli and parts of Rumelia in force. From then on, they moved steadily north and west into the Balkans, though with a complicated series of checks and reverses as, for example, when Tamerlane attacked from the East, defeating and capturing the Sultan Bayezid I near Ankara in 1402.

The tribute the Turks required was not just gold and silver. They

145

also wanted slaves and soldiers and so Murad I had founded the janissaries sometime in the 1370s. These were Christian youths paid as tribute by the Turkish-occupied territories. Most were trained as a corps of professional soldiers, but any who were obviously talented, were educated into Islam and could become viziers, the sultan's senior advisers. Being professional soldiers, they had a ferocious reputation, for European armies in the fifteenth and sixteenth centuries were often still peasant levies, ill-armed, reluctant and badly commanded. In due course, the janissaries became the bane of the Ottoman empire for they wielded such power that they chose and deposed sultans at will and wrought havoc where they pleased.

When they were not having to worry about their eastern flank, Turkish successes in Europe were fairly consistent. When Sigismund, king of Hungary and Holy Roman Emperor – he was the son of Charles IV of Bohemia – took up the crusade preached by Boniface IX in 1394, he led an army made up of contingents from all over Europe. After capturing Vidin, he moved on to Nicopolis, forcing Bayezid to raise the siege of Constantinople. The Christian forces were routed with tremendous losses. Some of the army managed to escape across the Danube, but many drowned and the Tsar of Vidin, Stratsimir, was captured and carried off to Brussa where he was killed. Thereafter the internal rivalries within Christendom ensured that there would be no unified response to the Turkish threat. Sigismund himself was occupied with the Hussites, though he did succeed in strengthening Hungary's military frontiers sufficiently to delay the Turkish conquest for a century.

By 1453 Constantinople had fallen and southern Serbia was under Turkish control. By the end of the century the Turks had moved through Croatia and into southern Austria. By that time too, the principalities of Moldavia and Wallachia had become vassal states. In 1526 under Suleiman the Magnificent they defeated the Hungarians at Mohács, the king, Louis II, being killed and Buda captured. In 1529 and 1532 the Turks were besieging Vienna, encouraged by the Empire's old enemy, France. Although they never took Vienna, they were able to partition Hungary, thereby proving a continual threat to Western Europe's frontier for a further two centuries.

It would be difficult to over-estimate the historical consequences of the Turkish success, for it shifted the balance of power in Europe from the centre to the periphery. With the discovery of the New World and the opening up of new trade routes, Eastern Europe was no longer crucial to the West. The struggle for dominance moved to the Atlantic seaboard. By the time any kind of peace returned to much of Eastern Europe it was too late to catch up. The massive depopulations wrought by plague and war meant that social and economic evolution had so stagnated or even, in some cases, been reversed, that the subsequent history of Eastern Europe has to be understood in the light of that interrupted development.

Vidin was under Turkish rule until not much more than a century ago, having been liberated by Romanian forces in February 1878. The Turks did not allow any native aristocracy to survive. What endured through those centuries of occupation was a stubborn, peasant culture, kept alive by the Orthodox Church which the Turks tolerated. Bulgarian history, therefore, has suffered a kind of protracted hiatus, in common with most of the Balkans, which results in a tendency to idealise the 'freedom' of the pre- and post-Turkish periods with little to remember in between. Such chasms in historical experience, in a sense of who you are as a nation, must leave deep and abiding scars. It is in that light that recent Bulgarian policies to expel or deracinate their Turkish population has to be seen. The flight of more than three hundred thousand refugees into Turkey in the past year is a measure of just how deep some of those scars have gone.

WHAT I had not expected in Vidin was the extent to which people seemed to be enjoying themselves. In Prague I saw unhappiness and aggression in many faces and Belgrade seemed relentlessly frantic. Even if people did not seem specifically unhappy, they did not exude contentment. Here, in some strange way, they did, and that impression was confirmed by several visitors to whom I subsequently spoke. Claudio Magris in his *Danube* attributes it to the capacity of a long-subject people to take comfort in the immediate pleasures of life. Whatever the reason, whatever the poverty, people smiled more, walked more slowly and generally seemed more amiable.

147

Admittedly, there was a public holiday to mark some anniversary of the Christianising saints, Cyril and Methodius, inventors of the Cyrillic alphabet. It would be difficult to imagine an official holiday for such an esoteric pair in Britain, but the Bulgarians cherish what history they have. Vidin's new town square is a large oblong in which the central area is given over to an attractive modern fountain and a war memorial. The square has been laid out in patterns of brick and fawn-coloured tiles. Its spaciousness, water, shrubs and trees make it a pleasant place to stroll or meet friends and in the early evening a great many people were doing just that in a leisurely *corso*. One end of the square is dominated by the high-rise offices of the Communist Party, but the other sides are lined by a theatre and concert hall as well as by administrative offices. Just round the corner from the square a brass band was playing marches with enormous zest, while, in the shade of the concert hall's entrance, a small orchestra was performing modern classical works, assisted by a rather good sound system. While these two groups of musicians were playing, a third was setting up a ferocious-looking barrage of speakers along the Danube embankment. This was a pop group, retailing the latest in Western decadence to the obvious interest of a crowd of admiring teenagers.

With no inherited class system to monopolise culture as the possession of a few, Bulgarians seem to take a more enthusiastic interest in cultural activities than their western peers. A large number of young people were waiting in the square for the theatre to open and almost all of them had dressed up for the occasion, the young men in dark suits and ties, their girlfriends or wives in their best frocks. Some of the young women looked very elegant in tight mid-calf length skirts, probably home-made. Black and red were favourite colours and most of the women carried flowers. With the difference of age, it could almost have been a British audience of the 1950s.

In sharp contrast to the care with which many of the strollers had dressed, the shopping street which ran off from the square was tatty and badly supplied. Few goods were available and those that were, were shabby. The lack of goods did not seem to inhibit people from window-shopping and several stall-holders were doing a brisk trade selling plastic trinkets. Not as brisk, however, as the chip shop or the ice-cream stand. Outside the immediate centre, the dilapidation of many of the buildings was

148

depressing and there were the usual eyesore – rows of multi-storey flats clad in dark-grey concrete.

The bar of the Hotel Bononia was a cool, darkened room with ceiling fan and quiet pop music and was obviously much favoured by the locals. Wine could only be had by the bottle, so I had a bottle of the excellent, local dry white wine, cool and not at all acidic. At about a pound a bottle, I felt under no obligation to drink it all. The Bulgarian authorities, unlike their Czech and Romanian counterparts, pursue a sensible policy with regard to foreign exchange, giving tourists a rate which hardly makes a black market worth while. In Romania, on the other hand, they insist on a ridiculously extortionate rate which drives everyone on to the black market, thereby frustrating their own greed.

By the time I had drunk a couple of glasses of wine, it was dinner time and I adjourned to the Bononia's restaurant. This was a long, wide, function hall, lit by huge chandeliers in which only a small proportion of the bulbs functioned. The floor was tiled and the tables ranged down the sides of the room. One table was set for forty or so people and the others for a dozen. One simply took a place wherever was available. At the far end of the room a band was in the process of setting up: guitar, drums, electronic keyboard and a mandolin. It was not, as yet, specially busy. The young waiter who arrived promptly at the table brought no menu. I asked for what there was and he told me I could have salad and slivović to begin and shashlik to follow with wine or champagne. There was no beer.

When the excellent slivović arrived, it was in a tumbler containing about a quarter pint of the fiery stuff. At the next table two young men, perhaps twenty years old, were drinking Russian champagne – which is not at all bad, though quite unlike its French version. They had clearly been there for some time and in the course of my dinner they drank their way through several more bottles until they were amazingly drunk. The quantities of alcohol consumed by all around me were prodigious and two people were carried out at different stages of the evening, having drunk themselves insensible. No one, so far as I saw, became quarrelsome or difficult. In a Scottish or Irish setting, equivalent quantities of alcohol would have produced mayhem.

The salad was a plateful of sliced cucumber in a sharp dressing. The shashlik which followed was none too warm and rather insipid – the meat had not been seasoned in any way – but was perfectly edible. What was extraordinary, however, was the wine, for which I was quite unprepared. Called *Gamza* it is produced at Nove Selo, a village not far from Vidin. Ruby-coloured with brown overtones, it was full of fresh flavours, mainly raspberry and rhubarb. It was like a particularly good burgundy but lighter than any burgundy I have tasted. It was so good, indeed, that I spent the rest of the evening finishing the bottle.

For an hour or so the band played Western-style pop tunes before switching to local music, the mandolin player giving some very dexterous performances. Now a crowd got up from the long table and began to dance, dragging their more reluctant friends up with them. The dances were mainly circle-dances of the kind I associate with Greece. But the music now sounded more Turkish than Western. Everyone knew the steps and when the band played a tune, some of the diners would sing along with them. I left them to their celebrations as they were still warming up. When I woke at five-thirty to the sound of blackbirds, a crowd of young people were still laughing and chattering on the benches in the little park beside the hotel. The rock concert which I had managed to sleep through had obviously been a success. Breakfast was a large cup of black, China tea from Shanghai, lumps of a soft, white, salty ewe-cheese, a rough salami and half a loaf.

One of the younger Serbian writers I had met, an immensely egotistical and arrogant young man who had never been to Bulgaria, had warned me against going there. When I asked him why, he replied: 'Because they are so poor and primitive and ignorant.' Poor certainly, but I greatly preferred what I had so far seen of Bulgaria.

O N the surface, Bulgaria's post-war history has been broadly similar to that of its Warsaw Pact allies but the similarities are deceptive. Like all the East European nation states I was to visit, the national revival began with a literary awakening in the early part of the last century. To some extent those literary awakenings were the result of the slow penetration of Western European ideas from the Enlightenment, but romantic nationalism soon split away from any early intellectual association it had with liberal and egalitarian aspirations. In the Balkan states the decay of Turkish power and the expansion southwards of Russian and Austro-Hungarian influence were the preconditions for fully-fledged national movements.

A peasant revolt, suppressed by the Turkish authorities with great ruthlessness and the massacre of over fifteen thousand Bulgarians, led to a Europe-wide agitation on Bulgaria's behalf. W. E. Gladstone's pamphlet on the Bulgarian atrocities helped shift British opinion in favour of the Bulgarians. First Serbia and then Russia declared war on Turkey, and the Western Powers, fearful of Russian influence, intervened. By the Treaty of Berlin of 1878 Bulgaria became an autonomous principality, though still subject to Turkish sovereignty.

Russian influence, however, remained paramount: so much so, that when Prince Alexander wished to return from exile after a palace coup in 1886, he was refused permission to do so by the Tsar. Next year a new prince, Ferdinand of Saxe-Coburg Gotha, was elected. The new state's foreign policy was heavily influenced by the fact that many ethnic Bulgarians lived under foreign rule, especially in the Southern Dobruja and in north-east Macedonia which Bulgaria regarded as *Bulgaria irridenta*. Ferdinand declared Bulgaria a sovereign state in 1908 and in 1912–13, along with Montenegro, Greece and Serbia, declared war on Turkey. It was a quick victory and drove the Turks from most of their mainland holdings, but the allies fell out over the Macedonian spoils. Bulgaria attacked her Serbian and Greek allies and lost disastrously, so Serbia and Greece split Macedonia between them and Bulgaria lost the Dobruja to Romania.

It was the hope of recouping these losses which led the pro-German Ferdinand to enter the First World War on the side of the Central Powers in 1915. Widespread discontent with the war forced Ferdinand to abdicate in 1918 in favour of his son, who took the title Boris III, the numeral reinforcing the idea of a continuity of Bulgarian history. Boris was a shrewd politician and from 1935 onwards ran the country as a royal dictatorship. In 1940 the Germans offered him the Dobruja in exchange for which he allowed German troops to use Bulgaria as a base for their attacks on Greece and Yugoslavia. He refused, however, to declare war on Russia.

King Boris died in 1943 and there have always been suspicions that the Germans got rid of him. After his death, a more pliable pro-German government was formed around the regents who controlled the government on behalf of the young Tsar Simeon. Opposition to the war, however, was strong in Bulgaria and the opposition parties formed an umbrella organisation called the Fatherland Front. After a last-ditch attempt at neutrality in 1944 which Russia found 'absolutely insufficient', Bulgaria switched sides and the Red Army entered Bulgaria unopposed. The communist leader Dimitrov, who had been exiled in Moscow for many years, was able to return and in 1946, after a referendum, the country was declared a republic.

During the anti-Tito hysteria of the late 1940s, the Bulgarian communists carried out a series of purges which continued with great ruthlessness into the early 1950s. Unlike Hungary and Czechoslovakia, Bulgaria never questioned its basic loyalty to Moscow and this provided a degree of continuity and stability unusual in Eastern Europe. To some extent, that could be attributed to the lingering affection many Bulgarians felt for Russia as their prime liberator. But it must also have had something to do with the fact that standards of living did not slump in the way they did in post-war Czechoslovakia. Bulgaria was not industrialised before the war to any great extent and the people did choose a socialist orientation, however much they may have deplored its abuses. From the late 1970s, a certain relaxation in communist stringencies became possible and peasants were permitted to own their own plots of land. Until his removal in 1989, Todor Zhivkov was the longest-serving of all the East European bosses, having held more or less undisputed power since 1961.

During the 1970s and 1980s there was no history of dissidence in Bulgaria as there was in Czechoslovakia or in Poland. Wherever it appeared, it was extinguished. In the 1980s, however, Zhivkov reversed his previous policy of rights for minorities. Bulgaria's Turkish minority, about a million of them, was to be assimilated in an effort to create a homogeneous Bulgarian state offering no opportunity for interference to any outside power. The Turks lost their separate educational, cultural and religious facilities. Protest demonstrations in May 1989 were violently suppressed with large numbers of people injured and at least sixty dead. The EEC cancelled a trade treaty and the Western press reacted with great hostility. Zhivkov's days were numbered. All through the summer the number of refugees streaming into camps across the Turkish border kept the spotlight on the government's actions, while internal opposition within the Communist Party built up around Peter Mladenov, a long-time friend of Michael Gorbachev. What other protest movements existed, were relatively small and centred on ecological issues. By November the dissident movements had gained enough confidence to hold their ground and a coup within the politburo forced Zhivkov's resignation and replacement by Mladenov. Free elections were promised for 1990.

THE E79 runs from Vidin to Sofia. For a main road, the quality is poor. At times it is little more than a winding, two-lane country road fretted with potholes, but the need to drive more slowly is, from the point of view of looking around, an advantage. For the first hundred or so kilometres to Mihajlovgrad, there are no towns of any size and cars are few and far between. In the villages, there are no obvious shops, no advertisements, but lots of individual plots, many with a few vines. The roadsides are a riot of colour. It is a countryside of low hills, heavily farmed. Anastasia was in need of a good wash and I was lucky enough to come upon a roadside stream where I could park.

The pool where I collected water was fringed with irises and alive with sapphire-coloured dragonflies. It was also raucous with the *brek-a-kek-kek* of frogs, just as Aristophanes describes it. Each time I approached for more water, the plopping noises grew frantic and, invisible among the rushes, a protest of quacks and gurgles set up, as loud as any dozen obstreperous ducks.

I had been watching a buzzard circling over a distant hill when, from the corner of my eye, I caught a flash of colour. It was a pair of bee eaters (*merops apiaster*) swooping and diving like overgrown swifts in a blaze of colour. They are spectacular birds and beautiful to watch with their chestnut head and nape, blue-green belly, yellow rump and throat and black eye stripe. Their long, curved wings with their dark fringes make them look like flying fans and I watched for half-an-hour before they moved on elsewhere.

Approaching Vraća the mountains begin to look more daunting as you swing round south-west towards Sofia and enter the central section of the Balkan range. Some of these tops rise to over six thousand feet, though with their rounded, grassy slopes they look less fearsome than their craggy Scottish equivalents. The last section of road before Sofia runs through the impressive gorges of the river Iskar. The road has been driven straight into the mountains in a series of three tunnels, each more than a kilometre long, and across bridges spanning deep ravines. It represents a considerable feat of civil engineering and the heavily wooded mountains looked as wild as anything I had seen. Near Sofia a pair of storks flew across the road. These were the first I had seen. Patrick Fermor writes of seeing great flocks of them in Hungary. I had not seen any. Pollution and the destruction of their favoured haunts has reduced their numbers enormously since the 1930s.

Following the main road for Sofia city centre took me straight to the Balkan-tourist office from which I was able to book a room in the Hotel Hemus on the south side of the city. The young man in front of me at the accommodation desk was an American. As we chatted, it emerged that he had just spent some time touring Romania. I was keen to find out whatever authentic information I could and he was pleased to have a chance to debrief so we arranged to dine together later that evening.

It was a pleasure to be able to spend an evening speaking English again without any of that stilted quality which inevitably creeps in to conversation with non-native speakers. If not careful, you end up speaking a kind of pidgin in an effort to simplify or by allowing foreign constructions to take over from what you would naturally say. We ate at the Vitosha, an up-market tourist hotel within sight of Mount Vitosha which dominates the southern skyline. Nowhere in Bulgaria is especially expensive for westerners and it was also an agreeable piece of self-indulgence to be back in thoroughly comfortable surroundings for an evening. Matthew had just graduated from Stanford and was having a few weeks in Europe to celebrate. He confirmed for me that Romania was perfectly feasible. He had also been in Prague and in East Germany so it was interesting to compare notes and impressions.

Perhaps the most striking thing about central Sofia for a driver, is how easy it is. There are relatively few cars and it is perfectly possible to park within a few hundred yards of the town centre. It was like stepping back a generation to the days when cars did not entirely dominate city life. I saw absolutely no sign of litter of any kind and the plentiful gardens and parks were well maintained. All the public buildings seemed to have soldiers stationed outside them. With conscription I suppose they have to find something for them to do.

Much of the downtown area consists of wide, cobbled avenues lined with elegant, turn-of-the-century buildings in assorted styles. The influence of Austro-Hungary is, surprisingly, much in evidence, perhaps due to the tastes of their German princelings. You can walk round the principal sights of the centre in a couple of hours. The late-nineteenth-century Alexander Nevsky Church must be among the most impressive in south-eastern Europe with its plethora of domes and vast interior, spacious enough for several thousand worshippers. It was dedicated to the Russian soldiers who fought in the War of Liberation in 1877-78.

One of the more bizarre monuments, presumably in emulation of Moscow, is Dimitrov's mausoleum outside which two soldiers, no more than boys, stand guard in their Ruritanian, ceremonial uniforms of black trousers with a white stripe, wine-red jackets heavy with elaborate silver facings and a kepi-type cap with a huge feather in the front. They have to stand absolutely motionless for an hour at a time, unlike the palace guards in London who can at least change positions at more regular intervals. They must have been exhausted and bored silly. Not long after my visit, the corpse of Dimitrov was surreptitiously removed from the mausoleum by the authorities as no longer in keeping with the new Bulgaria. He probably died a timely death in 1949. It meant he did not have to be purged or lose status in the worst phase of Stalin's paranoia. His enormous *kudos* in the communist movement stemmed partly from the courageous way in which he stood up to Nazi torture and intimidation at the Reichstag fire trial. He was one of the very few ever to walk free from a Nazi court, mainly because of the international publicity which attended the trial, after which he took himself to the Soviet Union.

Having a limited appetite for sightseeing, I went to the Sheraton for coffee. It was still a holiday, and everywhere else was closed. The Sheraton was as Sheratons are – much the same everywhere. In their Wiener Café, the walls were lined with photographs of the café at the turn of the century. It has been restored to its original decor and very elegant it was. They advertised American coffee, which turned out to be unavailable, but for a dollar you could have a good capuccino and a large glass of excellent, chilled apple juice.

155

There were orchids on the marble tables and gilt everywhere. The menu was a delight with 'crepes norman' – with apples of course – and other frivolities. On the street outside, three young soldiers were queuing up to weigh themselves for a minute sum of money on an old man's battered set of bathroom scales.

M Y target was Veliko Tarnovo, Bulgaria's ancient capital prior to the Turkish occupation. Almost out of petrol – not a clever idea in Bulgaria – I left the highway at the little town of Prevec, Zhivkov's birthplace. Happily, there was no queue *and* they had petrol. Just beside the pump a heavily built man in a red sweatshirt, somewhere in his early fifties spoke to me and grinned. I missed what he said and he switched to execrable German. He wanted to know where I was heading. When I said Veliko Tarnovo he more or less invited himself along for a lift. After a moment's hesitation I nodded and he got into the back. Gradually I worked out from a combination of German, Russian and sign language that he was going to Pleven, that he was on holiday and that his *Kind* (child) was studying English at Veliko Tarnovo. He kept up a steady stream of conversational pleasantries, repeating the same thing over and over again, but with no increase in intelligibility. My initial doubts about him – for he looked something of a bruiser – soon evaporated. He was careful not to disturb any of the rubbish in the back of the car, so much so, that he looked quite uncomfortable until I stopped and rearranged my assorted junk. I could at least manage 'I want to buy some mineral water' in Russian and he indicated a place to stop in the first village we passed through. They had no mineral water but we got several bottles of orange squash, for which he insisted on paying.

Since it did not much matter to me where I was on any particular day, I offered to drop him in Pleven. By this time I had worked out that he was a truck-driver who was on his way home for a few days' break having had to leave his truck in Sofia. His next trip would be to Frankfurt, and, having no transport, he would have to make his own way back to Sofia to pick up his load.

156

Communication was difficult but cheerful. Whenever he was stuck with something I just did not understand, he aided communication by waving his hands about and grinning.

When we got to Pleven he was insistent I come to his house for coffee. We duly arrived at a typical East European apartment block in light-grey concrete. The interior staircase was unattractive but clean with a lift that did not work. He lived on the third floor. When he opened the door a girl of three or four in her underwear danced up and down until he lifted her onto his shoulder. Behind her, his wife stood in the hallway. As he took off his shoes to enter, I did the same.

Within a few moments I was seated in front of bottles of home-made lemonade and tiny biscuits while his wife made coffee which she served in minute cups. Next to appear was the little girl's mother, who looked herself to be not much more than twenty-one. Then the *Kind* appeared and was introduced. His son was in his early twenties, had studied English at the university at Veliko Tarnovo and spoke a completely correct, if rather formal, English. I was at once offered a meal and asked if I would like to stay to see the town. Their hospitality was old-fashioned and utterly charming. Grandfather, meantime, to whom I had given the lift, was recounting the difficulties of our communications with great hilarity.

It was a small two-bedroomed flat shared by the four adults and child, furnished comfortably and unpretentiously, much as I would expect to find in any respectable working-class home in Scotland. Despite its evident overcrowding, it was tidy and scrupulously clean.

Boris, the son, made a living as a tour guide and freelance teacher of English. His wife had only recently returned from a visit to the Netherlands and the year before they had both managed a holiday in Budapest. He was obviously an energetic and optimistic young man. Asked what he made of the recent reform process, he replied that he did not much like the Soviet attitude towards the Baltic states. His father was much less willing to be critical and praised Gorbachev and the reform movement as wonderful developments about which everyone should be happy.

Boris wanted to see Bulgaria distance itself from the Soviet Union. He explained that Bulgaria was quickly developing a fair number of private businesses but still on a very small scale in relation to the national economy. He thought most people were pessimistic about the economic outlook but determined that the changes already in train should continue and even be speeded up. A recurring theme in his conversation was the fact that, as society became more competitive, one would have to be alert to its shifting opportunities. Boris's wife worked as a receptionist in a local tourist hotel. Most of their visitors were Russians who came on state-subsidised tours, though they did also get some Dutch and French tourists. British visitors were a rarity. They shook their heads when I explained that I was going on to Romania: 'We ought to be friends' (with Romania), Boris said, 'But they have so many difficulties and problems. And often nothing to eat.'

Pleven was the scene of a decisive battle in 1877 in the War of Liberation. The Turkish commander, Osman Pasha, was based at Vidin. The Russian and Romanian armies were moving south towards Plevna (Pleven) and, arriving just before the Russians, Osman Pasha repulsed their first assault and began to fortify the town, his troops (twenty thousand of them) working night and day. The Russian forces were bolstered by fresh troops from Turnovo and numbered almost double the defending forces. Osman Pasha again repelled a Russian assault inflicting heavy losses on the attackers. Under orders not to leave his position, he failed, however, to pursue the Russian forces.

The Russians then called in additional troops from the Romanian armies and assembled more than seventy thousand troops against Osman Pasha's forces, which had been increased by troops forced out of Lovcha to a total of thirty thousand. A further assault again failed. The battle had now gone on for nearly two months and the Russian and Romanian losses amounted to 18,000 men.

Finally, command of the siege was given over to General Todleben. At the end of October Osman Pasha was forced to surrender. By the end of the siege Osman Pasha had held up almost the entire army of liberation. Total casualties amounted to more than fifty thousand and after Plevna surrendered, the war was quickly over. The modern town is not very beautiful and its chief attraction, especially for the Russians, is its scattering of memorials and relics of the siege.

I had already decided to abandon my plans for Veliko Tarnovo and to push on instead to Ruse (Rousse or Rustchuk). As it was a considerable drive I declined my friends' offers of hospitality. They insisted on accompanying me downstairs. I needed water for the windscreen washers, since driving at any speed in the

Balkans in summer quickly clogs the wipers with insect goo. The ground level of the apartment block consisted of a series of small garages. Boris and his father opened theirs, revealing a battered Lada for which, they said, it was often difficult to get petrol. They produced water and a hose and hosed down Anastasia for me and, with smiles and handshakes all round, waved me away.

THE road from Pleven to Ruse cuts across the rolling country-side of the Danube basin. It is fertile land, much cultivated. So thickly were some of the wheatfields impregnated with poppies that they looked from a distance as though they had been coated with a crimson wash. Not far from Ruse I was waved down by a Bulgarian policeman waving a little red lollipop. When I stopped and went to see what he wanted, I was met with a stream of unintelligible remarks, punctuated by expressive gestures. He looked the classic caricature of the Bulgarian; pot-bellied, balding, heavy-jowled and with great, drooping mustachios. I knew perfectly well I had been speeding. Eighty kilometres was the limit and Anastasia was trundling along quite happily at eighty miles per hour. Nevertheless, I had no intention of indicating any understanding whatsoever. Eventually, waving his lollipop, he drew an '80' in the dust on Anastasia's bonnet. While all this was going on, cars would zoom past. He would wiggle the lollipop after them but no one stopped and he shook his head in mournful acceptance. Then someone he obviously knew drew alongside on a massive Kawasaki motorbike. Whether he was another policeman or not, I could not tell, but the cyclist roared off in flagrant outrage of any speed limit. He tapped his head to indicate 'crazy' and returned to my passport. I was fined five leva, about fifty pence, and waved cheerfully on my way. I later discovered that I should have been fined one lev for each kilometre I was in excess of the limit.

The Hotel Riga in Ruse rises above the Danube some fifteen storeys high. It is modern, comfortable and even has plugs for the wash-hand basins and showers. The view from the top storey was impressive. To the north, you looked across the Danube to the smoky haze of Giurgiu in Romania. The Danube is split here by a sizeable island and the far shore revealed only low marshes. To the west and south the Danube and the town stretched into the distance. At evening, in a faintly purple haze, the lights along the elegant Danube boulevard were reflected in the dark waters, creating an effect of tranquillity.

That effect is misleading for Ruse is Bulgaria's fourth largest city and its most important port on the Danube. It is a major economic and industrial centre as well as being the principal route into Romania. It was early evening by the time I had settled in to the hotel and in the town square the *corso* was in full swing. As in Vidin and Sofia, the immediate town centre has been pedestrianised. The main street leading to the square was sprinkled with busy cafés and, once again, many of the younger people had dressed up, though fewer of the women carried flowers. A Clint Eastwood film was showing at the local cinema, though the stills in the foyer were all in black and white. Along the north side of the square a long row of flower stalls had been set up. There was that same ease among the people which I had sensed in Vidin.

The receptionists at the Riga all spoke either French or German and one of them recommended the Leventa restaurant, a couple of miles outside town on the low hill topped by the TV transmission mast. The Leventa had begun life as a Turkish fortress and was a substantial building on ground level with numerous cellar rooms. Each room was devoted to the cuisine of a different Danubian country. It seemed silly not to opt for Bulgarian. I ordered a sharp, lemony potato soup, rather in the style of *avgolimono*, but much heartier, with slivers of carrot, noodles and lumps of potato. It had been made with a chicken-based stock and finished with cream and chopped parsley. And very good it was. The wine, Karlovski Musket, was dry and fruity and went equally well with the pieces of deep-fried carp and tomato salad. It was a good meal and at sixteen leva, about £2, it would have been good value by any criteria. A band was playing in one of the neighbouring rooms, fortunately not the one I had chosen, since it was rather loud. They played gypsy-style foxtrots and tangos. It all sounded very *entre deux guerres*. No one seemed to mind the children running about, obviously enjoying some kind of tag.

On the way to the Leventa by taxi, the driver remarked on some particularly atrocious driving by saying 'Bulgarian driving', and again, in the restaurant, I heard a waiter say 'Bulgarian manners' at some piece of bad behaviour. I heard equivalent remarks on several occasions during my time in Bulgaria. It is not something one would hear in Scotland or England and, I rather think, confirms something of what Ivana mentioned with regard to a sense of inferiority about national identity. My friend the truck-driver had been anxious to know whether I thought badly of Bulgaria in view of its poverty. Certainly, there seemed to be a sense, confronted with a Westerner, that Bulgaria did not have a high standard of living, but I suspect the insecurity had more to do with the fear that they might be thought Asiatic. Nowhere at all did one see any sign of celebration of the Turkish elements in Bulgarian society, though after half a millenium they must be considerable.

Back at the Riga, I sat on the balcony for an hour watching the strollers along the Danube embankment while around me fireflies hovered like a confetti of wind-blown stars.

A young Austrian with whom I got into conversation had been working in Ruse for nearly a year. His company had sent him to supervise the installation of machinery for a timber processing plant. He liked Bulgaria, but explained that the workers were in some cases '*etwas orientalisch*' (rather eastern). They would disappear for a few hours for a siesta if they felt like it. Others, however, especially the technicians, he said, were highly skilled and industrious.

ON the banks of the little Rusenski Lom, which flows into the Danube at Ruse, and about ten miles south of the town, there are several caves cut into the wooded cliff face. These form the Rock Monastery of Ivanovo and date from the thirteenth century. Because it sounded a difficult place to find I engaged the taxi-driver, Marin, who had driven me to the Leventa the evening before, to take me there. The only condition was that I wait half-an-hour so that he could go home and tell his wife. He duly arrived half-an-hour later with his three-year-old daughter. We did eventually find the track for the caves after Marin had stopped and asked a shepherd for directions. The sky had become very overcast and lightning was forking on the horizon. Marin

drove with demented zest, cornering at angles to the horizontal
I would hardly have believed possible.

A rough path led up the steep, wooded hillside. Marin had lived
in Ruse all his life but had never visited the caves and was keen to
know whatever I could tell him of their history. He spoke only a
few words of German, though he could understand most of what
I told him. Carrying his daughter on his shoulders, he followed
me up the steep path. The cave, we discovered, was sealed with
a metal grille, but by crouching down and craning upwards one
could see the very faded remains of the Byzantine ceiling frescos. It
was rather disappointing. We continued on to the clifftop, passing
on the way a broad shallow cave which the guidebook said had
been inhabited in the neolithic period. It commanded a spectacular
view across the gorge and the surrounding hills and must have
afforded advance warning of the approach of enemies. The whole
cliff indeed formed an impregnable fortress, provided one were
stocked with food and water. A few fat drops of rain were
beginning to fall and I would have returned to Ruse, but Marin
was keen to push on to the medieval fortress town of Cherven
which I had also wanted to see.

During the Russo-Turkish War of 1876–77, Ruse proved an
unassailable fortress. In earlier centuries, however, it had been
less secure. The Romans had a settlement here and in their wake
a small town grew up. The Danube plain surrounding Ruse offers
little in the way of natural protection and in the waves of tribal
movement which followed on the collapse of Rome, the little
settlement was several times destroyed. In need of a more secure
site, the inhabitants of Ruse moved to Cherven.

It is a natural fortress, a peninsula of limestone jutting into a
deep valley, assailable only from one direction. You approach the
ruins through the village of Cherven which stretches along the
valley floor and up its sides. The village is dotted with trees,
many of the houses supported at the front on stilts. Straw is
laid out to dry on many of the roofs and the streets are busy
with hens. Two old men were giving a donkey a haircut in
what passes for the village square. The individual garden plots
are laid out in neat rectangles around each cluster of houses. In the
newly restored sunlight, freshly washed by the shower of rain, it
looked a sheltered idyll from another age.

Steps have been cut into the limestone cliff leading up to the
ruins. Lizards were sunning themselves on the rocks, darting to

safety as we climbed. Little remains of the town. The Turks besieged it and, having eventually taken it, razed it to the ground. A few stumps of walls and a restored entry gate are all that remain, overgrown and smelling of wild thyme. It was a sad place, which seemed to have retained some trace of its unhappy end. Marin had not known of its existence. Looking down the rock peninsula it was easily possible to imagine an army encamped there and the dismay of the townspeople. There were no other visitors for, important city though Ruse is, it is not a tourist town. The sounds of cockerels and donkeys came floating up from the village and on the surrounding hills shepherds were herding their sheep across the slopes. Swifts, ravens and bees were the only other moving things.

Two of Marin's friends had emigrated to the United States, which was what he wanted to do. He envisaged it as a place where money ran in the gutters. He thought the communists were finished, whatever happened, and that, whoever took over, their main job would be to turn Bulgaria into a wholly European country. He claimed that the Party had been very corrupt, that Zhivkov had once spent five million dollars in a Los Angeles casino.

I WASTED a morning trying to get a telephone line to Bucharest before deciding that I would cross the border the following morning, come what may. Walking round the town, I saw a number of people going into a shabby grey-concrete building resembling nothing so much as a semi-derelict warehouse. It was about the ugliest building in Ruse, which is basically a late-nineteenth-century town, full of attractive neo-baroque villas and art nouveau public buildings. Following the crowd, I found myself in an amazingly busy supermarket. Why put up a notice to say what the building is when everyone knows? It was as dirty inside as it was shabby outside, but the throng were undeterred. About half the shelves were bare. The rest were lined with jam, tinned fish, tinned meat, jars of preserved fruit, bottles of sauce, local wines, soap, buckets, sandals, cooking utensils, dried pulses and not much else. Many of the jars were filthy and lacking labels.

Some empty freezer chests stood along the back wall. I would not have allowed a cat to piss in them in case it caught something. There were separate counters at which one could buy meat, though there was none on display. People queued up for their portion. Milk and butter were also available but no cheeses.

By comparison, the supermarket in Belgrade where I had stocked up, poor though it was by western standards, was an Aladdin's cave of goodies. What is depressing for the westerner is not just the lack of choice, but the absence of colour, of presentation, of all the packaging hype we take for granted and never realise is there until it disappears. The crowd was good-natured, buying whatever there was to buy. A female supervisor, a woman in her fifties, was stationed in the doorway to check, I think, that no one made off with the goodies. She was attempting to direct the crowd to go in one side and out the other, but with absolutely no effect and her remonstrations were spoiled by the fact that she stopped occasionally to smile at someone she recognised while the hordes pressed on.

Saturday is the day for weddings. I saw two sets of bride and groom walking towards the town hall in the square, accompanied by their two witnesses. The hotel restaurant had been set for a wedding party. It began at lunchtime and the dancing was still going on when I went to bed at midnight.

One side of the square was being renovated and protective hoardings had been erected around the front of the buildings. The local primary school children had been given the task of painting them, which they had done with tremendous colourfulness and vigorous design. Animals were a favourite motif and the long row of painted panels certainly brightened the scene. If I have one abiding impression of Bulgaria, it is summarised by those naïve paintings, their optimism and charm.

TORRENTIAL rain through the night and the pot-holed road to the Friendship Bridge is a foot deep in muddy water. It is chilly waiting for the queue of half a dozen cars to move forward. The car at the checkpoint is actually being dismantled. The couple with the car are taken away separately – for strip searches? Huge container lorries from Turkey pass through the neighbouring channel. A uniformed official asks for my passport and goes away. Twenty minutes later a tall, well-dressed man, who seems by his manner to be in charge, comes over with my passport. He seems relieved when he discovers that I speak French. He looks in the boot with its boxes of books and is clearly curious.

I explain that I am a writer. 'Do you have any of your books with you?' I do and he leafs through a copy of *Concerning the Dragon*. He hands the book back, smiling, satisfied: *'Je regrette beaucoup, monsieur, que je ne parle pas l'anglais. Je vous souhaite un bon voyage, au revoir.'* With that, he waves me through the still waiting queue of traffic.

It is a two-mile drive across Friendship Bridge, a grey-blue utilitarian structure completed in 1954. This morning the Danube looks the same cold colour as the bridge. On the Romanian side the gun-toting official who takes my passport is all smiles. Checking the visa is a matter of moments. Before handing back the passport, however, he whispers 'whisky'. I had been warned that bribes would be expected. Opening the boot, I extract a half bottle bought for the purpose. I put the bottle on top of a box of books. He reaches over and the bottle disappears into his satchel. The process is carried out with a degree of insouciance which makes it clear that it is entirely customary. He grins, hands me the passport and says: *'Danke und gute Reise.'* At my third attempt, I am in Romania. It is just an hour since I left the *Riga*.

Horses again replaced donkeys, pulling gypsy wagons or just being trotted along the road. The gypsy wagons were painted in intricate patterns of bright colour and the horses, sometimes two to a wagon, were decked out with streamers of red ribbon along their harnesses.

The outskirts of Bucharest were as dismal as in any East European city. Cars were few and far between. Even the town centre, however, had a cold, shuttered look about it, like a city in hiding. It was Sunday, and, as I later discovered, almost everything closes now that Sundays can be officially celebrated again. It was a spooky feeling, driving through these wide empty boulevards to the heart of the city, never seeing a lit shop or hotel or house. The drizzle which had begun as I crossed the border had stopped, but a cold wind was blowing.

The headquarters of the Romanian Automobile Association has, they claim, a twenty-four-hour duty service, but the premises were locked and empty. With some difficulty, I eventually found the British Embassy which is housed in a fine turn-of-the-century villa in a narrow street near the town centre. The staff were on holiday but the duty security officer was immensely helpful. I had no decent map of Bucharest, nor was it possible to buy one. The embassy, he explained, got theirs from Budapest. He made a number of phone-calls to hotels for me, but no one in Bucharest, it seems, answers telephones or the lines are simply unavailable. In due course, he was able to book me into the Hotel Bucharest without ever actually saying that I was from the embassy. It is a large, expensive hotel just off Calea Victoriei, two minutes walk from University Square and Communist Party headquarters in that section of the centre where the heaviest fighting of the revolution took place. It was mildly disconcerting to enter an hotel so dimly lit that from the outside it looked closed. My room was comfortably furnished, though without radio or television. I was later told that it had been a favourite haunt of the Securitate and that all the rooms were subject to camera surveillance, not, as one might expect, in the bedroom, but through an elaborate system of wooden slats which comprised the bathroom ceilings!

I was hungry and wanted something to eat. I was directed to the café-style restaurant which served breakfast and light meals. The system of service as I worked it out was as follows: you go in and take a seat in one of the four-place bays which run the length of a long, narrow room. The serving counter runs along the opposite wall. The waiters stand in a corner and ignore you for as long as they please. If you are unknown and have not bribed anyone, this can be until the café closes. Meanwhile, a steady stream of persons will pass through the restaurant towards the kitchens at the back and emerge carrying parcels. I had only been there a few minutes when an army officer, a police officer and a pimply recruit with a machine-gun, strutted briskly towards the kitchens. A few minutes later all three emerged with their parcels. The restaurant's real trade was run by the waiters and kitchen staff who exchanged food parcels for bribes. To be part of the game, you had to know someone. As for hotel customers, they were simply a nuisance or possible clients for the black market exchange of money or Western goodies. All these proceedings, as at the border, were conducted more or less openly. Nor was complaint a sensible or even practical way of dealing with the need to get something to eat. In Romania, there is no one to complain to, since no one in any given state-run business stands outside the structure of corruption. I was eventually approached to see whether I wanted to change any money. I did and even got something to eat – a perfectly decent omelette. In Romania the concept of *baksheesh* has been elevated to the status of a social principle.

I spent a cold afternoon walking round central Bucharest. Although in its maze of little back streets the town houses some fine neo-classical and neo-baroque villas and palaces, more recent buildings are dismal indeed, all concrete monumentalism and quite anti-human. Even more depressing, was the abject poverty evident from the shop windows, which were, as often as not, empty. Just round the corner from the Hotel Bucharest is the large open square of the Piaţa Republicii, its old name, which was restored after the revolution. Here Carol II built his palace in the 1930s, with the idea of leaving a clear field of fire across the square. The palace became Party headquarters and it was from here that Ceausescu addressed that last fateful rally from which he expected the customary mass obedience and which led to his downfall a few days later. It was from its roof that a helicopter lifted him and his wife when they decided to flee. Like the other buildings around the square, it was pock-marked with bullet holes from high-velocity rifle fire. Just down the road the remains of the National Library, which was burned out during the fighting, are framed with scaffolding as the repair work gets under way. The square was deserted. But a few hundred yards away across the broad boulevard of General Magheru, there were crowds in University Square.

An anti-communist rally is taking place and among the crowd some are carrying flags with the centre cut out in token of the detestation in which the communist regime is held. Near the centre of the square there are a few *ad hoc* crosses beside which wreaths have been laid, marking places where people were killed in the fighting. Another, more elaborate, memorial has been erected at one side of the square and says 'Eternal glory to Eroiler Neahului who died for freedom on 21st–22nd December.' A little tin shelter with votive candles has been placed beside the cross which is decked with fresh flowers. Further round the square, in front of the concrete slab which is the Hotel Intercontinental where the world's TV crews have been and are still based, is the tent city; a scatter of makeshift tents set down in a patch of muddy land and housing those protesters who claim that the

Iliescu government is still crypto-communist. It looks cold and miserable.

These were the hard core of protesters who served as a rallying point for numerous others in moments of crisis and whom the Iliescu government was desperate to be rid of. They did, finally, clear them out by setting brigades of miners on them, wielding clubs and iron bars. In the course of the next three days I was in University Square several times. It never failed to produce a sort of electricity which I think was felt by anyone who went there. Some weeks later, on my way through France, I came across a volume of photographs published in memory of a young French photographer, Jean-Louis Calderon, who was killed during the street battles of December. The photographs had all been taken in the few days of the revolution in the third and fourth weeks of December, 1989. Many of them are horrible. Most are intensely powerful and it was moving and eerie to look at these images of central Bucharest as though they had leaked through time from Stalingrad or Warsaw. It seems doubtful whether the final numbers of dead will ever be precisely known, but the figure appears to be in the low hundreds. Revolution has a logic of its own and the events of December were fuelled by rumour and counter-rumour of huge massacres. Similarly, though on a much reduced scale in Prague, it was the rumour of deaths caused by police brutalities on the night of 17th November which fuelled the mass demonstrations of the following days. No one in fact had been killed but, in the logic of events, that hardly mattered.

When the world suddenly becomes fluid, as it does in a revolution, people's first requirement, after physical safety, is information, and in central Bucharest people queued to buy news-sheets. Meanwhile in the underpass below the square, which was also the entrance to the *metro*, it was business as usual for the touts hoping to change money. A bedraggled gypsy woman stood on the steps trying to sell a single bunch of flowers. By contrast, the 'Mad Cobbler's Palace' with its thousand rooms was merely obscene. It was so much a symbol of the former regime that everyone I met in Bucharest urged me not even to visit it, as though doing so would be an acknowledgement of something they wanted to deny.

The fragmentary and fragile character of what had been achieved was brought home to me later that afternoon when the telephone in my hotel room rang. It was an American girl who, for no evident reason, had been connected to my room. She was telephoning from the other side of the country, trying to get in touch with colleagues working for a refugee organisation who, she thought, were staying at the Hotel Bucharest. It never occurred to her in her anxiety that it was odd to hear a British voice at the other end of the telephone. The mother of one of her colleagues had died and the daughter was needed at home in the States. I promised to find out if I could whether her colleagues were in the hotel and pass on the message, but dealing with people at the reception desk was like trying to swim through treacle and, eventually, I had to give up, none the wiser.

I HAD arranged that evening to meet the Romanian poet Petre Solomon. We had met several weeks earlier in London at the home of the Romanian exile Myron Grindea, who edits the literary journal, *Adam*. Petre arrived in the hotel lobby promptly at six o'clock. He is in his late sixties, solidly made. His roundish face usually wears a rather serious expression, but years drop away when he smiles. He wanted to take me to dinner. He had not eaten out in Bucharest, he said, in years and did not know what was possible. His first choice – in the Calea Victoriei – had closed, but his second, in a little side street, was still there and looked as if it was doing good business.

The room at ground level was full but Petre was able to get us a table downstairs. At the other tables were several young people, better dressed than any I had seen in the streets and looking much more cheerful. Two kinds of meat were available, ox liver and pork. One could have white wine. Red was not available. The service was prompt and friendly and Petre thought the restaurant was privately owned by a small co-operative. We were glad to get in, for outside it was pouring with rain again.

Petre had only just returned from the visit to Paris, London and Amsterdam on which I had met him. He had been invited to Paris by the publishers of a new edition of his poems. He had gone to Paris by train. On the day he was due to cross the Hungarian-Austrian frontier, the Austrians (in a panic about the large influx of gypsies and other destitute refugees and economic migrants from Eastern Europe) had imposed a visa requirement on Romanians. The new regulation had immediate effect so that he, together with about a hundred others, some of whom were elderly or ill, were taken from the train. Petre refused at first to leave, explaining that he was a writer and had engagements in Paris. This cut no ice with the Austrian official, a big, bearded man, Petre said, who started to shout at him: 'Get off the train, shit, or I'll put you off.' It brought back memories, Petre said, of his time under the pro-Nazi regime which governed Romania during the war.

The Hungarian authorities then took the Romanians, free of charge, back to Budapest so that they could obtain transit visas from the Austrian consulate. They waited there in a railway station until the early hours of the following morning when they went to queue at the consulate. Petre got his visa, but had to stay an additional and expensive night in Vienna and had lost two days of his journey. He subsequently asked his French publishers to arrange for him to fly home so that he would not have to pass through Austria again.

(It is curious how Austria has come to be seen in the West. It is a nation deeply xenophobic, which set out several times to provoke Serbia into war, finally succeeding in 1914. It was staunchly pro-Nazi from the mid-1930s onwards and put down the workers' rising in Vienna in 1934 with great brutality. It has recently elected an ex-Nazi as its president and yet, in the popular imagination, Germany is held to be solely responsible for the two world wars.)

Petre came from a Jewish family. In 1939 Jewish students were expelled from Romanian universities and sent to forced labour camps. Petre claimed that many Romanians did not want to see the 'prosperous and well-respected' Jewish community exterminated, but Romania has a long history of anti-Semitic feeling. It was only in 1923 that Jews were granted citizenship rights in Romania and in the 1930s there were frequent anti-Jewish demonstrations. There was a large influx of Jews into Romania in the aftermath of the First World War, most of them coming from the Soviet Union. Indeed, one of the reasons why King Carol's girlfriend, Magda Lupescu, was so disliked, was that she was a Jewess.

After the opening of the Russian front in 1941, German troops were stationed in Romania. Strangely, a Jewish university was opened and Petre was able to enrol there to study French and

English. The enthusiastically pro-Nazi Antonescu regime which governed Romania after the flight of King Carol in 1940, was intensely anti-Semitic. In the spring of 1944 Petre had the chance to get out of Romania through contacts he had with the Zionist movement, although not himself a Zionist. He went first to Turkey and then to Palestine: 'I also just wanted to see the world. I was twenty-one and very sad at having to leave my family and sweetheart. Of course, you see the world differently at twenty-one.' He grinned and said: 'I enjoyed Istanbul.' In Palestine he was interned for two weeks by the British and remembered the Palestine Police as 'very brutal'.

Petre did not return to Romania until 1946. 'The Germans,' he said, 'did not get round to organising a massacre of the Romanian Jews and gypsies. The front was too close at hand.'

Petre believed that the mild winter of 1989 had helped the revolution: 'During the Ceausescu winters no one had fuel. There were continual power cuts and food shortages. People thought to themselves: "We won't survive another hard winter without heat." The milder weather enabled them to go out on to the streets, especially in Timişoara. On Christmas Day, with the execution of the Ceausescus, the revolution had completed its first stage. On that day the weather broke and we had the first snow of the winter. If you believe in God . . ..' He let the sentence trail off.

Petre thought the trial of the Ceausescus was a mistake, a habit left over from the days of 'Stalinist justice'. For that reason, he said, the trial which had just begun of Nicu Ceausescu, the dictator's playboy son, would be specially interesting since Nicu was intelligent, well advised and quite capable of conducting his defence if he were not interrupted by the judge. His defence was to be, substantially, that he had opposed his father's policies. (The trial continued until October 1990 when Nicu Ceausescu was sentenced to twenty years imprisonment.)

As to the 'Mad Cobbler's Palace', Petre explained that in March 1977 a severe earthquake destroyed substantial parts of Bucharest. The most stable quarter, as well as one of the most interesting, which survived the earthquake, was seen by Ceausescu as the ideal site for his thousand-year posterity. Consequently, he obliterated that section of Bucharest. Petre's explanation for what made a Ceausescu possible, was that the system allowed and even encouraged it: 'Ceausescu was a nothing. Not a peasant. Not a worker. He had been a political activist from the age of sixteen or so, an apparatchik, a careerist politician. So he actually knew nothing. He and his wife were complementary monsters. He had the will power. She had the cunning. There was one legendary occasion when the minister for health went to see him and complained that the country had no drugs of any kind, not even aspirin, and that, as a result, people were dying needlessly. Ceausescu shouted at him: "You come here and bother me with this trivia and shit when I am struggling with an historic destiny," and threw him out.'

I discovered that Petre had met Hugh MacDiarmid in Bucharest on two occasions, once on the bi-centenary of Robert Burns's birth. MacDiarmid, he said, had made a great impression in Bucharest. We discussed the ambiguousness of MacDiarmid's communism and Petre observed, thinking of Marx and Hegel: 'It is foolish to lump together and then blame two early-nineteenth-century thinkers for the mess in which Eastern Europe now finds itself.

'Any befouled estuary, even the Danube, may rise from some unpolluted source.' He continued. As for poetry, 'The regime hated poetry, but did not think it was very important, so any kind of subtlety eluded them. They would, for example, censor any reference to God but leave other, more damaging items, untouched.' Petre's way of coping with the strains and stresses of the regime was to write in French or English as a kind of therapy.

I was later to hear the same from another Romanian writer. 'This,' he said, 'enables me to escape from the frenzies of actuality.' The circulation of any book of poetry was officially restricted to a few hundred copies. 'But of course,' he said gleefully, 'that is enough to inflame an entire country.'

A number of long-time exiles had recently returned to Romania in order to take part in the elections and among these was Ion Ratiu, the former leader of the Peasant Party. Ratiu had fared disastrously in the elections. He accused the authorities, and particularly Iliescu, of vote-rigging and intimidation. Petre thought that Ratiu and his friends had simply been out of the country for too long and had lost touch: 'The country has changed. Many young people have been forced to leave the land as a result of the collectivisation process which was completed in 1962. They have been forced to live in urban ghettoes in a hellish, sterile parody of a life in which there was nothing for them to do and in which they could not even lead a genuinely urban existence. They could not and did not wish to return to the land. They were no longer peasants. Ratiu was simply an elderly irrelevance to these people and his class attitudes were mocked even in the villages. In one village where he went to campaign, he was met by geese with bow-ties round their necks.' (Ratiu always sports large bow-ties.)

The problem about the protestors in University Square, Petre thought, was that they helped Iliescu because Romanian society was deeply conservative. After the revolution many people feared a slide into anarchy which, they thought, the protestors represented. Therefore, they voted for Iliescu as a clever politician who did not represent an entire break with the past. He knows the system and is, Petre believes, a genuinely repentant communist.

It was still raining heavily by the time we left the restaurant and adjourned to the Hotel Bucharest for a drink. Petre was fundamentally optimistic that better times lay ahead for Romania, though he thought there would be tremendous difficulties.

ROMANIAN history can be summed up as a long series of catastrophes interrupted by the occasional disaster to relieve the monotony. As a modern nation state its history, like Bulgaria's, is not much more than a century old. Also, like Bulgaria, it has no tradition of democracy.

Until 1774, the year of the Treaty of Kuchuk Kainarji between Turkey and Russia, what is now Romania consisted of two principalities, Moldavia and Wallachia, while Transylvania was part of Hungary, though it too had once been independent. Wallachia from the end of the fourteenth century, and Moldavia from the end of the fifteenth, had been vassal states of the Ottoman empire. From the late seventeenth century onwards, both principalities had been under the sway of Phanariot Greeks. These were Islamicised Greeks of the Phanar (lighthouse) quarter in Constantinople, appointed by the sultans as hospodars of the principalities. ('Hospodar' is simply the Romanian version of the slavic *gospodar* or 'lord'.) These hospodars ran the principalities

173

on the basis of having paid enormous bribes to the Porte for the privilege. Their average rule was for about three years, so they had to make their money very quickly. Corruption and extortion became a way of life in societies in which repressive violence had been endemic for centuries. The peasantry were mere helots, there to be exploited, and the native aristocracy, where it had not been exterminated, was assimilated to Turkish rule.

Towards the end of the eighteenth century, Russia began a period of rapid expansion with the aim of making the Black Sea a Russian lake and, ultimately, gaining access to the Mediterranean. Moldavia and Wallachia were importantly situated pawns in that game, while the Western Powers manoeuvred among themselves to exclude Russia from the Balkans. They thereby found themselves propping up a decadent Ottoman empire while at the same time espousing the values of liberalism or, more often, romantic nationalism. Ideology usually, but not always, took second place to *realpolitik*. At the same time, Austria-Hungary hoped to expand south-east into the Balkans.

By the middle of the nineteenth century, Russia had so far succeeded in her aims that she had secured from the Porte a quasi-protectorate in Moldavia and Wallachia and was able to insist on a degree of rationality in the governance of the principalities. Throughout the period from Kuchuk Kainarji until the Crimean War, a sense of nationality had been developing in the principalities and this, as in so much of Europe, found expression in uprisings in 1848. After Russia's defeat in the Crimea and the progressive erosion of Ottoman authority, a process which continued throughout the nineteenth century as the Western Powers and Russia sliced away its European possessions, the Western Powers ended the Russian protectorate. In 1858 permission was secured for the principalities to be administered jointly in important economic areas and in the following year they elected a single prince, Alexander Cuza, a native boiar.

Cuza's policies were liberal though his style was autocratic. He emancipated the peasantry from forced labour and confiscated church lands, thereby offending deeply vested interests. By 1866 he had made himself so unpopular with the ruling caste that he was obliged to abdicate and in his place, with the support of Napoleon III, Charles of Hohenzollern-Sigmaringen was elected. The principalities joined Russia in the war against Turkey of 1877–78. The liberation of Bulgaria was a comprehensive defeat

174

for the Porte and the Russians imposed the treaty of San Stefano. Afraid of such a considerable increase in Russian influence in the south-eastern Balkans, the Western Powers called for a general conference which resulted in the Treaty of Berlin of 1878 by which Romania gained international recognition. By the same treaty, Russia was granted Southern Bessarabia, an area to the north-east of Moldavia inhabited mainly by Romanian speakers, whereas Romania, by way of compensation, was granted the Northern Dobruja, which was in turn taken from Bulgaria. These grants were to come back to haunt Europe. The official declaration of a kingdom had to wait until 1881 when the childless Charles (or Carol I) nominated his nephew, Ferdinand of Hohenzollern, as his successor. Russia deeply disapproved of Charles as likely to be pro-Austro-Hungarian, and was not fully reconciled to the dynasty until the early years of the century. Russia's fears were justified. In 1883 Charles signed a secret treaty with Austro-Hungary and Germany for their joint defence. During the second Balkan War of 1913, Romania occupied the Southern Dobruja and retained it in the subsequent settlement. The secret treaty was renewed early in 1914. In June of the same year the Tsar and his family visited the king at the Black Sea port of Constanța.

When war broke out, the Allies offered Romania the crucial bribe of Transylvania, predominantly Romanian, but part of Austro-Hungary for centuries. The Central Powers offered the return of Bessarabia. Charles died in the same year, his death, it was said, hastened by Romania's failure to honour the secret treaty. Ferdinand, who succeeded him, was married to another of Queen Victoria's ubiquitous grand-daughters, Marie of Edinburgh. Romania entered the war on the Allied side and occupied Transylvania, the Banat as far as the river Tisza and Bessarabia as far as the river Prut. Greater Romania had come into existence.

Romania has to be seen as a composite entity with the principalities on one hand and Transylvania on the other. Their histories are quite distinct, for Transylvania remained quasi-independent – and at times completely independent – long after the principalities had become mere vassal states of the Ottomans. Part of that difference originates in geography. Transylvania is a mountain-island in the Central European sea. It is therefore more defensible than anywhere else, and provides, in its highland fastnesses, a refuge in times of trouble. That is how the Moldavian state came to be founded by people who had fled to Transylvania, filtering down from the mountains at a time when an expansionist Hungary was establishing itself, and the Catholic religion, in Transylvania in the thirteenth century.

Roman Catholicism and the reformed religions made no impact on Moldavia and Wallachia. So long as the Turks controlled them, any such development was impossible. Transylvania was another matter. In the thirteenth century Transylvania was frontier territory for Hungary. As the young kingdom consolidated and expanded, three 'nations' were recognised as having rights in Transylvania and Hungary: the Magyars, the Szeklers and the Saxons. Only these 'nations' formed the *populus*, those who in Rome would have been citizens or, in Athens, members of the *polis*. Only members of the *polis* had any political say and were exempt from taxation. The *plebs* were not recognised as citizens and in Transylvania these *plebs* were mainly Romanian-speaking Vlachs. The Saxons had been invited to settle in what is now south-western Romania in the early thirteenth century. Their political rights were specified in King Andrew's Golden Bull of 1222, the Hungarian equivalent of Magna Carta. The Szeklers, a group ethnically kin to the Magyars, had settled the frontier areas of Hungary, including Transylvania. (*Szekler* has the root meaning of *frontiersman*.)

To abbreviate an extremely complex story: during the sixteenth century, many Magyars became Protestant, mainly Calvinist, while the Szeklers tended to become Unitarians and the Saxons, Lutheran. The great mass of the peasantry, meanwhile, remained disenfranchised and Orthodox with neither religious nor civil liberties. In essence, that remained the case until 1848. During the seventeenth century in the so-called 'golden period' of Transylvania, the Transylvanians paid a nominal allegiance to the Turks, for after the death of Michael the Brave, the Habsburg emperor Rudolf II, educated in Spain by the Jesuits, was intent on converting his subjects to Catholicism, by force if need be. The Transylvanians elected Stephen Bocskay prince in 1605 and under his leadership extracted from Rudolf a constitutional guarantee of religious liberties which, even in Hungary proper, was never wholly lost. It made Transylvania a bastion of religious liberties during the seventeenth century and a stronghold of Protestantism. None of this affected the Orthodox Vlachs.

Under another prince, Gabriel Bethlen (1613–1629), Transylvania became a power of European significance, since it formed an eastern counterweight to the Catholic-Habsburg territories of Central Europe during the Thirty Years War. By 1691 Transylvania had been reunited with Hungary, and in 1699 the Turks renounced all sovereignty there. The reunification, however, left Transylvania quasi-independent with its own gubernatorial functions in Kolozsvár (Cluj). Transylvania was really under the direct rule of the emperors rather than via the Hungarian Diet in Budapest. Even after 1848, that remained so until the formation of the dual monarchy in 1867 abolished the administrative distinction between Transylvania and Hungary.

Calvinist and Roman competition for the souls of the leaderless Romanian Orthodox, resulted in 1700 in many Orthodox priests joining the Uniate Church. This meant that they could keep their traditional rites, gain a small measure of official recognition and exemption from serfdom in exchange for some 'minor' changes in creed. Those changes were precisely the issues which had divided the Eastern and Western Churches centuries before, but this new adherence to the Roman creed at least kept the Calvinists from further encroachment. It also created the beginnings of Romanian nationality by virtue of the fact that it gave a protected status to an organisation with which those who were ethnically Vlach and linguistically Romanian could identify. It was not until 1809 that those who resisted the Union were granted the right to elect a bishop who spoke their own language, and not until 1863 that the Romanians were allowed to separate from the Patriarchate of Serbia and develop their own cultural institutions.

Transylvania and the principalities were united at the end of the First World War. After the collapse of the Russian front the German forces, under Field Marshal August von Mackensen, defeated the Romanians and imposed, briefly, a punitive settlement. The country was war-exhausted and there was widespread starvation. The surrender of the Central Powers in November 1918 restored Greater Romania, extending as far into the north-eastern Carpathians as the Bukovina. Hungary bitterly contested the Romanian gains in the west, but by 1919 Romanian troops were occupying Budapest and the Hungarians had to submit.

Post-war unrest was quelled by the prime minister, General Averescu, who also pursued land reform policies. These were well intentioned, but many of the plots made over to the peasants by expropriation were too small to be economically viable and no credit was available for equipment or seed. There had already been a peasant rising in 1907 in protest at the exploitation of the peasantry by Jewish moneylenders. Those anti-semitic feelings deepened through the 1920s and 1930s, especially following on the economic crisis of the early 1930s when the infamous price-scissors (the rise of manufacturing prices and the fall in agricultural prices) decimated the Romanian economy which was almost wholly agricultural.

Ferdinand's heir, the egregious Carol, eloped in 1925 with the Jewish actress, Magda Lupescu, giving up his rights to the throne in favour of his son, Michael. He was, in any case, already married to Princess Helen of Greece. His father died in 1927 and a regency was formed. In 1930 Carol returned to claim the throne. His aim from the beginning was complete royal authority. His competitors were an organisation called the Iron Guard. Founded by the student leader, Corneliu Codreanu, it was a fascist organisation, strongly pro-Nazi and anti-Jewish. It based its appeal on a primitive chauvinism and peasant rights with the motto: *omul si pogonul* (every man an acre). The 1930s in Romania saw a confused series of power struggles between the crown and the Iron Guard with other parties and powers complicating the matter until the whole conflict became a bloody mess. The Iron Guard assassinated two prime ministers between 1933 and 1939, and Codreanu and thirteen of his associates were murdered on Carol's orders while being held prisoner. Both sides were ruthless and violent but, ultimately, the Iron Guard over-played their hand.

There was an element of pro-Western sentiment in Romania. The Romanians think of themselves as Latins and their language is eighty per cent romance-based. The fiasco of Munich, however, undermined any confidence that the West would stand up to Hitler and Mussolini, and the Molotov-Ribbentrop pact pushed Romania further towards the Axis. In March 1939 a trade-treaty with Germany was concluded, much to Romania's disadvantage. Rich in oil and cereals, Romania was strategically important to the Axis. In 1940 Carol formed a new government containing elements of his own National Renaissance Front and the Iron Guard.

A series of foreign policy fiascos, however, forced Carol's abdication and left Romania committed to the Axis powers. He had been forced by the Axis to cede Bessarabia and Northern Bukovina to the Soviet Union in July 1940, and in August Bulgaria was given the Southern Dobruja while Hungary was awarded the western half of Transylvania. Greater Romania was reduced to about two-thirds of its land mass and lost about a third of its citizens.

The new regency under Prince Michael and General Antonescu suppressed the Iron Guard with considerable vigour in early 1941. This was done with Hitler's approval, despite the ideological links, since he needed a stable Romania and the Iron Guard seemed incapable of self-control, since they fed off the most primitive of political passions. Antonescu's regime was pronouncedly anti-Semitic.

Michael brought about a *coup d'état* in August 1944 with the Red Army at his borders. In September, an armistice was signed with the Allies and in November Romania entered the war against the Axis, thereby ensuring the restoration of its pre-war boundaries, with the exception of some necessary concessions to the Soviet Union – in particular, Bessarabia and the Northern Bukovina. Antonescu was hanged in 1946.

Stalin was not prepared to envisage any anti-Soviet governments in Eastern Europe. Soviet security considerations came first. The Communist Party had been banned in Romania since 1924, and when its Moscow-based exiles returned in 1944–45, they could number less than a thousand members in the country. With Soviet support, however, and using various disruptive techniques, they soon established their hegemony in the new government. By 1948 they were in power and able to conduct the kind of show trials then taking place throughout Eastern Europe. Prince Michael abdicated and left the country in 1947. In 1948 a series of Soviet-Romanian joint corporations were established, whose main function was to siphon Romanian raw materials to the Soviet Union. In 1949 the process of agricultural collectivisation got under way.

The leader of the communists was Gheorge Gheorghiu-Dej. In the early 1950s he began to assert a degree of independence from the Soviet Union and that process speeded up after Stalin's death. He instituted a collective leadership in 1953 and dissolved the joint corporations. In 1955, as part of an internal power struggle, he nominated three of his protégés to the politburo, one of whom was Nicolae Ceausescu.

Ceausescu succeeded Gheorghiu-Dej in 1965 and quickly purged any possible rivals. He was popular with the West since he seemed to be prepared to stand up to the Soviet Union. When the Warsaw Pact invaded Czechoslovakia in 1968, Ccauscscu, speaking from the balcony of the Party headquarters in Piaţa Republicii, condemned the invasion in forthright terms.

Gradually, the regime ran into greater and greater difficulties. Agricultural collectivisation produced very poor results. As in the Soviet Union, it was massively inefficient and provided no motivation for the peasants. The large-scale industrialisation, aimed chiefly at heavy industry, became less and less competitive on the world scene as the 1970s and 1980s progressed. The internationalisation of capital and of the market in primary resources, left all of Eastern Europe languishing with outdated plant and even more outdated planners, not to mention extraordinary levels of industrial pollution. Ceausescu's regime was fiercely nationalistic but also developed a personality cult which permitted any whim of the dictator's to become national policy in the same breath. The difficult economic situation of the early 1980s led to a determined effort to clear their international debt and an austerity programme of savage rigour was introduced. So much so that, in a primarily agricultural country, there was little food in the shops.

WHEN I met Myron Grindea in London, I promised to deliver some items to his brother-in-law, Rudolf Pietreanu. Rudolf is slightly deaf and hearing-aid batteries are not easy to come by in Bucharest. Rudolf arrived at the Hotel Bucharest at ten o'clock. After the heavy rains of the day before, it was a mild, overcast morning. We went to the bar in the hotel lobby and chatted over brandy and good capuccino coffee. He is an imposing figure for his eighty years, tall and broad and genial and highly presentable in a suit of old-fashioned cut and good cloth. His liveliness made it difficult to believe his years. He speaks no English but an elegant French learned in the 1920s as a student in Nancy. Starting off as a mathematician, he had become an economist with a particular interest in statistics. With his rather aristocratic charm and good manners, he was a reminder that not everything in Romania had always been dismal.

Inevitably, we chatted about the revolution and the Ceausescu regime. I was curious to know what had allowed it to develop as it did and, in illustration of its eccentricities, Rudolf told a number of stories. A new museum was to be built to house a history of the Communist Party and Ceausescu wanted it to be ready in time for 23rd August, the date which marks the overthrow of the Antonescu regime. There was to be a large-scale military parade at which Ceausescu would take the salute. A week or so before the 23rd, Ceausescu noticed that the power lines for the trolley-buses crossed the square outside the museum and spoiled the purity of the view. These lines served some 350,000 people with three lines running to the town centre and two to the Gara de Nord. He ordered them to be removed at once, remarking that people could find other ways of getting about. The resulting chaos can easily be imagined.

On another occasion, a bridge was to be built to link the Place de L'Opera to the Cotroşeni quarter of the city. His security cavalcade had, as usual, diverted all the traffic. Ceausescu asked what was being built and, on being told that the volume of traffic was too heavy for the existing road and bridge network, commented: 'But I've been here for half an hour and not a single car has passed.'

Ceausescu's speech was, apparently, that of an uneducated man and he would frequently mispronounce words. Anyone foolish enough to point this out to him was unlikely to stay in favour for very long and so sycophantic were some of his associates, that they would adopt his mispronunciations for fear of offending him.

Rudolf had studied in the 1930s at the mathematics department of the University of Bucharest and his first inkling that there was something really strange about the Ceausescu regime, he said, was when all the professors of mathematics from his old department left the country. In the medical faculty, posts were awarded to Party members, irrespective of their qualifications.

Just before Christmas, Rudolf and his wife had returned to Bucharest from London, where they had been visiting his sister and brother-in-law. Childless themselves, they wanted to bring back presents for their nephew and grand-nephew. Knowing how the system worked, they prepared substantial bribes for the customs officials. They made up two parcels; one for a man and one for a woman. In one, there were chocolates, Kent cigarettes, eau de cologne, cash and coffee. The first official they dealt with at the airport was presented with his bribe and he pointed them to another, saying: 'Go to that woman over there.' Rudolf's wife then opened a suitcase and presented the second official with her bribe, saying: 'That is for you.' They were then waved through without further examination and without paying the tax due on the video cassettes they had imported, which would have amounted to 250 lei on each cassette.

As a young man, Rudolf had served in the cavalry reserve and was an enthusiastic horseman. When it was discovered that he was partly Jewish, he was dismissed. During the process of agricultural collectivisation, in which Russian tractors replaced horses, horses were no longer considered necessary. They were also expensive since they consumed fodder. Accordingly, more than 100,000 were slaughtered. Rudolf's anger when he spoke of the matter was the only moment when his urbanity gave way. There were no spare parts for the tractors.

Because he was half-Jewish, Rudolf had been sent to a forced labour camp. His estimate was that about 150,000 gypsies had been killed or deported by the Germans, with official co-operation from the Antonescu regime although, strangely, Antonescu would not permit the mass deportation of Romanian Jews. Antonescu was one of the few men able to stand up to and out-talk Hitler.

It was during his studies at Nancy that Rudolf first encountered the writings of Marx: 'He was very intelligent but almost wholly focused on social issues, believing that people would be happy if they could own more. He had a splendid Utopian vision, but failed completely to take account of human nature.'

Rudolf had supplemented his allowance while in Nancy by booth-boxing: 'About Christmas 1925 I began to box in a local sports festival. That was in Piatra Neamt. I was to go two three-minute rounds with a local ruffian. My mother, as wife of the town's bank manager, was heavily involved in local charity work. She was sitting in the front row of the arena, knowing nothing about my being there. I knew bugger-all about boxing, so I got hit first with a left, then with a right. My mother jumped up and shouted: "Don't you hit him," and, of course, the audience roared with laughter. Things went from bad to worse. In the second round I was being hammered and she shouted: "Go home, you idiot." After that, wherever I went, the locals would shout "Go home, you idiot". It was supposed to be a friendly match but I had a good punch and knocked the other boy out at the end of the second round. In Nancy, for a stake of a hundred francs, my friends and I could win five hundred. We had a good time on the five hundred francs.'

Rudolf offered to take me along to the Writers' Union building in Calea Victoriei. It had been an aristocrat's palazzo in the last quarter of the nineteenth century, all gilt and marble, now only half-lit. We discovered that the Union had moved to other premises along the road. We left a message there and I, regretfully, took my leave of Rudolf and his fund of stories.

F LORIN Bican is secretary to the president of the Writers' Union, Mircea Dinescu. He had received my message and rang me at the Bucharest. We arranged to have dinner that evening. Florin is thirty-four, bearded with dark hair, and an unhurried manner. He arrived dressed in jeans and wearing a red silk neckerchief. He is as near as one will find in Romania to a hippy, though the laid-back manner masks an alert mind. Florin suggested we eat at Manuc's Inn, one of Bucharest's best-known eating places. It was originally built as a caravanserai by Manuc-bey, a rich merchant. On the way, we visited the remains of Prince Dracul's palace. Dracul, better known to history as Vlad the Impaler, was, in the words of Seton-Watson: 'A man of diseased and abnormal tendencies, the victim of acute moral insanity.'

Vlad IV was put on the throne of Wallachia by Matthias Corvinus in 1456, recognising Matthias as his suzerain. The sultan Mohammed II, the Conqueror, demanded tribute from Vlad of 500 young men and ten thousand ducats. Vlad refused to pay. Mohammed's emissary had instructions to take Vlad prisoner but was himself outwitted by Vlad and duly impaled on a stake. When Mohammed invaded Wallachia in 1462, in Seton-Watson's words:

> Vlad, after a bold but unsuccessful raid upon the Turkish camp, fled before him. Legend tells that even the ruthless Conqueror was moved to tears when he visited the scene of Vlad's hideous exploit and saw a whole valley desolate yet peopled with its thousands of

stakes, on which still hung the mangled remains of impaled Turks and Bulgars.*

Vlad fled to Hungary where, for reasons unknown, he was imprisoned by Matthias for a number of years before being briefly restored to the throne of Wallachia in 1476. He was murdered in the same year.

All that remains of his palace are a few archways and pillars and a cellar used as a museum where the skulls of some of his victims are displayed.

Manuc's Inn is set round a large courtyard planted with trees. It is a three-storey building dating from 1804 and all the way round the upper floors run elaborately carved wooden verandahs. There were a couple of gypsy wagons in the yard when we visited it. It was the only restaurant in Bucharest where I was able to get red wine. I was unwise enough, however, to believe the waiter who said that steak was available. What I got may have been dead cow, but it could not by any stretch of charity be called steak. It was a composite of fat and sinew from some unrecognisable part of the bovine anatomy, still suppurating blood. Carnivore though I am, this particular delicacy was beyond me. Florin, wiser in the ways of Bucharest, and in any case a vegetarian, had a plate of cheese and salad vegetables.

Florin's English was excellent. He had studied Russian and English at university but was not allowed to teach English and so taught Russian for a number of years. Like almost everyone else I encountered in Eastern Europe, he was deeply anti-communist. 'What helped make Ceausescu possible,' he said, 'was that many peasants were removed from the land and came to Bucharest and to the other cities. Once in that urban context, they lost their bearings. It was an unfamiliar world for them so they either succeeded very quickly, or they became terribly anxious to please because they had no self-confidence rooted in education or in success. Their strategy for survival became one of conformity and the scarecrow of a system which has grown up here exploits just that weakness.'

Florin says that he has always felt himself assailed by an essentially hostile reality. In Ceausescu's Romania, paranoia seems to have been a reasonable response to actual conditions. English,

*R. W. Seton-Watson, *A History of the Romanians*, Cambridge, 1934.

therefore, was an escape, and his half-hour in the British Embassy library once a fortnight was 'like stepping into another civilisation entirely'.

Florin was deeply sceptical of Iliescu's democratic credentials, especially since Iliescu used the same categories and phrases in his public pronouncements as Ceausescu had done. 'Ceausescu's grasp of the "big lie" as an effective political technique was unreal,' he continued. 'Interviewed recently by a Soviet journalist, he had been asked why the shops were empty. He replied that there were plenty of goods available. It was just that the Romanian people despised ostentation. Later in the same interview he was asked how it was that his son, Nicu, had become his official successor. Ceausescu's reply was that the Romanian people had chosen him because he was the best candidate for the job.' The irony of Ceausescu being tackled on such issues by a Soviet journalist had not been lost on anyone. 'The Romanian attitude,' Florin said, 'is not to try to make things better but to pray for the avoidance of a yet greater catastrophe.'

Florin had been at the demonstration near the TV building when the shooting began at six o'clock on the evening of the 22nd December. It had taken everyone by surprise for, until then, it had seemed as though the revolution had been achieved peacefully. He had gone home, feeling sick with apprehension for what was to follow. The next day tanks could be heard passing his house. He spent the day going from place to place, trying to find out what was happening, but 'everything was chaotic and in doubt'.

THE building to which the Writers' Union had recently moved was, like its predecessor, a nineteenth-century palazzo in Calea Victoriei, in this case a splendid example of mock baroque. Even the semi-gloom of Bucharest lighting could not disguise the circular sweep of marble staircase which opened onto a broad balcony running round all four walls. The ceilings were a confection of gilt *putti* and faded paintings. The building had been maintained and heated even through the worst of the Ceausescu winters because Elena Ceausescu wanted to turn it into a Palace of Chemistry.

Florin was waiting for me in his office. He had agreed to act as my guide/interpreter for part of my stay in Romania. I would pay his expenses which, so long as I could pay in lei, would be minimal. and he would get a trip to northern Moldavia and Transylvania. His secretary was booking hotels for us in Tulcea at the entrance to the Danubian delta and in Iaşi the old capital of Moldavia. She was also preparing an official document stating that on Writers' Union business, we were entitled to pay in lei. It was important for me to insist on that point, for it transformed a fiendishly expensive trip into something manageable. The official rate of exchange was sixteen lei to the dollar. The going rate on the black market was anywhere from seventy to a hundred and twenty.

Once the paperwork had been completed, we bought Florin's secretary a bunch of flowers and headed for the Union canteen where we had arranged to stock up on some foodstuffs not likely to be readily available: cheese, some Czech pâté, mineral water and tinned meat. At the fruit and vegetable market nearby, we were able to buy radishes, cucumbers and green pimento peppers. It was impossible to get bread that day, or wine, or onions and only with much persistence were we able to get hold of a bottle opener and some ground paprika for sprinkling on the cheese. There was no fruit to be had and we were fortunate to get what we did. I had taken the precaution before leaving Britain of packing small jars of salt, herbs and pepper.

Over lunch in a café/restaurant – I had learned to order chicken since it seemed to withstand culinary destruction better than anything else – Florin told me about a party given by his boss on New Year's Eve the year before the revolution (1988). Dinescu, the Writers' Union president, was already unpopular with Ceausescu, but kept himself 'clean' by not doing anything really forbidden. It was forbidden for Romanians to meet with or speak to foreigners unless they reported the conversation to the Securitate. Dinescu had invited to his party most of the Western ambassadors, cultural attachés, press representatives, and so on. Florin, whose wife had just had their first child, was also invited along as Dinescu's assistant. He spoke with the wife of the German cultural attaché and the British ambassador's wife. A few days later when he returned to his office, Florin was asked to go to Securitate headquarters. There he was interviewed as to what exactly had been said at the party. He told them the details of how the British ambassador's wife had advised him to change nappies. He was not believed, but they did nothing about it. He also related how a fellow student at university in Iaşi had had the misfortune to have the same name as a famous Romanian hero of the Middle Ages. The young man was stopped by Securitate officers one day. His papers were, unwisely, at home. When he gave his name he was promptly beaten unconscious.

Before leaving the hotel that morning, I had heard an English voice in the coffee bar. It belonged to Tony Drummond who worked for Eurovision. He had been in Bucharest for a number of weeks setting up transmission facilities for the world's TV crews so that the elections could be adequately covered. He was waiting, impatiently, day after day, for trucks to arrive to transport the equipment to Prague to cover the elections there. That meant, of course, that he had to have dealings with various Romanian authorities. He detested Bucharest, was weary of the graft and corruption, and found the general dirt and inefficiency depressing. As he lived in Geneva, the contrast must have been startling. He is a tall, quiet-spoken man, much travelled and with a lively sense of humour, though his time in Romania had eroded it somewhat. He spoke of that spiral of hostility one can fall into in such circumstances which, in turn, generates hostility and frustration. As we were chatting we were approached by one of the touts who habitually hung about the foyer of the Bucharest. These thuggish-looking characters were neither more nor less than *banditi* and were clearly into whatever rackets would turn a dishonest lei. My way of dealing with them was to ignore them or, failing that, simply to walk away. Not so, Tony. The fellow asked if he wanted to change money. Tony said: 'What rate?' To which the reply was 'eighty'. Tony laughed at him: 'I can get twice that from any of your friends. What about 200?' Two hundred lei was well above the going rate and after a moment's hesitation the fellow left us alone.

We had arranged to have dinner that evening in the Bucharest. When we met in the lobby bar Tony was being drawn into conversation by a youngish bearded man who said he was a teacher of philosophy. He spoke a hesitant and ungrammatical French, explaining that he had been in Bucharest to obtain permission to start up an import business for cosmetics. As it was too early to go to dinner we sat at a table in the bar and continued the conversation. I was curious to know what a Romanian philosophy teacher taught. I asked him whether he was familiar with the writings of J. R. Searle or John Austin, two writers in whom I have a special interest. No. Had he heard of Wittgenstein? No. I could not resist telling Tony the story of the English philosopher G. E. Moore going to Buckingham Palace to be invested with his OM. In the carriage on the way home he looked very glum and Lady Moore said to him: 'What's wrong, Moore?' To which he allegedly replied: 'The king has not heard of Wittgenstein.'

I must have made some reference to Hungary, for this sparked off from the young man a fierce diatribe about the Magyars. His eyes glazed with hatred and passionate conviction: *'Ils sont, vous comprenez, comme les Niponais, Asiatiques.'* He was quite oblivious of the Japanese couple at the table behind him. Pressed upon the point, he descended into incoherence and Tony and I decided to adjourn to dinner, leaving him to his hatreds.

Strangely, this Magyar-Vlach hostility is shared to some extent by both peoples. The Hungarians feel themselves to be surrounded by a sea of Slavs and other races with whom they have no affinity. It is certainly true that their language has no affinity with the Indo-European languages by which they are surrounded. The Romanians, or some of them, feel that they are an outpost of Latin civilisation set in a hostile sea of Asiatic Magyars and Slavs. The truth is that both peoples inhabit a part of the world which has been overrun, depopulated, repopulated and overrun again so many times through their histories, that any notion of racial integrity is merely absurd. Huns, Avars, Magyars, Turks, Cumans, Pechenegs, Bulgars, Vlachs, Ruthenians, Saxons, Austrians, Greeks and just about every other European and Asian people have contributed to the stew. What provides a national integrity, where it can be said to exist at all, is language and an acknowledgement of a common history. But the fierce hatreds, alas, are unlikely to vanish. Communism kept them below the surface, as it suppressed all forms of dissent and much individuality. Now that the cork has been taken from the bottle, it may be that all sorts of evil spirits will roam abroad and none more dangerous than that romantic nationalism which defines itself by the hostile exclusion of others from the community of what counts as human.

As we chatted over dinner, Tony pointed out to me that some of the characters appearing in the restaurant were those same touts who hung out in the foyer by day. Changed into dark suits and ties, they were scarcely recognisable. Not only did they have the best tables, but the restaurant manager was clearly anxious to accommodate them in whatever way he could. Some 'arrangement' had evidently been agreed. I thought of a remark of Florin's earlier in the day: 'Romania, you know, is the fifth wheel on the European cart.'

I HAD arranged with Florin that we should set out for Tulcea just after five in the morning. By four-thirty I was ready to leave and was carting my luggage into the foyer. The young man working as night-duty receptionist offered to make me a coffee. He knew from my passport that I was British and had perhaps seen me the evening before in the company of some of the press corps who were based in the Bucharest. He spoke a stumbling but adequate English and explained that he was a student supplementing his income by working part-time at the hotel. He went on to say that several former senior Securitate officials had been in the hotel the night before and had got very drunk. They had boasted of how in the morning they would be taking part in an operation to clear University Square of its 'troublemakers and layabouts' on orders received directly from the president's office.

I think he expected me to pass the information on to my friends in the press corps. I had no notion what credence to give to his story, but I passed it on to Florin and suggested he telephone some of his friends. We discovered later that an attempt had been made that morning to clear University Square. The attempt had been thwarted when the police found themselves confronted not only with an unexpectedly large number of demonstrators, but with television cameras and newspaper-men. It was my impression that not much remained secret in Bucharest for very long. Only a few weeks later the demonstrators in University Square were cleared out with fierce brutality by miners brought in from the Jiu Valley. The police, evidently, were not sufficiently pliable.

Like Florin, the young man thought nothing much had changed and that the 'revolution' was a ploy by those in power to dump

189

Ceausescu who had become a liability. It is a difficult matter about which to form any opinion. I think Romanian politics is a peculiarly filthy business, but that a genuine effort is being made to introduce reforms. There exists in Romania no untainted class of persons capable of revitalising a system poisoned by decades of acquiescence and corruption. The issue of how reforms can be introduced in such circumstances is far from simple, for who will administer new laws which may well militate against the interests of a deeply entrenched and profoundly compromised *nomenklatura*? Where no pure spring is available, dirty water may be better than death by dehydration.

The landscape through which we drove that morning had been scoured clean by two nights of torrential rain. It was farming country, good for wheat and maize, the latter widely used for animal feed, especially for poultry and pigs. In this part of the world, pigs are the peasant's food factory. There need be no waste with a pig which, once killed, will provide fat and meat for several months. The nearer we got to the Delta, the more frequent were the storks, perched on their nests on top of the roadside telegraph poles or standing forlorn-looking in the fields.

We crossed the Danube again at Giurgeni. It flows fast here, wide and dirty-brown, its embankments heavily wooded. Now we are in the Dobruja. In the town of Hirşova the apartment blocks are even less prepossessing than usual, three-storey buildings with a peculiarly low ratio of window to wall area. After Hirşova the road takes us through a strange landscape of low hills and marshes, lively with birds. We stop at one small lake, fringed with rushes. A little egret is standing patiently in the shallows. A few yards away coots and a flurry of new-hatched chicks paddle to safety, while a kestrel hovers in the middle distance. Farther off, two grey herons, motionless as statues, stare into the waters. The road is lined with walnut trees and beyond the roadside are peach orchards and acacia woods.

I hoped to be able to take a boat through the Delta to the open sea and we had been given the names of a couple of people who, we hoped, could arrange transport for us. Romania, alas, is not so simple. Once we arrived in Tulcea and made contact with the people we were supposed to meet, we discovered that there was a seaman's strike in progress. Nevertheless, we were told, something would be possible. While something was being arranged, we checked in at our hotel. Half-an-hour later we heard that a small boat would be available at twelve dollars an hour, payable in hard currency. Half-an-hour later, the price had gone up to sixty dollars. Half-an-hour later, the price had risen to three hundred dollars. There was general surprise and dismay when I insisted on having my passport returned by the hotel receptionist and checked out. If I could not reach the Black Sea via the Danube, I would head for Constanţa. Florin seemed as surprised as anyone that I was not prepared to barter and bargain and arrive at 'an accommodation'. The idea of doing business in any other way seems simply not to arise. It was already mid–day and I had been driving for six hours. Nevertheless, I had determined to reach the Black Sea that day and reach it I would. As it turned out, Florin did not like Tulcea and was happy enough to leave.

Between Tulcea and Constanţa, on the edge of Lake Sinoe, are the remains of Histria, a settlement founded by colonists from Asia Minor in the seventh century BC and which endured for nearly twelve hundred years. It was an important trading centre dealing in wines, oils and cereals. The Romans occupied it in 72 BC and dredged the harbour which had silted up over the previous two hundred years. It was a sophisticated place, with a water supply piped from some thirty kilometres away through ceramic and stone pipes. The Goths destroyed a large part of the town in 248 and again in 270. By early in the next century it had been abandoned. It was resettled under the Byzantines, but never flourished again, being too exposed to the successive waves of invaders who occupied the Dobruja between the sixth and tenth centuries.

What you see there now, apart from the great sweep of the lake with the Black Sea, tantalisingly, just over the horizon, are stumps of wall and column and a few wheatears flirting among the ruins. It is difficult to imagine these shards as the remains of a thriving town. Much more exciting was the herd of wild horses romping among the marshes which fringe the road to Histria. They were grazing the long marsh grasses and cantered off as we approached, bucking and cavorting with sheer energy. The marshes too were a haven for birds, the great white egret, the little egret, the bittern and a great variety of ducks and waders. It was blowing a chill breeze and we watched the birds from the shelter of Anastasia. I was so intent on trying to identify a flock of ducks, that I paid little attention when the car began to rock from side to side. I put it down to the breeze, though it would take a hurricane to rock

191

Anastasia in that way. We discovered later that these had been the tremors of an earthquake reaching 6.8 on the Richter scale and that several people had been killed. On our way back to the main road, we passed a wheat field where thousands of swallows were feeding, tracing huge swirls of dark movement. Their flight was too intricate for the eye to discern any pattern beyond the sudden surges and eddies when several thousand birds would rise or fall in a single sweep.

Much less attractive were the industrial plants we passed as we approached Constanţa. At Năvodari one began to see why it might, literally, be called the Black Sea. These were large-scale exercises in pumping filth into the air and earth, wholly, it seemed, without restraint. I have never encountered such unconcern for pollution as in Romania. The cars and trucks burning low-grade fuels were bad enough. One would not drive close behind a Romanian truck for long for fear of being asphyxiated. But the petro-chemical plants were obscene in the scale with which they poisoned everything around them. Florin pointed out to me that some forms of pollution were regarded as healthy and that the government encouraged such vulgarities as poems in praise of the blackness of a river, that being a sign of the wealth of coal they were able to extract. The idea that resources might be developed in a more benign way still seems the merest sentimentality to many Romanians. In a society which thinks only in terms of scarcity, environmental considerations come far down the list of priorities. It is difficult to imagine those attitudes changing unless they are forced to.

Equally unpleasing is the Danube-Black Sea canal, which reaches the sea just south of Constanţa. The project was begun in the late 1940s and suspended by Gheorghiu-Dej in 1954. It was built by the forced labour of political prisoners and is described by Joseph Rothschild as 'a cloaca of immense human suffering and mortality'.* The project was revived by Ceausescu and completed in 1985. The figure of a hundred thousand lives has been given as the cost of its construction, many of them conscripted peasants.

Constanţa was named after Constantia, sister of Constantine the Great who founded the city in the early years of the fourth century. It is Romania's most important port on the Black Sea and its three-mile-long waterfrontage of wharfs, warehouses and

*Return to Diversity, 1989.

grain elevators makes it clear that it is a busy if unattractive place. A series of skyscraper blocks in various stages of construction intended as tourist hotels stretches along the northern part of the seafront, adding to the general scene of ugly disrepair. Much of the town dates from the period immediately after the war of 1878 and would be attractive if cleaned. Black is not my favourite colour in buildings.

A steep stairway takes you from the edge of the town down to the beach. It is depressing to walk across the filthy sand and see just what a mess has been made of what could have been a beautiful resort town, as it once was, for there are numerous curative springs in the area. This was as far east as I could go unless I set out for fabled Colchis, for the Argonauts are supposed to have landed there.

Someone who, against his will, certainly did land here and never ceased to complain of the fact, was the author of the wonderful *Metamorphoses*, Publius Ovidius Naso, more usually known as Ovid. It was Ovid's misfortune to celebrate and satirise the dissipations of an essentially frivolous phase in Roman society at a time when the Emperor Augustus, intent on moral reform, hoped to restore Rome to its ancient virtue, as he saw it. Ovid's *Ars Amatoria*, bland enough by contemporary standards, deeply shocked Augustus and led, in 8 AD, to the poet's banishment to provincial Tomis. Neither Augustus nor his successor, Tiberius, was disposed to revoke the banishment, a favour for which Ovid pleaded for the rest of his life. He found the inhabitants of Tomis a barbarous lot after the refinements of Roman society in one of its most brilliant moments. Ovid was not the last poet to land himself in political hot water, but he was certainly one of the least boring.

After looking at the statue of Ovid outside the Archaeological Museum, we made our way to the Casino. A frivolous confection of disparate styles, it was cobbled together for Elizabeth of Wied, wife of King Carol I, and better known as Carmen Sylva, her pen-name. She was more than mildly eccentric, a would-be Sappho, who wanted the pavilion built so that she could stage an entertainment for Tsar Nicholas and his family who visited their Romanian relatives in June of 1914. The occasion turned into a general fiasco and the Russians stayed for only a day. That was long enough, however, for Carmen's 'allegorical tableaux' to collapse around the performers, for Marie of Edinburgh to quarrel with the Tsarina, for the Tsarevich and the young Prince Carol to have a spitting competition, and for Marie to remark: 'Nicky is Tsar of all the Russias – and my cousin – but nothing can make him look like anything but a cook.' All in all, it was a truly family occasion. The Casino now houses a restaurant. While we looked round, the staff were assembled in the foyer betting on a coin-throwing competition. *Plus ça change.*

WE set out for Iaşi at eight o'clock. For the first time since I had crossed the Romanian border, the sun began to edge through the cloud-cover, illuminating, from moment to moment, a landscape shrouded in mists. We crossed the Danube again at Giurgeni. Soldiers were stationed at either end of the bridge for no very obvious reason, though we were not stopped by them. We passed through a succession of little villages on the road to Braila, each with its resident storks. Most of the nests were perched atop telephone poles and, in the dangling tangle of twigs, sparrows built *their* nests undisturbed by their giant neighbours. The villages were full of animals; horses and chickens, pigs and geese and goats. It is difficult to believe that anyone goes hungry in a country so rich in livestock, cereals, fruits and vines. In the village of Mihai Bravu I stopped to photograph the storks. Mihai Bravu (Michael the Brave) was a Wallachian prince who came to the throne in 1593. He began his career by imprisoning a horde of Turkish tax-collectors in his palace and then burning it to the ground. Together with some Cossack forces, he seized the fortress at Braila and even captured Ruse. Despite his defeat of a Turkish army sent against him in 1595, Wallachia was overrun and Bucharest plundered. Some help came from Sigismund Báthory, prince of Transylvania and, for the moment, it suited the Turks to agree a truce. Their attentions were elsewhere in their final assault on Győr, which they captured, and Buda which, on this occasion, they did not. In 1599, with the support of the Habsburg emperor Rudolf II, Michael ousted Sigismund's successor from Transylvania and proclaimed himself prince. In the following year he seized the Moldavian throne, thereby uniting the three components of greater Romania. His success was ephemeral, for he was murdered in 1601, but as a legendary figure who defeated the Turks and united Romania, he provided a hero for nationalists of the nineteenth and twentieth centuries to hang their aspirations on. He was a ruthless careerist, neither better nor worse than his contemporaries, but that matters little to the sentimentalisers of history.

Florin told me that Braila was famous for its knife-wielding thugs, a considerable achievement, surely, in Romania. After Braila we left Wallachia and entered southern Moldavia. We passed some lovely acacia woods, their thin, long trunks creating a sense of delicate airiness in the wood.

Not far from Birlad we passed a cluster of sheds surrounded by a high wire fence and stacked between one of the sheds and the fence was a pile of large, handsome wicker baskets. Others were hanging from the eaves. A middle-aged woman was seated on the grass by a shady tree beside the shed. I asked Florin if he would buy one of the baskets for me. The woman explained that they were for export only and that they were not allowed to sell them. Florin, pointing to Anastasia, explained that it was for a foreigner. However, the foreman was down at a nearby railway siding supervising the loading of a consignment of baskets. Perhaps if we saw him . . .. She then summoned a cheerful little man to take us along to the siding. He was wearing his work apron and was in his late fifties; scrawny, with bright blue eyes, protruding teeth and an incessant grin. He removed his apron and carefully arranged his thin hair, putting on a cloth cap before shaking hands. He was shabbily dressed in poor-quality clothes. The railway siding was only a mile or so along the road and the little man became very subdued once in the car. His boss was a hefty fellow, also in his fifties, but instead of a cloth cap he sported a grey felt hat and dark, battered-looking suit. He confirmed that the baskets were not for sale, but he would give us one as a present. Back at the factory, he took us into a long shed where hundreds of baskets of different shapes and sizes were piled high and asked me to take whichever I wished. I had given Florin a couple of packets of Kent cigarettes to give to the two men as a gesture of thanks. Kent are a kind of universal currency and, having been forewarned before entering Romania, I had taken a carton with me. The foreman was immensely pleased with his present and insisted on adding a second basket to the first. We were told to wait in the car and a few moments later the baskets were brought out wrapped in big sheets of grey paper tied with string. I had chosen a large, strongly made basket, ideal for the mushrooming for which I now use them.

We stopped for a late lunch at the roadside and ate our cucumber and cheese and cherries in the shade of a quince orchard. Since we set out that morning, we had driven north along the westernmost edge of the great plain which stretches away to Soviet Asia, and for much of the later part of the day we were only twenty miles or so from the Soviet border. Not long after lunch, we were waved down by a policeman. He was a young man, perhaps thirty years old, tall, broadly built and with a swaggering and disagreeable manner. He said something in Romanian and, assuming he wanted to see my papers, I produced them. He examined them carefully and then said something which I did not understand.

He kept repeating himself, clearly getting agitated. In any questionable situation I have found it wise only to acknowledge English since an inept understanding of anything else could lead to problems. Florin, meanwhile, sat in the car. Since we were getting nowhere, I declined to acknowledge Florin's reluctance and suggested he interpret. We were then invited to accompany the policeman to his office a few yards away, but otherwise in the middle of nowhere, 'for further discussions of the matter'. It seemed that he thought I had been driving dangerously and was going to fine me 250 lei which would be a lot for a Romanian, but for me amounted to about three dollars. However, he wanted to know whether I understood why I was being fined. I had no idea since, as far as I knew, I had been driving perfectly safely. In fact, I had overtaken a truck on a clear stretch of road which had – at one time – had filter markings and therefore prohibited overtaking. I eventually said that I understood what he was telling me. He and Florin then began a lengthy conversation.

He wanted to know what I did. Florin explained that I was a writer. Did I really write books? Of course. Then Florin produced the official document from the Writers' Union. In post-revolutionary Romania, writers occupy a doubtful position from the point of view of policemen. Too many of them are suddenly too senior in the government to trifle with and Florin's boss, Mircea Dinescu, had become an influential figure in national life. Whatever the reasoning, the fine, it was announced, was waived and by the time we left his manner had become distinctly less authoritarian. He told Florin to tell me that we should be more careful. I thanked him politely (in English). He was not a pretty piece of work and I should not like to have been a peasant who had fallen foul of him.

In the last twenty miles before arriving at Iaşi, we passed through a hillier terrain, planted with splendid deciduous woodlands. These low hills are the foreword to the eastern rim of the Carpathians. Then, all at once, we were high above the city and the valley of the Bahlui river, on the left bank of which the capital of Moldavia is situated. The Soviet border runs only ten miles to the west along the line of the river Prut, and to the north lie the Ukraine and Byelo Russia.

On the outskirts of the town – somewhat to my alarm – we passed a petrol queue several miles long. We booked in to the Hotel Unirea, standard East European shabby but with a larger proportion than usual of touts hanging about the foyer. By the time we had settled in, it was late afternoon and, as it was pleasantly warm and sunny, we set out for a quick walk round the town. Florin had been a student in Iaşi and there was no difficulty about finding our way around. Of Iaşi's many churches, it was the seat of both an Orthodox metropolitan and a Catholic bishop, perhaps the most interesting is the Church of the Three Hierarchs.

Built in 1640 by the local prince, Basil the Wolf (Vasile Lupu), the exterior walls and twin towers are completely covered in intricate carvings of geometric and floral motifs. In the following year Basil established Moldavia's first printing press in the grounds of the monastery. It was also the site of the first school to use Romanian rather than Greek as the language of instruction. You enter the church through a vestibule beyond which the two octagonal towers each form a section of the nave. From the dome of each tower, the face of Christ the Pantocrator gazes down on the worshippers. Set into the walls are the tombs of Basil the Wolf and Alexander Cuza, first ruler of the united principalities. It is an extraordinary example of Byzantine art.

Passing a supermarket, I wanted to look round. It was a somewhat depressing activity. What goods there were were shabby, and the food hall was even more spartan than the one I had seen in Ruse. As we wandered round, Florin was approached by a young gypsy. It was difficult to tell his age but he was perhaps in his late teens. He wanted Florin to write a letter for him. His future parents-in-law refused to let him marry their daughter until he had a television. In order to be allowed to buy a television, he had to write a letter of application to the store manager but he was illiterate. While Florin wrote out his letter for him, a process which seemed to involve elaborate and protracted debate, I sat in the sun and wondered how such a shambolic system had survived for as long as it had.

Dinner, in a restaurant called The Select, was an abject affair. There was no wine or beer to be had, but we did manage a bottle of peculiarly nasty pink 'champagne' which resembled nothing so much as sweetish soda-water with gas. The only truly edible component of the meal was a salad of cucumber and onion which they had failed to destroy. There was grilled chicken but one would have needed a taste for cardboard properly to appreciate it. There was neither coffee nor mineral water.

What irritated me, apart from the dirty table-linen and cutlery, was the *needless* squalor and incompetence. The ingredients were perfectly good, if limited, but no one gave a damn and the unhappy-looking waitress seemed harassed and tired. Romanians regard complaint as a complete waste of effort and, given the system they inhabit, they are probably right. Anyone faced with a complaint will merely shrug and, if pressed, say: 'Don't blame me, I'm not responsible.' But no one is responsible. The buck never stops and people survive by withdrawing any interest from their public activities. The result is a vicious spiral of apathy and demoralisation.

Back at the hotel, I extracted a bottle of excellent Bulgarian brandy from Anastasia. Having had too much spare money the night before leaving Ruse, I had bought two bottles of good, old brandy from the barman in the Riga, doubtless at a handsome profit to himself. In the course of the next couple of hours Florin and I worked our way through most of the bottle as we traded attitudes on the causes of the demoralisation I saw everywhere in public life.

Florin's response was to try not to think about it too much, lest depression take over, and to live as privately as possible, which meant family and, above all, a life of the imagination. My view was that this national schizophrenia between public and private worlds was itself a cause as much as an effect and that, in France or Germany, people would be less passive about the abuses to which they were subject. Is that mere wishful thinking? What seems lacking in Romania is any general sense that individuals

can change the way things are *in any degree*. It seems too long ago
to lay the blame at the door of centuries of Ottoman occupation
when passive endurance was a way of life. All the Romanians
I spoke to desperately wanted to be thought Europeans, but in
practice they were, both culturally and as individuals, intensely
introverted. Their world was Romania and they seemed not to
worry much about what the larger world made of them, perhaps
as a way of avoiding too harsh a look at how things really
were. Here exactly was where history and the individual were
indistinguishable and, therefore, enigmatic. It was only later that
I came across the Romanian proverb: the sword does not lop the
bowed head. My own impatience with such attitudes was also
a cultural habit and how can you 'imagine being someone else'
without also taking over their attitudes?

Florin had to return to Bucharest next day, and this meant being
in a town with decent rail or air services. I wanted to spend time
in Transylvania. Florin had friends in the Cluj (Kolozsvár) area
with whom I could find accommodation – despite the distance,
that seemed the place to make for. The problem was: not much
petrol in Anastasia and even less in Iaşi, where there had been none
for the previous two days. We decided to try the next town on the
off-chance that there had been a petrol delivery. We set out just
after five o'clock heading west for the little town of Tirgu Frumos.
There is no difficulty locating garages in Romania. Any large town
will have a garage on the edge of town on each main road. In small
towns or villages, if there is a garage at all, it will be on the main
through road at one end of town. By the time we reached Tirgu
Frumos, the sun was up and promised a fine day. The garage did
not open until nine, but a local confirmed for us that there was
in any case no petrol, although 'a delivery is expected today or
tomorrow'.

There might have been enough of a reserve in Anastasia to take
us on to Roman, the next town of any size, but, if not, then we
would really be stranded. With what Florin clearly thought was
Western naïvety, I suggested we call at the local police station for
help. Florin disappeared inside and emerged ten minutes later with
a promise of petrol. The duty constable had telephoned the garage
attendant who would open a reserve pump if we would go to
the garage and wait for him. Half-an-hour later the policeman
arrived to discover us still waiting and went off to fetch the
attendant. Ten minutes later both arrived, chatting and smiling

and, apparently, not in the least put out. Florin, meantime, had gone to do what Romanians get to be very good at – scrounging – and came back with a loaf of freshly baked bread. The garage forecourt was unchained and Anastasia was replenished – with a higher octane petrol than was usually available – and we were ready for the day. After I paid for the petrol, in cash and not in the officially mandatory but unofficially unwelcome coupons, I offered my benefactors packets of Kent but they refused them. The policeman finally accepted one from the packet. With handshakes all round, we set out for Transylvania.

The sky was a wash of pale blue and the road lined with cherry and walnut trees. By eight we had crossed the Siret which rises in the highlands of Ruthenia in the Soviet Union and runs into the Danube at Galaţi. On the outskirts of Roman, power lines march across the rolling countryside while all the local transport appears to be by horse and cart. Despite the absence of traffic, the authorities in Roman have introduced a one-way traffic system Byzantine in its obscurity and positively malicious in its absence of road signs. Eventually, we emerged from it to cross the Moldova into a countryside of upland plateau where the rounded hills support only a thin covering of grasses, giving them a curiously shaven look. We stopped by a maize field to watch a large flock of storks feeding on grasshoppers. Somewhere near where we stopped, between Roman and Piatra Neamt, Stephen the Great of Moldavia fought the battles of Rašboieni (1476) and Scheia (1486), which marked the last real Moldavian resistance to the Turkish advance.

Stephen acquired the Moldavian throne with the aid of Vlad of Wallachia. His strength lay in the fact that Moldavia still supported a free peasantry whose tenure rested on military service. His weakness lay in the inability of the Christian princes to unite against the Turkish threat. Matthias Corvinus in Hungary was more interested in his westward schemes, while Casimir of Poland was absorbed in the Baltic. Stephen repeatedly attempted to form a Christian league, but his efforts came to nothing and on his death-bed he advised his successor to come to honourable terms with the Turks. The Hungarians in particular, in failing to support Stephen, made a rod for their own backs only a few years after his death when, at Mohács, they had to withstand the full weight of the Turkish assault.

If there is a single overwhelming consequence to be drawn from the Turkish assaults on and occupation of Eastern Europe, it is that its effect on the peasantry determined much of the course of subsequent European history. In Bulgaria and the Balkans generally, as well as in the principalities, the peasantry became helots, a servile populace with little to gain from a strong defence of their territories, exploited as much by native boiars as by the Turks. In Hungary, the free peasantry disappeared, leaving only the nobles as representatives of 'the nation of St Stephen'. In consequence, Hungary became the most feudalised of European countries, run by a clique of landowners until 1848. As a result of that disastrous weakening of the concept of the nation, the Austro-Hungarian dual monarchy became the creature of a nobility intent on the defence of its interests and incapable of adapting to changing circumstances. In the period before 1848, many of the smaller Hungarian landlords had been ruined and their estates assimilated by the larger magnates. That displaced gentry formed the administrative corps of the empire in place of the non-existent middle classes. Their loyalty was to a reactionary ideal which identified itself with the court and was its creature. That stratification of classes underlay Austro-Hungarian policy-making until the shambles of the First World War swept them all away. Even in Germany, the ruin of the free peasantry between the wars of religion and the Thirty Years War had the most profound consequences for the rest of Europe. The lack of a socially powerful middle class not only delayed industrial development, but encouraged the caste-conscious militarism which became the curse of Central Europe.

As we approached the ancient town of Piatra Neamt we had our first real sighting of the Carpathians, a steel-blue ridge serrating the horizon. The countryside to the west of the town with its wooded grassy slopes and the reservoir formed by the river Bistriţa, reminded me of nothing so much as the side of Loch Earn in Perthshire, even to the fingers of mist creeping over the rim of the hills. A little further west, the valley of the Bistriţa is disfigured by an enormous paper-mill set down, apparently, where it has been calculated to do the maximum visual damage. Just past the little town of Tarcau we entered the Bicaz Gorge, a pass through the Carpathians at places only a few yards wide and where the surrounding mountains rise to six thousand feet. At one section the road has had to be cut directly into the rock, which has been left as an overhang, with the furious rush of the Bicaz stream channelled to one side. At the narrowest point, the limestone walls converge to a near tunnel known as the 'neck of hell'. As the Gorge began to broaden again, we entered a landscape of limestone fangs and pinnacles sometimes just twenty yards across, but rising hundreds of feet. It resembled a landscape copied from some sword and sorcery tale.

After leaving the Gorge and passing by the side of Lacu Roşu, a drowned valley created by a landslip damming the Bicaz, and where you can still see the tips of pine trees jutting from the water, the road winds tortuously up into the mountains. A red-gold dog fox darted across the road in front of us and every mile or two we could see hawks and eagles hunting above the wooded slopes. At the highest point on the road we emerged from the forests into alpine meadows of short grasses, flowers and shrubs. The sward was studded with alpine violets and as we walked up the slope above the road, a kestrel was hunting far below. Having crossed the eastern rim of the Carpathians, we were now in Transylvania.

Down in Gheorghieni, the look and feel of the place was different from anything I had encountered in Moldavia. The houses were painted in different colours, green and beige being a standard combination, and the architecture was more like that of Austro-Hungary. Many of these northern Transylvanian towns are still substantially Hungarian-speaking and, since the revolution, had been the scene of disturbances between Romanian and Hungarian ethnic groups, especially around Tirgu Mureş.

In his later years, Ceausescu pursued a policy of destroying villages, especially in Transylvania where Hungarian irredentism was at its strongest. The recent riots were a natural expression of that conflict now that the Securitate lid had been removed. But it was not just the buildings in Transylvania which seemed different. The people behaved differently. When Anastasia passed through any town or village (and it became more marked as we moved westwards) the younger people would stand by the roadside showing the Victory sign, while older people would wave or smile. In these remoter areas, foreigners must still have been a relative rarity and any welcome offered to them perhaps understandable as a defiance of the previous regime and its acute xenophobia.

We stopped in the village of Lazarea to discover where we

might find a coffee. While Florin went a-hunting, I sat in the park. I had a bar of Swiss chocolate and was being watched by two little boys. The less shy of the two gradually worked his way towards the bench on which I was sitting. I offered him a piece of chocolate and then the other came forward and he too was given a piece. The elder and less shy sat on the bench and began chattering away in Hungarian. His companion went away. After a few minutes the child had succeeded in working out that I was 'angol' and that the chocolate was Swiss. No mean feat since the wrapper was in English. I was sorry I knew no Hungarian. When Florin returned it was to announce that he had found a café where they would make us coffee. It was busy with working men downing tumblers of brandy and seemed more cheerful than anywhere I had encountered hitherto in Romania.

By noon the line of the Căliman Mountains stretched to the north. We stopped for lunch by the side of the Mureş, the verge a gala of wildflowers and the hills rising steeply behind us. A pair of eagles circled in the distance and on the cliffs above us ravens were flapping from ledge to ledge. Lunch was our by now customary collation of bread, mineral water and assorted salad vegetables. I have rarely enjoyed food as much as I did these picnic simplicities, and after eating we gave Anastasia a much-needed wash.

As we followed the line of the Mureş we could see from time to time tiny blue-painted shielings perched high on the mountainsides, like houses out of a folk tale. The villages we passed through would have been entirely picturesque, but for their befoulment by Ceausescu-ordained apartment blocks planted in their midst. Three or four storeys high, they dwarfed the other village structures and were the cheapest, nastiest buildings I had seen. Constructed out of poor-quality concrete, they had few windows and no heating, so that their inhabitants had had to punch holes through the walls and build *ad hoc* chimneys out of oil drums. Ceausescu may have been extraordinary in the extremity of his authoritarian whims, but the underlying idea of forcing people to conform to what suits central planners is widespread and produces slums wherever it is allowed free rein, whether in Glasgow, Bucharest or in Transylvanian villages. The excuse is that such impositions are 'progressive'. In fact, they grossly oversimplify historically evolved diversities, often of great sophistication and at the price of misery for their victim.

We reached Cluj in the late afternoon and were able to fill up with petrol after a wait of only thirty minutes. Our goal was the village of Petreşti, where Florin had several times stayed with a peasant family, Mr and Mrs Rotar. By the time we arrived, it was almost seven o'clock. I had been driving most of the day, since five-thirty, and was gaga. Florin found the house and was made welcome by Mr and Mrs Rotar – their name means 'wheelwright'. The gates were opened for me to reverse Anastasia into the yard. I failed to see a grassed-over ditch on the opposite side of the road and, as I drew forward, the front wheels dropped into the two-foot ditch with an appalling thump. My heart sank faster than the wheels and I had nightmare visions of irreparable damage and weeks of useless hassle. Rural Transylvania is not the place to have a mishap in a Volvo. Or anything else. Nor did it help that I felt a complete fool.

After peering under the chassis and failing to see any damage, I tried reversing out, but the wheels could get no traction whatsoever. Then we tried forcing bundles of twigs under the wheels. But the ditch was too steep and Anastasia too heavy. Next, it was suggested that a couple of water buffalo be used to drag her out, but they were not yet back from the fields. Just then the son of one of the Rotars' neighbours came on the scene. He was an agricultural engineer, Mr Pîrvu, and was visiting his parents. There was a brand new tractor just two houses away, the only one in the district. It had just been purchased on credit by a couple of his friends. Mr Pîrvu went off and two minutes later appeared driving a tractor so new, I do not think it had ever been used. In another two minutes Anastasia had been dragged out of the ditch entirely unharmed. After profuse thanks all round, Anastasia was parked safely in the yard.

While Mrs Rotar prepared something to eat, Florin, Mr Pîrvu and I set out to find the village schoolmaster to discover whether there were any French, German or, better still, English speakers in the village. Florin had to leave the next day and was anxious not to leave me stranded without an interpreter. It was a lovely walk in the warm twilight through streets which hardly ever saw a motor car and where everyone said '*buna seara*' as we passed. The schoolmaster was not at home, but his wife insisted we come in and have a glass of *ţuica*, which stretched to three glasses in the space of half an hour. Ţuica is the Romanian equivalent of slivović, usually made from plums. The farmers collect their crop and then, after it has been weighed, send it to a state-run distillery. The state takes thirty per cent of the distillate and the rest is returned to the village where it is divided *pro rata*, according to the original weight.

There was, it seemed, a local teacher who had studied English and Florin noted down her name and address. On the way back to the Rotars', Mr Pîrvu explained to Florin as much as he knew of the history of Petreşţi. I had missed the evening return of the water-buffalo, for a number of them were now scattered along the roadside and by the stream, shaggy, primitive-looking creatures. We joined the Rotars in their tiny, earth-floored kitchen, dominated by the big yellow oven which took up half the room. We ate bread and cheese and goose sausages. I fetched the remains of the Bulgarian brandy and was soon half asleep.

BREAKFAST in the tiny kitchen consisted of water-buffalo milk which tasted very rich, with an agreeable mustiness about it and boiled duck eggs, cut in half and scooped out with a spoon. Bread accompanied every meal, heavy and yellow and made from a mixture of wheat and maize flour. Mrs Rotar made seven loaves at a time in the big stone oven. Mrs Rotar was busy feeding the geese, ducks and chickens which paraded up and down the yard. They had two houses, one on either side of the yard. A little blue-painted one-storey house next to the kitchen where she and her husband lived, and a larger house (which they did not much like) across the yard. When their son, Nicu, was at home, he lived in the downstairs part of the big house, which consisted of three rooms and a bathroom. The little house had been too small for a family. Just inside the gates was the artesian well. The arm of the well was broken, but as the well was only about thirty feet deep, a bucket and chain provided for all their domestic needs. For larger quantities, they had water from the hill from a tap at the bottom of the yard. Next to the little kitchen were a vegetable garden and a couple of fruit trees, beyond that the pig's hut and run. Below that again, was a ditch, another patch of garden and the hillside. Below the big house were two long sheds for storing hay and for the chickens and geese. Mrs Rotar's days passed in looking after the animals – they were not well enough off to have a buffalo cow, but they traded eggs for milk. By the time she had cooked, cleaned and been to church, the day had vanished.

THE schoolteacher who had studied English lived in the village of Deleni, about three miles away up a narrow single-track road. Florin's flight to Bucharest from Cluj was to leave at two o'clock and he had to be at the airport an hour earlier. The schoolteacher's name was Ileana Mărincean, but when we found her, it was to discover that her English was even rustier than my Russian, about which she was greatly embarrassed. Her niece, Delia, however, spoke fluent English and was studying nearby at the University of Cluj. The niece was expected that evening; if I returned then, we should meet.

I was given directions for a short-cut to the road for Cluj which took us along a dirt-track designed, at best, for horses and carts, through a series of maize fields planted along the sides of what were, at times, quite steep hills. It was a wonderfully surreal drive across a landscape which had certainly never had a Volvo pass through it and I was only sorry there was no one to be entertained by the sight.

Delia did not turn up that evening. I drove her mother, Elena, and Ileana to Turda in an effort to find her, but the buses from Cluj run so irregularly that public transport is haphazard to an extraordinary extent. Each evening at dinner Mr and Mrs Rotar would teach me a few more words such as *apă* (water), *pahar* (glass), *varza* (cabbage), so that by the time I left I had a small but useful vocabulary. They were a kindly couple, both, I guessed, about sixty. She was small, stout and cheerful, he more reflective and thin. I managed to get some bottles of red wine from the hard-currency shop in Cluj, and each evening we would demolish at least a bottle with dinner. As Mr Rotar had high blood pressure an occasional glass was all he would take, but she drank with gusto, though she would not take wine before she had been to church.

SUNDAY. Mrs Rotar cooks on top of a stove attached to the oven. The oven is about five feet high, built of stone, plastered and painted yellow. The stove has a circular lid which she removes and sits a pot in the top of the hole. Whatever she has to cook, has to be prepared on that single surface: this is done by stacking pots one on top of another with whatever requires the longest cooking time in the big pot at the bottom of the pile. Breakfast this morning is bread and home-made pork sausages, dark-skinned and spicy. Mrs Rotar gets in a flap if I don't eat enough. After breakfast she heats some water for me to shave with and goes to change into her Sunday clothes. It is Pentecost and I have agreed to accompany her to church. Pentecost, the descent of the Holy Ghost among the apostles, is one of the chief festivals of the Orthodox Church.

Sunday best is a black skirt and cardigan, black headsquare, stockings and shoes. It is a fine sunny morning and as we stroll the few hundred yards to the church, there is already a trickle of old women flowing towards it. The church is new, having only been completed at the end of the seventies. It has been built not only in traditional style, but as an exact replica of its eighteenth-century predecessor, which finally expired after several bouts of fire and earthquake. It was forbidden to build new churches under the Ceausescu regime but, in this case, special permission was granted through the intercession of a local priest who was distantly related to the Ceausescu clan. Most of the work was carried out by the villagers themselves and was paid for by each family contributing according to its means. The basic structure is simple: a tower, the base of which is the vestibule and staircase leading to a gallery, and a nave, supported by six columns, partitioned at the far end by the iconostasis to create a sanctuary. The exterior is painted a pale green. In front of the vestibule is a porch round which, in Byzantine style, have been painted in brilliant colours medallions of the faces of important saints.

The interior has not yet been dimmed by the candle-reek of decades or centuries and it too is a riot of bright colours, lit by three electric chandeliers. There are narrow wooden stalls along the side walls of the nave and gradually these fill up, men to the right, women to the left. In the fenced area in front of the richly decorated iconostasis, there are two crosses. These are suddenly lit up by a string of tiny bulbs like fairy lights and a few moments later the murmur of praying worshippers is smashed by the opening notes of the liturgy sung through a *loud*, loudspeaker system. The liturgy is chanted behind the iconostasis by the priest and his acolytes. The congregation takes no part in this continuous antiphony which represents a tradition dating back to the early second century.

The initial impact of the liturgy *is*, literally, stunning, but as the minutes pass into hours – the service lasted just over two hours – it becomes hypnotic, for it never stops and, musically at least, shows no progression so that it inhabits a timelessness. Throughout the service, people continued to arrive and after the first hour the nave was full. The older men wore black suits and soft hats which they held in their hands, but the young men wore suits of light grey or brown. Virtually the whole population of the village must have been present. Three times in the course of the service the priest left the sanctuary and processed the length of the nave while the congregation knelt on one knee, some of the old women kissed the sleeve of his robe as he passed, swinging the censer. His vestments were richly embroidered in gold thread. Three times he vanished again behind the iconostasis. Not understanding the liturgy, I found the service a combination of garishness, solemnity, noise and hypnotic sound, and was powerfully struck by how unlike Roman and Protestant services it was, most obviously in the complete lack of participation by the worshippers.

Finally, the congregation filed out into the violent sunlight, forming up into a procession behind two religious banners. As Mrs Rotar's legs would not allow her to walk any distance, I accompanied her back to the house.

Looking at the physical and emotional structure of the service, all the crucial events happen behind a screen, glimpsed only in a shadowy way by the congregation. The Orthodox Church regards priesthood as conferring a touch of divinity, which distinguishes celebrants from the mere people. From time to time during the service, these privileged beings emerge from behind a screen and move among a kneeling mass before disappearing again. Save as audience, the congregation plays no part in the service. They are entirely passive.

The analogy with Romanian political life is striking. The crucial events are performed by privileged beings behind a screen. They emerge into the world of the masses only to announce to them their fate. The relation between invisibility and power, as in the myth of Gyges, the shepherd who found a ring of invisibility which enabled him to become king, is as old as history. A mystique is the more easily fostered by invisibility and inaccessibility. A peasantry steeped in such models can hardly provide the stuff of democratic transformation and is rather more likely to engage in prolonged passivity followed by violent *jacquerie* which is, in fact, a pattern of Romanian history. There must be a stage where one's condemnation of corrupt political systems rests not on impatience with its passivity, but with the obvious misery it inflicts on so many people, even if they solace themselves in their misery.

Since Pentecost was a special occasion, lunch was more elaborate than usual, and I had watched Mrs Rotar the evening before taking cabbages from the brine in which they were preserved and soaking them in fresh water, preparatory to making *sarmaluţa*. These are rolls of cabbage-leaf from which the spine has been removed and stuffed with a kind of maizemeal porridge, seasoned with minced meat, which can be pork, or pork and beef, and hot pepper. Rice is sometimes used but maizemeal is traditional. These *dolmades*-like rolls, about the size of a tennis ball, are stacked in a clay pot and the pot is filled with the juice of the preserved cabbage and some pieces of dill and cooked very slowly. They taste delicious. These were accompanied by *slanina*, slices of smoked pork fat which, though it may sound horrid to western ears, tastes very good, pieces of roast goose, *brînză*, a ewe-milk slightly sour cheese, and the ubiquitous bread (*pîine*). There was always a plate of radishes and spring onions on the table. We ate from a tiny wooden table which, much of the time, also served as platter. The meal began with a goose-soup with noodles and thereafter one ate the assembled goodies in any order.

BACK at Deleni, I arranged to drive the Mărincean family to Cluj that evening to their daughter's flat. By then, it was late afternoon and I wanted to see the Turda Gorge which lay a mile south of Petreşti. Alĭn, Delia's sixteen-year-old brother, offered to act as a guide, partly, I knew, because he was keen to have a ride in Anastasia. We drove through Petreşti and then down to the entrance to the Gorge. Part of the track had been washed away on a section of fairly steep incline and a small loose scree had slid from the hillside to cover it. At its steepest, the angle of incline was just short of forty-five degrees and the combination of the tilt and the scree, convinced me that we would be fortunate indeed not to slide down the twenty-metre slope into the stream below. Since it was impossible to retreat I had to inch Anastasia forward. By the time we had negotiated those fifteen to twenty metres, I was bathed in cold sweat and felt I had aged by about a year per metre. And it had to be negotiated on the way back.

Inside the Gorge the cliffs rise on either side to almost a thousand feet in places. A few hundred yards in are a number of deep caves which once sheltered outlaws and now colonies of bats, of which Alĭn was distinctly nervous for all his fearless leaping from rock to rock. About three kilometres long, the gorge offers a lovely walk. A vulture was nesting high up on the cliffs, but I could not get a proper look at it.

Alĭn studied English and Russian at school but was too shy to speak English in front of his family. As we walked, we exchanged words of English and Romanian for the various trees and objects we encountered. The cliffs offer fine but dangerous rock-climbing, as witnessed by a memorial to two Hungarian climbers who died there in 1974. At the far end of the Gorge is a state-run *cabană*, a sort of café, selling lemonade, beer and sweets. It was busy and blaring out some Romanian pop song. By the time we had had a lemonade and renegotiated the Gorge, it was time to take the family into Cluj.

We found Delia in a flat in one of the uglier parts of Cluj, a typical wasteland of crudely built apartment blocks. As in every other private house I had been in, the interior was as well looked after as the exterior was shabby, a kind of visual equivalent for the public/private dichotomy which I had found everywhere in Romania. She was not much over twenty, slim, black-haired, pretty and incessantly garrulous. She did speak excellent English and, like many of her contemporaries, put British students to shame with her degree of mastery of a foreign language.

The family pressed me to eat with them and to stay for a few days. I accepted the meal, but declined the bed as politely as I could. They were, I think, puzzled by my refusal. They knew the Rotars, of course, though not well. They knew, therefore, that they were a poor peasant family while they themselves were much more prosperous. In any society less demented than Ceausescu's Romania, the Mărinceans, with their intelligence and energy, would have prospered and become the members of a middle class. As it was, their house was furnished in a much more modern way than that of the Rotars. They had two buffalo cows and a bay horse as well as the usual collection of poultry and a pig.

Back at their home, the father, Gheorghe, who was rather shy since he could not understand English or Russian, offered me a glass of his home-made ţuica and, with Delia translating, came out of his shell a little. He told me that there was already a legend that Ceausescu was not dead, but only hiding. While the women prepared supper, he took me to see the buffalo cows being milked by his wife, Elena. The cow's tail was tied to a rafter. This one cow yielded eight litres a day, half of which the family sold and used the rest themselves. The sow had just littered with eight piglets. Before the revolution, he said, each piglet would fetch twelve hundred lei but now only four hundred, a large drop in the family's income. Back in the house, he taught me the Romanian toast Narok and we ate. The food was the same as at Mrs Rotar's and Elena wanted to know whether her sarmaluţa was better than Mrs Rotar's. I replied that both were very good – as they were.

The family were keen that the revolution should continue. The older members thought that Iliescu could be trusted, but Delia was sceptical. Their living-room was dominated by a photograph of Delia's grandfather. His wife, Maria, had raised the family on her own ever since her husband had gone with the Romanian armies to Russia. He had disappeared at Stalingrad. Maria was still a powerful, energetic character, though she kept herself rather in the background. Her hands were coarsened and red with years of work and I never saw her but that she was washing, cooking or feeding animals, a routine she clearly kept up from morning till night. I was a complete stranger to them, with no connection to their lives. Nevertheless, they made me welcome and only seemed concerned if I declined their hospitality.

EACH morning, while Mrs Rotar prepared whatever was for breakfast and looked after the animals, I liked to sit on an old blue-painted bench in the yard and write up my diary. It was pleasant to sit in the hazy morning warmth and the yard was a sort of dictionary of peasant life: Mr Rotar sharpening his scythe, the geese with their entourage of goslings strutting about in a solidarity of stupid ill-nature, the kittens staging mock battles with each other, Mrs Rotar keeping the pig at a distance with her stick. The pig is afraid of her stick but as soon as she has filled its trough and retreated, it made a mad dive to guzzle the lot in as few seconds as possible. I felt myself becoming more aware of light and shade in a place where electricity was not so much used: eating in the tiny kitchen in a cool gloom and then walking into the hot glare of the day. My room is always cool for the curtains are kept drawn against the sun. These sharp transitions focus the dilemma of European philosophy with its metaphors of 'inner light', 'illumination', 'interiority', all of which presuppose that it is dark *inside*.

I had offered to take the Mărincean family for an outing. Alin had to go to school, but that still left Gheorghe, Delia, Elena and Ileana. Romanians *en famille* are a noisy lot, all talking at once. Gheorge insisted on filling the tank from his store of petrol and we set off at ten, first to Turda, not a very attractive town apart from the main square which has some handsome eighteenth-century frontages – merchant houses by the look of them. Once out of Turda, I was directed along an avenue of tall poplars towards the haze-shrouded Apuseni mountains. We soon crossed the Arieş river which we were to follow for the rest of the day. The river is a pale jade-green colour and the hills rising steeply on either side are heavily wooded. We passed a goatherd with his flock of forty or so; the leading billy-goat, a brown and white, shaggy monster with a five-foot span of upcurving horns.

The roadside is a continuo of elder and acacia blossom with passages of dog-rose and birch, but as we move further up the valley, pines become the dominant motif. A peasant couple were walking the road in traditional dress: he in white woollen trousers, white embroidered shirt, black waistcoat and straw hat; she in black skirt, white blouse and purple over-jacket. Many of the houses were wooden shacks and the hillsides were dotted with the tiny blue-painted shielings with thatch roofs I had seen earlier.

Ileana wants us to stop in the village of Lupşa where she knows of a local museum she has never visited. Ileana is the sharp one of the family, quick-witted and sharp-tongued. She can only walk slowly having a bad limp from a twisted foot. Her room in the house at Deleni is lined with books which she showed me with obvious pride. I had the impression that books matter more here and her shelves were well stocked with Russian translations of modern dramatists, novelists and philosophers.

There is no answer from the museum which looks very closed, but a local man sees us and hammers loudly for several minutes until the door is opened. Mr Albu, who runs the museum, is eighty-two. He had been sleeping. He is the museum's owner, founder, curator, collector, etc. The collection of local materials is housed in what used to be the village schoolhouse where he taught for fifty-seven years. He is a tall, stooping man, gaunt but sprightly. He has devoted a lifetime to creating this collection and receives no state help of any kind. It is an extraordinary collection, far larger than the old man can look after or catalogue properly and spread over the seven or eight rooms of the schoolhouse. It smells musty but is packed with wonders. There are Roman artifacts – they mined these mountains for gold in the first and second centuries AD. There are household objects, some of them centuries old, ritual objects, farm implements, clothes, tools and implements for beekeeping, fishing, logging, ploughing, hunting, weaving and killing. There is a medieval window made from stretched, transparent gut; a wooden chain-rope used for dragging trees from the forest with oxen. There are mementoes of Avram Iancu, a local patriot chieftain of the 1848 uprising who, after its failure, went mad and wandered the mountains on the run. The villagers would leave out food for him each evening, one household a bowl of milk, another a piece of bread, and so on, as in the Irish story of mad King Suibhne. There were stakes and a spindle on a rope for sorcery.

The last local witch, he said, had died only twenty years ago. He knew her well, but her family were ashamed that she was a witch and have not continued the tradition. He showed us a heavily embroidered blanket of many colours used by local witches to cure syphylis. The patient lay naked on the blanket in a room where a small window directed the sunlight onto his body, throwing the colours of the blanket into him. Mr Albu had seen it done and knew that it worked. There is no space to display much of the collection and the local costumes were simply hung on racks – hundreds of them. Some of the shepherds' jackets which he drew out were wonderfully embroidered. He was enormously pleased to have a foreign visitor and before I left insisted on presenting me with a lump of gold-ore mined from the Apuseni.

At Arieşeni we stopped for *ojina*, a cross between lunch and dinner. Gheorghe collected dry sticks and moss to make a fire, while Ileana and Elena laid out the food, which was exactly as it always was for these people: *brînză*, bread, radishes, spring onion, cucumber and some pieces of very fat mutton. Paprika is sprinkled on the cheese and meat. For Gheorghe and myself there were thimble glasses of *ţuica*, while the women drank a kind of home-made squash. Pieces of *slanina* were speared on sticks and held over the fire until they began to melt, the dripping being caught on pieces of bread. An outing of this kind was unusual for them, and their enjoyment was a real pleasure. It is difficult sometimes to remember just how much we in the West take for granted.

As we ate, the conversation turned to the revolution. They all hoped for better times ahead. According to Elena, by the end of Ceausescu's reign it was impossible to buy anything, not even a piece of cheese. Florin had told me that to buy a piece of bread you had to produce an identity card. Even then, if you were not local you might be refused, since some for you was less for a local.

Delia said that the worst aspect of the regime was that one person in three was an informer. You never knew who could be trusted and, therefore, trusted no one. Things were already more free, they thought, though the Romanian catch-word was still *n'avem* (we don't have any). The current debate in Deleni and Petreşti, however, was about land. After the revolution, the peasants had voted to de-collectivise the land. Of these, two-thirds had voted to run their own holdings, while the remainder wanted the collectives to continue. Those who wanted to continue could do so, but, as Gheorghe said: 'It did not work before. It will not work now, for precisely those who want to keep the old system (collectivisation) are those who were least efficient and most lazy.'

As we drove back towards Turda, the mountains lay pale and beautiful in the evening light, folded one behind another in pleats of shadow and sun. We stopped briefly below some towering buff-coloured cliffs. The only sounds were the onrush of the Arieş and a concert of birdsong.

Back in Deleni, I *had* to stay for 'something to eat' and when I returned to Petreşti Mrs Rotar would not believe that I was not fading away from neglect and hunger.

Alin had been disappointed not to be able to accompany us. He had to catch a bus each morning – the only one – at four-thirty. I had to ask twice to check I was hearing properly. Classes begin at eight and he tries to sleep in the bus station. Romanian bus stations must be among the least attractive inventions in the world. Prior to the revolution, classes were six days a week. Now they have been reduced to five. He gets home at four in the afternoon. He wanted a photograph of Anastasia to show to his friends, but misloaded his camera and spoiled the film. As I was leaving for Petreşti, I offered Alin and his father a ride to the edge of the village. There are no cars in Deleni, and after a few yards, showing Alin the basics of gear-change and so on, I swapped places and let him drive the half-mile or so to the track for Petreşti. It was hard to tell whether he or his father was the more pleased.

A COOL, cloudy morning, cool enough to need a cardigan outside. My birthday, and Petreşti is as good a place as any to spend it. Delia has to return to her classes tomorrow, so I drive her from Deleni to Cluj, taking the opportunity to say my farewells. Gheorghe presents me with a bottle of his *ţuica*. By the time we get to Cluj, it is raining heavily so we lunch in the hope that the rain will go off. I need petrol to get me to Hungary. Delia tells me that before the revolution the petrol ration was fourteen litres a month.

We go to the Belvedere for lunch. It is the best in Cluj and the most expensive, but, even so, the bill only comes to four dollars. We have a 'ham' starter which turns out to be a plateful of rough-cut garlic sausage and cucumber sufficient to feed a couple of people. Then a *çiorba de burta*, a sour soup made with belly pork and seasoned with cayenne and garlic – not at all to my taste – followed by deep-fried sweetbreads which were good. It was the first Romanian state-run restaurant I had been in where everything looked clean.

I remembered eating with László Kunos in the Fisherman's Bastion. As in most fashionable Hungarian restaurants, there was a band and the fiddler had seemed very accomplished. People at the next table asked him to play a piece which, László told me, was called the *Pácsirta* (skylark). It is a virtuoso piece in which the trilling of a lark is imitated – very effectively. The difference between the Fisherman's Bastion and Petreşti struck me as one of more than just space. They are only a couple of hundred miles apart. It is more a difference in time; between the slow rhythms of peasant life, slow to change, and the magpie-like flutterings of cities, which swallow everything and everyone with the same greedy disinterest. But the difference goes deeper still.

Cities create a loss of meaning, because disparate people, objects and events are juxtaposed in a merely abstract way, with no inherent connection to each other beyond spatial coincidence. Money, by operating as a medium of exchange between unlike objects and events, operates in a similarly abstract way. Market forces cannot operate on the basis of *real* singularity, for the truly singular is not exchangeable for anything else. It may be lost or gained, but it is immeasurable and a money price only violates it, for price rests not on the inherent qualities of the thing, but on a network of relative prices.

Even if we have learned to think of space in relativistic ways, that the earth is not the centre of the universe, we do not often succeed in thinking of time, of history, in that way. We still tend to think that our generation, our lives, are somehow at the centre of reality and that history radiates out from *us*. Religion subsumes that attitude in a kind of mass egotism, in which individuals are viewed in relation to a higher reality from which history (and futurity) radiate out. The 'escape' which city life offers some intellectuals, is often enough merely from that mass-egotism to the egotisms of 'private life' or bafflement. In the case of liberal intellectuals that bafflement often takes the form of a denial that there are any definite truths. Hard and fast truths have come to be seen as politically and emotionally unacceptable. But that is to misunderstand the function of words like 'truth' and 'falsity' in their varied contexts. Within the limits of any system of discourse, some truths are absolute. Outwith those systems, the issue simply cannot arise, *could* not make sense. Similarly, in the ordinary way of things, it makes no sense to deny or doubt most of what we know. To do so meaningfully, we have to change the rules, thereby changing the game. In the case of historical knowledge, we have to distinguish what has been learned intellectually from what we have breathed in through childhood and adolescence. If we could transform what we know *only* intellectually into an imaginative reality and drag what we feel *only* through the pulse into the light of criticism, we might be nearer to learning something both about history and our own historical relativity. The beginnings of morality, if Kant is right, lie in putting yourself in the place of another and thinking what it would be like to be (or have been) that person: German or Catholic or Jew, and acknowledging that the label is not the person any more than the tin is its contents. Our endemic egocentricity as persons, as a culture, is understandable but misleading. Without the imaginative transformation which shows us *how* misleading, there can be no ethical behaviour, only an unthinking obedience to rule. If the unhappy histories of Eastern Europe illustrate anything, it is that unthinking obedience is the mark of the victim. It destroys morality in both ruler and ruled.

DELIA was not optimistic about the future. She distrusted Iliescu and quoted a remark I heard several times to the effect that 'God has forgotten the Romanians'. There were a couple of sights I wanted to see in Cluj but, before that, Delia wanted to see one of her teachers, a 'philosopher'. Alas, anyone who had taught philosophy in Romania is almost by definition intellectually corrupt, since 'philosophy' consisted of the Ceausescu version of Marxism and nothing else. Like the king, Delia's teacher had not heard of Wittgenstein, something that, even in Romania, I found hard to believe.

We went, the three of us, to the Café Lux, Cluj's fashionable café. It provided good coffee. Delia's teacher spoke German. He claimed that Romania had been sold out by the Western powers at Yalta and, more recently, Malta. Because I felt that a little provocation might be in order, I suggested that his whine was rather misplaced: 'What, after all, do you expect since Romania sided with the Axis against the Allies? The Soviet Union was our ally. Why should their interests be sacrificed to those of our enemies? Why, in any case, should the West get you out of a hole your own passivity has dug?' This was not a line of argument he seemed prepared for, and he had little to say to it beyond an irrelevant repetition of the anti-Magyar trope ('They are Asiatics') which I had heard from that other 'philosophy teacher'. It was unfair to provoke someone I did not know, but I had heard this 'sell-out' theory of history too often in Hungary, Yugoslavia and Romania to have any patience with it.

The theory of the sell-out is itself a cop-out. The realities of Eastern Europe after the war were that Stalin would not tolerate non-communist governments and the West was in no position to do much about it, without continuing an already catastrophic conflict. No people in Eastern Europe can shrug off responsibility for their history any more than Scots can reasonably avoid the fact that Scotland now is what Scots men and women have made it. It is easy to sentimentalise history or to dismiss it as a 'mere abstraction' or to disclaim responsibility for it: 'I was not born then', a refrain one hears most often in Germany. But these attitudes miss the point that we are *also* history, we are *also* those bundles of belief, prejudice and gut-reaction which our cultural milieu has made us, and unless we can acknowledge to ourselves at least the worst of them, then we must simply reiterate the past. It is, ironically, Engels who remarks somewhere that those who scorn philosophy are most often those who remain enslaved by the worst, vulgarised relics of past philosophies.

Ideologies of hatred have never been far from the surface of European political life. In the seventeenth century, they took the form of religious hatreds, whether in Ireland or Bohemia.

In the twentieth they have tended to be more ethnically based. I see Eastern – and to some extent Central – Europe as a nest of potentially vicious ethnic, religious and national squabbles which are only likely to be exacerbated by the difficult economic times ahead. The Croats are at loggerheads with the Serbs. In Bosnia-Hercegovina Moslems are at loggerheads with Catholic Croats *and* with Orthodox Serbs. Albanians are being persecuted in Kosovo. Anti-semitism is rearing its head again in Hungary and in what was East Germany and Romania. The Slovaks want to be independent of the Czechs. Turks are being persecuted in Bulgaria. Austria, like Germany, wants to close its borders to the hosts of refugees who are likely to cascade from Eastern Europe and the Balkans.

Whatever the excuse for the ideologies of hatred, the logic of prejudice is unflinching. It is all very well for people to be 'entitled to their beliefs', but not if those beliefs insist on persecuting others. The logic of prejudice is that we deny to some other person/persons, a fully human status. We refuse to admit that they are 'like us', for, self-evidently, in one or more respects, they are not. We are white. They are Niggers. We are Christian. They are Yids. We are straight. They are queers. The excuse is irrelevant to the logic.

In each case, the slur, whatever it may be, dehumanises its victim, deprives them of a human soul; hence, the ever-repeated trope of animal imagery: Alabanians are 'just out of the trees' or Jews are 'bestial' or Asiatics are 'like animals' – all accusations I heard in Eastern Europe. In his splendid book *The Claim of Reason*, Stanley Cavell identifies this proclivity as soul-blindness or soul-refusal, the exact phrase.

But, despite this denial of fully human status, the 'person' we reject mimics in every other respect what we accept as defining humanity or human-being. He/She (It) uses language, inhabits a culture, looks like a person. So the real claim is that *one* attribute (blackness, membership of a particular religion or whatever) out-weighs and nullifies all the others. The upshot is that the mimic is a failed imitation of ourselves. We are the 'real thing'. That is why we feel threatened.

This egocentrism is often disguised to ourselves by being sunk in a group identity: a *we* is the real thing, thereby, at a single stroke, we both avoid personal responsibility *and* shore up our own identity. So long as the negative exists, the positive need not be questioned. It is a cop-out, a refusal to acknowledge our own triviality in the face of historical change and our own dismissal by time. This is what Pascal means when he writes of the terror of infinite spaces. Pascal's is the most uncompromising of gazes. He writes: 'We are fools to depend on the society of our fellow men. Wretched as we are, powerless as we are, they will not aid us; we shall die alone. We should therefore act as if we were alone, and in that case should we build fine houses, etc? We should seek the truth without hesitation, and if we refuse it we show that we value the esteem of men more than the search for truth.'

Pascal and Descartes were both children of the Counter-Reformation but headed in different directions – Pascal towards Kierkegaard and faith, Descartes towards Hume and scepticism. But the discipline Pascal requires of you, also requires faith. Without that, all that remains is stoicism – as illustrated by the later life of W. H. Auden.

ONE of the things I wanted to see in Cluj was the birthplace of Matthias Corvinus. He is regarded as one of the greatest of Hungary's kings, though he was of despised Vlach stock. I like too to point out that the drums which beat William of Orange across the Boyne were a gift from the Pope. History is less comforting than we often imagine. Corvinus' birthplace now houses a small art gallery. It is an attractive two-storey building with a little garden at the back where we sat for a few minutes in the sunshine. The centre of Cluj is substantially intact, much of it dating from the eighteenth century. As the capital of Transylvania, it attracted wealth and some fine buildings. Kolozsvár to the Hungarians and Cluj to Romanians, it was Klausenburg to the Saxon settlers who came here in the twelfth century. Ceausescu renamed it Cluj-Napoca since there had been a Roman town, Napoca, on the site but no one uses that name. The main square is dominated by the huge church of St Michael in front of which stands an impressive equestrian statue of Matthias. Now that Ceausescu has gone, the church is coming back into use, though there are fewer Catholics here now than when it was completed in the fifteenth century. The statue shows Matthias's horse trampling on the Turkish banner, but, in fact, Matthias was not one of the great crusaders against the Turks, being more concerned with his ambitions in Bohemia and Austria.

ONE of my evening pleasures in Petreşti was to watch the return of the water-buffalo. Each morning early they were taken out to pasture. It was a communal herd, numbering about a hundred-and-fifty beasts. Each evening, just before dark, they were brought back to the village and, as they passed each house, the cows peeled off from the herd into their own yard. The duty of herding them rotated through the village families. They are bad-tempered beasts, but impressive as they plod through the town, their necks stretched out, making deep groaning sounds. The villagers line the street as the buffaloes pass, the men with sticks to make sure that none wanders into the wrong yard. The dog at the Pîrvu house barks wildly if any of the cows stray towards his yard. In the late evening, some of the cows browse the grasses by the stream which flows through the centre of Petreşti. On this, my last evening before setting out for Hungary, there is a wonderful, crimson-flaring sunset. The ugliest building in the village is the store/café/pub, a concrete and tin imposition from the last decade. There is a minor brawl going on as I pass. My *buona sera* passes muster readily enough among the villagers, and if one had no Romanian, a knowledge of Italian would be more useful than anything else.

For dinner Mrs Rotar has made a *ciorba de macris*, a kind of sorrel soup, slightly sour and very good. The soup is accompanied by leaves of fresh sorrel on the side. It involves milk, eggs and a pork stock, but even after several days and a small Romanian dictionary, I cannot quite follow her explanation of the technique. The Rotars detest the old regime and Ceausescu and the Red Army. They hope for better days. I hope that if better days do come, they will not involve too sudden a loss of what they already have.

I TOOK Mrs Rotar to the market in Turda. She had a bag of eggs to sell and a bottle of lemonade to drink. Before she got into Anastasia, she commended herself to God with a short prayer, crossed herself and prepared to meet whatever fate lay in store. I could see from the corner of my eye that she was praying quietly to herself as we covered the ten miles or so to Turda. When I left her in the square, she told me to be sure to come back and beamed a huge grin.

Approaching Cluj from the south, you look down from the Fegat hills into the valley of the Someş, along which the town stretches. Long strands of mist stretched along the valley but, true to Romanian tradition, they turned out on closer inspection to be clouds of pollution. Leaving Cluj, I headed west towards Oradea and the western rim of the Carpathians. The villages looked increasingly Hungarian, painted green and ochre, and the domed towers of the Orthodox churches began to be replaced by the pointed spires of Catholicism.

Near the village of Dumbrava the mountains of the Bihor range began to rise in front of me. Several hillsides visible from the road had clearly once been terraced for vines but now lay neglected and overgrown. The day was overcast and rain threatened.

A mist hung on the mountains, heavily wooded with beech and oak, birch and walnut. There are many natural hot springs in this part of the Carpathians and near Bors you could smell the sulphur. At the border crossing on the Romanian side there was a long line of waiting Dacias but I had long since learned to ignore such queues. As the rules for foreigners leaving the country are completely different I simply drove up to the head of the queue. The process of passing the two checkpoints only took half-an-hour, most of which was spent on the Hungarian side where a surly official looked at my boxes of books with deep suspicion.

To my surprise, I was immensely relieved to be back in Hungary. Without the help I had received from Florin and others, and with no grasp of the language, coping with the difficulties of private travel would have been a nightmare. Now I found it a distinct relief to be able to go into a café and buy a coffee or glass of cola with no difficulty, no *n'avem*, no hostility and no hour-long delay.

Driving across the great Hungarian plain, the *puszta*, the succession of maize-fields and wheat-fields is only broken by the occasional line or clump of trees. Reaching Budapest, crossing the Danube and arriving at the Orion was like an encounter with old friends. I remembered László Kunos' parting remark when I was preparing to leave this country: 'When you get tired of other places, come back to Budapest.'